Preface

Review of Australian Research in Education (RARE)

The Australian Association for Research in Education (AARE) is committed to encouraging excellence in research in education and to dissemination of this research through its conferences, publications, awards and its program of research training. This is the fifth in a series of monographs that aim to meet all of some of the following:

contribute to the continuing development of high quality, relevant, and cutting edge research on Australian topics;

improve communication and understanding between educational researchers and users of research;

make a significant contribution to on-going discussions of research issues, priorities and directions, and

contribute to the wider dissemination of research, and in particular make the findings of significant research accessible to policy makers, teachers and postgraduate students.

The acronym RARE is particularly pertinent to the aims of this monograph series. It suggests AARE is publishing material that is unusual, valuable and important; that the editions are limited; and that there is much that is unique and interesting about the Australian educational research scene.

No. 1   *Australian Educational Research Journals: What They Do and How Well They Do It* (1989)
No. 2   *Educational Policy Development and Implementation* (1993)
No. 3   *Reflections on Educational Research in Australia* (1995)
No. 4   *Ethics in Educational Research* (1997)

Reviewing panel for RARE no. 5

Professor Sid Bourke   The University of Newcastle
Assoc. Professor Ray Debus   The University of Sydney
Assoc. Professor Shirley Grundy   Murdoch University
Dr Barbara Kamler   Deakin University
Professor Terry Lovat   The University of Newcastle
Dr Richard Walker   The University of Sydney

Acknowledgements

Many thanks to Sitha Kahagalle. Her desk-top publishing skills and her commitment were essential ingredients in the production of the camera-ready manuscript. Thanks also to the Dean of the Faculty of Education, Terry Lovat, The University of Newcastle, for his support for the project and his involvement as a reviewer. We sincerely appreciate the efforts of the reviewing panel, and most especially the contributors for their interest, their scholarly efforts, and their patience and co-operation.

Review of Australian Research in Education
No. 5

SUPERVISION OF

POSTGRADUATE RESEARCH

IN EDUCATION

Edited by

Allyson Holbrook

and

Sue Johnston

Australian Association for Research in Education
1999

First published 1999

National Library of Australia Cataloguing-in-Publication data:

Supervision of postgraduate research in education:

Bibliography
Includes index

ISBN 0 9585903 1 1

1. Education - Study and teaching (Graduate) - Australia.
2. Universities and colleges - Australia - Graduate work.
3. Teacher educators - Research - Australia. 4. Graduate students - Research - Australia. I. Holbrook, Allyson. II. Johnston, Sue. III. Australian Association for Research in Education. (Series: Review of Australian research in education : no. 5).

378.155072094

Design and Layout: Commodore Press Pty Ltd

Published by: Australian Association for Research in Education Inc. [AARE] 1999

Publishing Services: PJ Professional Resources Services Pty Ltd, Coldstream, Victoria

Proudly printed in Australia by Commodore Press Pty Ltd, Lilydale, Victoria.

CONTENTS

Preface

INTRODUCTION

PART I: Research Supervision - Setting the Scene

PART II: The Experience of Supervision

PART III: Personal Accounts of, and Reflections on, Doctoral Supervision

INTRODUCTION

The Many Facets of Research Supervision in Education

Allyson Holbrook
The University of Newcastle

Sue Johnston
The University of New England

Introduction

There is an increasing number of researchers interested in the administrative processes, educational strategies, outcomes, and cultural and mythological dimensions of postgraduate supervision. But there is also a much greater and growing number of potential and neophyte research students and supervisors who seek information about the nature of supervision, and the attendant expectations and 'mysteries' associated with postgraduate research. This monograph goes some of the way toward rendering the processes and the culture more visible and understandable, particularly within the field of education in Australian universities. It is not a handbook of 'how to do a PhD or professional doctorate', although very few of those are specifically published for an education readership. It is, by contrast, a book that intends to promote discussion, stimulate questions, challenge taken-for-granted assumptions, and offer insights.

The chapters are layered in such a way that they can address the different needs of the readership. For example, supervisors may direct new students to the section devoted to personal accounts and reflections (Part III) with an aim to facilitating dialogue and assisting in the process of negotiating expectations. Experienced supervisors will find challenges to the way they might handle supervisory relationships in the ethics section (Part IV) and the section on the experience of supervision (Part II). Similarly more experienced students may be encouraged by the issues raised in those sections, to re-evaluate their supervision and give voice to their concerns, or they may find solace and validation in the community of experience contained therein. Policy makers, administrators and faculty managers will find much of specific interest in the introductory and closing sections. Researchers interested in exploring supervision will find potentially fruitful lines of inquiry to pursue and an excellent coverage of the literature throughout.

This book draws together a group of authors, at different stages in career, including PhD candidature, who are at the frontier of research and debate on postgraduate supervision. The articles reflect a range of methodological approaches and perspectives and draw together material primarily concerned with the academic field of education in Australia. Yet the themes that are explored traverse boundaries of discipline and nation. To many experienced research students and supervisors in education much of this material will represent familiar territory. Nonetheless there is little empirical research in the field. The formation of academic identity in education, the supervisory relationship, even the learning and teaching strategies involved in training researchers are issues that, until recently, have barely been raised. This RARE (Review of Australian Research in Education) represents a beginning, a small step - in anticipation of rapid, and necessary growth in research and interest in the area of postgraduate supervision.

The relative recency of research supervision

Compared to the lifespan of universities, postgraduate research supervision is a contemporary phenomenon, particularly in Australian education. The first PhD in Australia was awarded by the University of Melbourne in 1946 (Connell 1993, p. 118), although the original PhD award had originated in Germany early in the 1800s, and was more rapidly taken up by America than it was in Britain (Nicoll 1996, p. 275; Partridge 1968, pp. 122-3).

Research degrees were comparatively rare among Australian academics prior to 1970. In 1940 teachers' college staff were sent a survey to ascertain their qualifications. Twelve had PhDs and, for just over half, the highest educational qualification was the Bachelors degree (Turner 1943, p. 48). By the 1960s the educational aspirations of the population were already changing, and the expectations of the university were too. There were demands for greater rigour, and more research output to meet heightened national aspirations, fuelled by the promise of science and technology and a vigorous economy. The federal government promoted research, especially in the sciences, and provided scholarship money for postgraduate students. Moreover, new universities were established (see Macmillan 1968, pp. 15-25). Sanders remarked in the early sixties that postgraduate enrolments were growing apace as 'more emphasis was placed on research'. Students were moving from pass degrees to Honours degrees to Masters degrees to Doctorate degrees, and the latter were expanding particularly 'rapidly' (1963, p.134; see also Aitkin 1991).

In 1960 there were 2,408 higher degree students in all Australian universities and by 1970 the number had grown to 9,648 (less than half were full-time). During the 1960s enrolments in higher degrees outpaced growth in undergraduate enrolments, growing from 6% in 1962 to 10.3% in 1972. In 1975 11.3% of university students were enrolled in higher degrees, by 1980 this had reached 12.6% (Connell p. 415). About 3% of candidates completed doctoral degrees between 1975-85, and there was a rise in Masters students to 9% (about two thirds were part-time) (Connell, 1993, p.118, p. 123, p. 415). Today the total number of postgraduate students in Australia is well over 100,000 (see Evans and Pearson in this book).

Masters degrees in education took the form of the MEd or MA. The first MEd was introduced by Melbourne University in the early twenties (Eunson 1973, p. 884; Spaull & Mandelson 1983, p. 93). At the University of Sydney an MA degree in education was possible from 1902, but after 1910 was available in the Department of Education at that university. An MEd was introduced there in 1947 (Connell 1983, p. 158).

In the sixties, according to the Director of the Australian Council for Educational Research, Bill Radford (1964, pp. 264-5), the Masters thesis was 'generally thought of, and seen by the university staffs, as a training in research'. Hence emphasis was 'placed on the training rather than on the significance of the topic or the contribution to knowledge made by the thesis'. By contrast the doctoral thesis was 'expected to make a significant and original contribution to knowledge'. Furthermore the topic required 'a more profound understanding of subject and of research techniques' than that for a Master's degree. As with the Masters degree the topic was chosen by the student, but candidature differed substantially in that 'most' Doctoral degree candidates were full-time. He advised that it was 'rare for anyone other than a member of a university department to be permitted to undertake the degree on a part-time basis' (pp. 264-5). In the late nineties the differentiation between a research masters and a doctorate is still much the same within the Academy, but far fewer students are full time, and more move straight into a PhD from an Honours or minor thesis level. In addition, and as evident in the later chapters of this book, the professional doctorate has been introduced and is growing in popularity. In the 1960s, however, educational research was still a small enterprise and postgraduate research provided a significant contribution to the total research endeavour (pp. 265-6),and this remained true for the 1970s-1980s (NBEET 1992, p. 17)

It was in the 1970s that educational research mushroomed in Australia as elsewhere in Europe, the United Kingdom, the United States of America and Canada (Bessant & Holbrook 1995, pp. 19-26). University faculties of education were set up in the new universities, and there was an increase in postgraduate enrolments, slow at first but accelerating throughout the late 1970s and through the 1980s as teachers returned to study. Between 1987 and 1991 the number of enrolments in research masters in education grew from 626 to 910 (45.4%), enrolments in masters by coursework grew 59.3% to 5,430 and PhD enrolments grew from 559 to 850 (52.1%) (NBEET 1992, p. 18). Given the growth in enrolments, and the economic rationalism and interventionism of governments in the nineties it is not surprising that questions of accountability and quality assurance have been raised with respect to postgraduate education, especially once it became evident that students were critical of their supervision, completion rates were often low, or the time taken to complete the degree was too long (Holdaway 1996, p. 60, pp. 67-70). In addition the strategic importance of research has created yet another slant on accountability which extends to the postgraduate area.

Since the 1970s there has been concern within the community of educators and researchers, and at federal and state government levels about what problems are being researched in education, the effectiveness of dissemination and the utilisation of educational research (Bessant and Holbrook 1995 pp. 50-51, pp. 226-33). This is not a uniquely Australian concern (see Hillage et al. 1998, Tooley 1997) and is unlikely to become less important in the near future. In Australia, more of the research effort in education is taking place in universities as state departments of education reduce their own research activities. Hence it would seem that more, rather than less attention will focus on university activity, including postgraduate research, at a time when that activity is becoming more diverse (including diversification of research degrees). Under such circumstances it is all the more important to understand the culture and practices of research training in education and the ramifications of new developments in doctoral degree structure (for example, see Brennan 1998).

In terms of quality improvement in the supervision process administrative solutions have been offered (manuals of procedures, lists of suggestions about contact, the formation of separate graduate faculties and the like) but they do not address the more deeply embedded cultural elements. Obtaining a PhD is more than generating a product, or perfecting a set of skills. The postgraduate experience, and especially the formation of academic identity much like academic collegiality (Tapper & Palfreyman 1998), is essentially intangible and is not defined by a clearly articulated pedagogy or institutional structure. Whether this 'intangibility' is essential to good research output and the creation of skilled and innovative researchers is as yet unknown. The relevance and importance of 'belonging' to the academic culture for students, constitutes an intriguing direction for future research. What is very clear, particularly in the articles in this book, is that students and supervisors are under pressure. The research role of universities has become at once more open, more important, more competitive and less resourced. Students and faculty also face inexorable pressures from within their home and work lives and these pressures cross over into the realm of academic life and supervisory relationships. It is the press of these factors and the subtleties of disciplinary induction that the authors of self-help literature for students and supervisors find hard to address.

Supervision by the book

There is an abundance of *how to*: *plan, organise, write and present a thesis* literature on the market. Few of these books specifically address students in the field of education (a notable exception is the work of O'Donoghue and Haynes (1997) written within the Australian context). What is most striking about them is that they tend to steer clear of supervisory relationships. The worlds they describe have rules and resources and run smoothly. They are populated (if peopled at all) with omnipotent, albeit extremely personable and caring, supervisors, and with students who have struck a single problem that is remediable (for example, Evans 1997). They are books of practical, clearly explained, and specifically situated advice. They are about decontextualised and resolved situations, not complex, messy reality. They give an impression of good management and control. Tears and tantrums, frustrations, phobias and personal agendas are missing, so are the supervisors who do not have the correct answer or students with unmanageable problems. Sometimes the supervisor is absent from the text entirely, giving the impression the student is on their own. Methodology texts tend to give the same impression. So students who are part-time and very dependent upon such sources of 'research culture', may well feel isolated and bereft, most particularly if the supervisory process is not going well.

Such literature also makes assumptions about the level of 'readiness' of the reader and their familiarity with appropriate genres of discourse. The words methodology and theory provide a case in point. They are used in multiple and often shorthand ways in academic conversation that frequently bear no relation to the advice manual or methodology text. As Knowles points out in this volume, there may be a gap in knowledge and expectations that can undermine feedback strategies between student and supervisor from the very start. In their recent book on supervision, Delamont, Atkinson and Parry (1997) highlight the dearth of basic knowledge that supervisors might expect (p.16). The latter is one of the richer and more engaging texts available. It is aimed primarily at the supervisor but could prove an aid to student understanding of supervisory expectations, understandings and tactics. Nonetheless, is not a text for the absolute novice in that it assumes a basic understanding of academic culture, as well as a desire to 'belong'.

Phillips and Pugh (1994) provided one of the earliest manuals that tackled supervisor relationships in some detail. It addressed the personal side of supervision and the pitfalls, raising awareness of the need to tackle the problems. The student is not delivered benign comfortable advice in that text, but is urged to be aware and be proactive and 'manage' their supervisor. Supervisors in turn are urged to be aware and flexible. There is more attention paid, however, to what is preferable rather than what is possible. And this brings us to the key problem of the written text. The problem with giving advice in text, no matter how many useful anecdotes are provided, is the lack of the dynamic that attends open discussion and clarification. As Delamont et al. point out, such literature needs to be discussed by all involved parties (p. 16).

With respect to the last point, the editors of this RARE wanted to provide a window to the worlds of both supervisor and student in education specifically, because so much of the abovementioned literature assumes full-time student status, on-site supervision, and small supervisory loads, which are not often the reality in education. Because so little specific research has been carried out in education many of the authors in this volume had to draw on larger data bases to isolate the education student data or, lacking that option, choose cases from other disciplines that would have pertinence to the education setting. Bearing this limitation in mind, and in order to promote meaningful dialogue between student and supervisor in education, we decided to include stimulus material (that could be used in a variety

we are unable to state what educational research is or is not? Moreover how narrow are the perceptions of what constitutes 'education'? There is sufficient provocation within the book to suggest the need for further work on clarifying the nature of education as a discipline and of educational research so that this understanding can be used to clarify the nature of postgraduate supervision in education.

Disciplinary knowledge is at the very core of taken-for-granted expectations of thesis supervision, its taken-for-grantedness and critique of same can both be found in these pages as competing and complementary discourses. The latter can be what neophyte researchers find so very confusing, and what established academics can find so hard to explain. Välimaa (1998) raises the question, why are the boundaries of the disciplines where they are, especially when one considers that the environment, for example social preconditions and availability of material resources not only set the essential parameters for the content of academic work but outline the nature of the research problems addressed as well. Such questions have a particular salience for academic education which has a tense history within universities and a fragile relationship within the teaching profession and with the major employers of its graduates - the education authorities. What research problems and topics are pursued, and what methodological approaches are used, bear more than a small relation to the political agendas of the period. Supervision too, is caught up in these movements.

The students: Profile and skills

Students in education have had a different profile to other postgraduate students, their contribution to the evolution of the 'institution' has to be considered. As Evans and Pearson point out in Part V, education candidates in the late twentieth century increasingly seek a form of doctoral work in which the emphasis is on developing professional expertise rather than academic expertise per se. The statistics indicate that they are more likely to be older and part-time than postgraduate students in other disciplines. Clearly, we need to know more about the students, their expectations, their needs, and their impact. Often they come to postgraduate research with extensive professional experience and with strong views about the practical questions they wish to research. What does this mean for the nature of postgraduate supervision in education? Issues of flexibility, the need to value their knowledge and experience, the importance of openly negotiating and clarifying expectations are all explored by authors in the book. Does more work need to be done in highlighting the profile of postgraduate students in education and using this as a basis for resisting pressure to compare completion rates across disciplines or import inappropriate solutions from very different contexts?

How postgraduate students learn and how in education teachers translate their understandings of learning to the postgraduate sphere are important as well as fascinating issues.

The learning environment and the teaching issue

Postgraduate supervision does not take place in a vacuum. Although the relationship between postgraduate student and supervisor is a critical factor impacting on outcomes, so too are the departmental and institutional characteristics. In this regard, policies and procedures are important givens for the smooth operation of postgraduate research, but they are not enough on their own. What is even more important is a culture or learning environment at both departmental and institutional levels which supports postgraduate students personally and professionally. We could do much more to understand the more intangible elements of a culture conducive to postgraduate research.

As in all disciplines, one important theme arising in the book is the question of where postgraduate supervision fits into the lives of academics. Postgraduate supervision seems to lie awkwardly, somewhere between teaching and research. For some academics, probably more so in disciplines other than education, postgraduate supervision is a clear extension of their research activities. But, the diversity of research questions and methodologies of postgraduate students in education means that there is sometimes a tenuous link to the research of their supervisors. For some academics, postgraduate supervision is seen as an extension of their teaching involvement and this stimulates questions about how postgraduate students learn and how supervisors can facilitate that learning most effectively. There are no clear answers to these questions because the process of postgraduate supervision has not yet been adequately explored in this light.

Models and structures

In several chapters within the book contrasts are drawn between traditional stereotypes of postgraduate supervision and the newer models which are emerging in our universities in response to changing demands. Traditional models of supervision are based on a single supervisor working with a motivated, well prepared student over an extended period of time. In reality, many factors distort this image. The diversity of students entering postgraduate research means that students bring with them diverse motivations, prior experiences, expectations, commitments and skills. Increasing numbers of postgraduate students and pressures on academic workloads are causing many academics to question whether supervising postgraduate students in traditional ways is cost effective. Furthermore, both students and academics are more mobile than in the past. Students can have several supervisors over the period of their candidature and may need to be supervised at a distance or in more flexible ways. All of these factors raise questions about whether the traditional model of postgraduate supervision is appropriate for new times. Do we know enough about alternative models?

And what of examination? Given the multi-disciplinary nature of education, particular problems arise. Students are advised on many fronts that they should play a role in choosing examiners, but what does this mean? How is their involvement operationalised, and how should they interpret their examination results? Moreover how well does examination stand up to scrutiny? Then what of the research? What happens to the 'contribution' to knowledge? Issues of dissemination and utilisation of research, and support for these activities during and after candidature need serious consideration. The eligibility for, and success rate of, education students in the award of government funded scholarships, requires careful monitoring as do the mechanisms by which they are awarded.

The student-supervisor relationship

Many elements of the supervisory relationship are already under investigation, and these elements are closely tied in with discipline, collegiality, research environment and the skills of the learner and teacher. It is a field that will continue to be an important one for research into postgraduate supervision, as new technologies and social developments proceed. Longitudinal studies are rare, and class, gender, ethnicity, internationality, and age are all raised by the authors of this book as little researched. Indeed, many authors noted the dearth of literature specifically in education. Thus it seems appropriate to end this introductory section with a list of potential research areas. In some, as indicated elsewhere in this book, a start has already been made but others are yet untouched.

On a final note, postgraduate research in education is at the very heart of the research endeavour in education in Australia. Its importance is appreciated by the AARE and support for it is one of their core objectives. Drawing on the thrust taken by Evans and Pearson and Green and Lee at the end of this volume, it is timely and important to ask ourselves where is this endeavour going in education, and where will we knowingly, or unknowingly, allow it to go?

Topic areas:
1. **Discipline and academic identity**
     the exploration of postgraduate pedagogy
     history and role of the PhD in education
     the transmission of disciplinary knowledge
     the construction of academic identity
     politics of supervision
     the dissemination and utilisation of completed research

2. **The students: profile and skills**
     transition
     reasons for topic choice/motivation to do a PhD
     choice of university/mode of research studies
     perspective on research and academic culture
     perception of how their research will be received

3. **The student-supervisor relationship**
    supervisory effectiveness/strategies
    causes of non-completion
    feedback
    exploration of difference
    cross-sex supervision

4. **Models and structures**
    the process of examination
    impact of the streamlining of entry criteria
    comparative study of models of supervision
    the nature, structure and impact of alternative modes of delivery
    the impact of new information technologies
    comparative analysis of experience of Masters, PhD and EdD
    distance supervision

5. **The learning environment and the teaching issue**
    the function/impact of the seminar, methods subjects
    longitudinal studies of knowledge and skills acquisition
    patterns in postgraduate research
    effectiveness of different administrative structures, e.g. graduate
    departments
    effectiveness of resource and support structures
    economic analysis of resourcing

References

Aitkin, D. 1991, 'How research came to dominate higher education and what ought
    to be done about it', *Oxford Review of Education*, 17 (3), pp. 235-247.
Bessant B. & Holbrook, A. 1995, *Reflections on Educational Research in
    Australia: A History of the Australian Association for Research in Education*,
    Coldstream, Victoria, AARE.
Brennan, M. 1998, 'Struggles over the definition and practice of the Educational
    Doctorate in Australia', *Australian Educational Researcher*, 25 (1), pp. 71-89.
Delamont S., Atkinson, P., Parry, O. 1997, *Supervising the PhD: A Guide to
    Success*, Buckingham, The Society for Research into Higher Education & Open
    University Press.
Connell W. F. 1993, *Reshaping Australian Education 1960-1985*, Hawthorn,
    ACER.
Connell, W. F. 1983, 'The professors—G. S. Browne and C. R. McRae', in C.
    Turney (ed.), *Pioneers of Australian Education Volume 3: Studies of the
    Development of Education in Australia 1900-50,* Sydney, Sydney University
    Press, pp.118-166.

Postgraduate Supervision in Education: An Overview Of the Literature

Sue Johnston
The University of New England

Introduction

The number of postgraduate students in Australian universities has increased significantly over recent years. DEETYA figures show 22,525 PhD students enrolled in universities across Australia in 1996 compared with only 9,298 enrolled in 1990 - nearly a two and a half fold increase. The growth rate has been so dramatic that some commentators have questioned the capacity of the system to cope with the current rate of expansion of PhD students and graduates (Harman 1996).

Education as a discipline and as a structural unit within universities has experienced some of the most dramatic of these changes. In fact, it is probably fair to conclude that few disciplines have been affected by the Dawkins' reforms in higher education more than education. No faculty of education remained untouched by the abolition of the binary system at the end of the 1980s. Most underwent significant changes, often with amalgamations of different faculties of education into single faculties in newly formed universities. Even those education faculties in universities which did not change in name and structure were faced with new competitors which now approached the market place with changed names, structures and status. Faculties whose 'bread and butter' had been teacher education began looking to diversify and place less emphasis on undergraduate teacher education programs (Kennedy 1994).

Along with changes in structures, names, status and functions came a new emphasis on research and postgraduate programs. Faculties of education with backgrounds as colleges of advanced education were now looking to compete for research funds and postgraduate students with the more established faculties from traditional university backgrounds. This meant not only improving the postgraduate qualifications and research potential of staff but also looking to increase enrolments of postgraduate students and ensuring that they succeeded through quality programs and support.

The dramatic changes experienced by faculties of education are confirmed by DEETYA figures for the enrolments of postgraduate research students in education during the 1990s. In 1990, only 654 students across Australia were enrolled in PhDs in the field of education and educational doctorates were not yet on the books. At this same time, 754 students were enrolled in Masters by Research in the field of education. Enrolments in 1996 contrast dramatically with these 1990 figures, with 2,035 enrolments in PhDs (more than a three fold increase) and 1,177 in Masters by Research in the field of education. Educational doctorates have now made their mark, with 79 enrolments recorded in 1996. It is important to remember that the changes have been of kind as well as number because with increased numbers of postgraduate students comes a more diverse and variable student population (Kamler & Threadgold 1996).

Along with these increases have come criticisms of fields such as social sciences, education and humanities because completion times and attrition rates for postgraduate students in these disciplines compare unfavourably with those in the more science-oriented disciplines (NBEET 1989). A longitudinal study of completion rates of social science PhD students in the United Kingdom, by Dunkerley and Weeks (1994), suggests that a 'staggering' 46 per cent of a sample of 1969 candidates withdrew from their studies (p. 156).

Such criticisms may themselves be considered problematic. Booth and Satchell (1996) suggest that the use of PhD completion rates as a performance indicator has some shortcomings because there is considerable variability of completion rates across subject areas, gender, educational background of students, and employment status of students. The profile of postgraduate students in education is substantially different from that of students in science-related disciplines, a point used by some to argue that comparisons among disciplines are not valid.

In spite of these reservations, there is a need to explore issues of quality in postgraduate supervision in education. Although there exists a relatively broad and diverse literature on postgraduate supervision generally, much of the field continues to remain under-researched and under-theorised. Australian researchers and writers have made significant contributions to the field but much work still needs to be done. This chapter reviews the literature related to postgraduate supervision and makes links, where possible, to the particular implications of this literature for supervision in the discipline of education.

Sources and focus of the literature on postgraduate supervision

In the United Kingdom, the impetus for serious investigation of the PhD within the discipline of the social sciences has come from the Economic and Social Science Research Council (ESRC), the main funding agent for doctoral education in the social sciences. With concerns about long completion times and high attrition rates as the main stimulus, the ESRC instituted changes to the organisation of doctoral studies in the field and also commissioned research studies to ascertain the source of problems and impact of these changes (Burgess 1994). Strict time limits were imposed and also training courses in research methods were made compulsory for students. The sanctions policy introduced by ESRC in 1985 meant that academic departments in which over 40% of ESRC-funded doctoral students failed to submit in four years incurred the penalty of loss of funding for doctoral students. Concerns about efficiency and productivity in doctoral studies are not confined to the United Kingdom. In the United States of America, Cornwell (1997) suggested that the productivity of doctoral supervisors should be made a matter of public record as a form of accountability and so that students would be able to act as more informed consumers.

An interesting and widespread stimulus for action on postgraduate supervision within Australia has been faculty or institution-wide surveys of postgraduate students. The outcomes of a number of these surveys have been reported within the literature or at conferences, often with lists of initiatives which have resulted from student feedback. King (1997) has reported on steps taken at Monash University based on surveys similar to those carried out in earlier years by Powles (1988) at the University of Melbourne. Postgraduate students' associations have also been a source of data, with reports such as that from the University of Newcastle (1995) providing a stimulus for action. Jones (1995) undertook a detailed study across departments at the University of New England, documenting student responses and examples of good departmental practice in the supervision of postgraduate students. It is likely that many universities and individual faculties employ these data gathering, quality assurance and monitoring procedures without necessarily publishing them for a wider audience.

The nature and purposes of postgraduate education

One of the major debates within the literature on postgraduate supervision has been about the nature and purposes of postgraduate education. Such debates have centred around whether the PhD is a form of supervised research training in which skills are the product or whether the focus is on the outcomes of the research in the form of the production of new knowledge or whether the whole exercise is a form of initiation into 'the fraternity of master researchers' (Moses 1988, p. 23). Hockey's (1995) study of supervisors' responses to the ESRC imposed changes to doctoral programs highlights the range of views held by supervisors about the purpose of doctoral study. Supervisors range from those who see doctoral study as gaining competence in research methods and therefore fitting with a training ethos to those who emphasise the role of doctoral study in extending the frontiers of knowledge and encouraging the creativity of the student. Supervisors who took the latter view lamented the time restrictions which had been placed on the completion of doctoral studies, maintaining that time limitations resulted in loss of research depth and creativity. Hockey (1995) found that sociologists were less likely to embrace the need for training in research methodology than their economics and business studies colleagues, suggesting that disciplinary differences are important in perceptions of the process for doctoral study.

Pearson (1996) argues that doctoral candidature should be seen as a time of learning the craft and artistry of the professional practice of research and scholarship in the field and contrasts this notion with the term 'training' which is so often associated with doctoral studies. Given the connotations of the term 'training', it is surprising to see it so commonly used for what is considered to be the pinnacle of university study. The focus on postgraduate study as a form of research training has also been criticised by Evans and Green (1995) who maintain that such a focus perpetuates the research/teaching dichotomy in universities and detracts from efforts to understand postgraduate supervision as an educational process. According to Lee and Green (1995), too much of the debate about postgraduate supervision, as well as its attendant research, has concentrated on 'matters of administration and procedures, protocol and policy, finance and governance' (p. 2) at the expense of exploring it as a teaching and learning process.

The call by Connell (1995) some years ago has really not been heeded. He argued that 'supervising a research higher degree is the most advanced level of teaching in our education system' (p. 38) and continued by highlighting supervision as one of the most complex and problematic forms of teaching. Yet, this complexity is often not acknowledged, with many academics failing to see postgraduate supervision as a form of teaching. Green and Lee (1995) suggest the need for a focus on postgraduate pedagogy so that some of the more problematic issues of how and what postgraduate students learn can be addressed. They base their case on the point that pedagogy draws attention to the process through which knowledge is produced rather than limiting the consideration to simple teaching methods.

In summary, although there have been calls to conceptualise postgraduate supervision as a teaching/learning process or in pedagogical terms, there is still a tendency to equate it with research training and with the research responsibilities of the academic role. This means that educational issues, such as curriculum, teaching methods, teacher/student interactions and the learning environment of postgraduate supervision can be easily ignored, with an expectation that the postgraduate student will supposedly 'absorb the necessary know-how by a sort of intellectual osmosis between great minds' (Connell 1985, p. 38).

Disciplinary differences

A number of studies in the field of higher education have indicated the distinctive differences among disciplines studied and taught within universities. Becher (1989) described academics as members of distinct tribes which have their own rituals, languages and procedures and which defend their respective territories. It is interesting that none of these reported studies across disciplines has focused on comparisons of the discipline of education with others. Groupings for such studies usually include humanities and the social sciences which are contrasted to the sciences. Parry and Hayden (1994) used Becher's (1989) disciplinary categories to compare and contrast practices related to postgraduate supervision across a range of disciplines. Their observations suggest that supervisors in fields similar to education are more likely to value independent thought, creative ideas and critical analysis of traditional views and therefore are more reluctant to force particular perspectives on their students. For some, this translates to a 'sink or swim' approach in which students unable or unwilling to make their own way are left to 'fall by the way'.

A study in the Scandinavian context by Kyvik and Smeby (1994) highlights disciplinary differences in the supervision of research students similar to those reported by Parry and Hayden (1994). Their study found that postgraduate students in the humanities and social sciences were less likely than students in the natural sciences to choose research topics that related to their supervisors' research interests. A significant implication of this difference was shown to be that increased research productivity for supervisors was linked to postgraduate supervision in the natural sciences but much less so in the social sciences and humanities. Kyvik and Smeby (1994) attribute these differences to knowledge structures and research organisation in different disciplines. Because knowledge structures in the social sciences and humanities are less hierarchically organised and there is more scholarly disagreement among researchers, postgraduate students are more likely to formulate their own research problem and undertake their work more independently than the collaborative, research team approach common in the sciences. Such conclusions suggest fundamental differences in research and postgraduate supervision among disciplines and that efforts to introduce practices which originate in the sciences into disciplines such as education might not be successful.

Whittle (1992) draws comparisons between postgraduate supervision and research in the arts and sciences. Her portrayal of supervision in the arts probably approximates that in education, with characteristics of low student satisfaction, a high proportion of part-time candidature, low tendency to publish and attend conferences, less frequent meetings with supervisors, greater chances of feelings of isolation for students and a less 'hands-on' approach by supervisors.

The perspectives of postgraduate students

Several studies draw on data collected in interview or survey form from postgraduate students to portray the experience of postgraduate study from the students' perspective. The study by Johnston and Broda (1996) was situated in a faculty of education and highlights the problems students experience as they move from undergraduate study or postgraduate coursework programs into postgraduate research programs. The study draws attention to the relative lack of structure provided to students, the sense of isolation experienced by students, confusion about the resources available and changes to power relationships with staff as students move into postgraduate research degrees. These findings are similar to those reported by Eggleston and Delamont (1983) who found that postgraduate first set of motives is intellectual and is manifest in supervisors who see supervision as anchored in the supervisor's attainment of intellectual knowledge or as a means of furthering the discipline. To these supervisors, the research outcomes of the student's project are seen as important for the discipline and for the supervisor's own development within the discipline. There is also a sense of responsibility to the discipline for the induction of new academics to the field. The second motive is functional, such as that related to perceptions of tangible benefits, material or otherwise. Particularly in the sciences, postgraduate students contribute to the supervisor's research output and joint publication is a common outcome so supervisors may see their role with postgraduate students directly benefiting their careers. The third motive is subjective, such as those central to the self-esteem of supervisors in their academic role. For these supervisors, work with postgraduate students is seen to be a recognition of their status as senior scholars.

Phillips and Pugh (1994) have drawn attention to a possible mismatch in expectations held by supervisors and postgraduate students. Supervisors tend to emphasise the intellectual aspects of postgraduate research while students emphasise the interpersonal and support aspects of the supervisory relationship. Johnston and Broda (1996) highlighted how students seek both reassurance and direction from their supervisors while also wanting a high degree of control over their research - a balance which is not easily achieved. To overcome such difficulties, some writers have suggested the use of checklists, contracts and guidelines for discussion, all of which have the purpose of making these expectations explicit and the basis of negotiation of shared understanding between supervisor and student (Grant & Graham 1994; Ryan 1994; Yeatman 1995).

Given the increase in postgraduate student numbers, there are many academics supervising students for the first time. McMichael (1993) conducted a study of concerns about supervision expressed by Australian and Sri Lankan supervisors who were new to the task. Supervisors from both countries expressed concerns about establishing their credibility, creating a satisfactory research base and providing a climate in which research could flourish. The required standard for theses, workload and time management issues were also of concern to these inexperienced supervisors.

Much of the literature which explores the nature of the supervisory relationship acknowledges the complexity and the intimacy of the relationship between supervisor and student. Data from the perspective of supervisor and student highlight the link between the quality of the relationship between supervisor and student and the quality of the outcomes of postgraduate studies for the student. Along with relationships of this length, complexity and intensity come issues of power. Although Aguinis, Nesler, Quigley, Suk-Jae-Lee and Tedeschi (1996) maintain that the topic of power relationships in postgraduate supervision is 'seriously under-investigated' (p. 268), several studies have reported findings in this area. Although the US study by Aguinis et al. (1996) demonstrates the complex effects of power relationships, it also concludes that student outcomes are more likely to be positive when the relationship with the supervisor is based on expert power rather than coercive power.

Work by Elton and Pope (1989) in the United Kingdom emphasises the value of collegiality in the relationship between supervisor and postgraduate student. Collegiality is seen to be important because postgraduate study is a form of preparation for an academic career and because postgraduate students should be treated as adult learners who have a right to and can benefit from autonomy in their learning. Acker, Hill and Black (1994) studied thesis supervision in the social sciences to determine whether supervisors used a managed approach or a negotiated approach to supervision. The managed approach was more directive and involved following a set series of steps or procedures organised by the supervisor. The negotiated approach took into account the individual differences and needs of students, with mutual expectations negotiated and changed according to input from both supervisor and student. The study revealed that negotiated approaches were more often used by supervisors in social sciences although elements of both approaches were often present.

There is little doubt that issues such as gender and culture impact on postgraduate supervision, yet relatively few studies focus on these issues. Over, Over, Meuwissen and Lancaster (1990) have reported a quantitative study which attempted to determine if publication rates during and after PhD candidature were affected by variables of same-sex or cross-sex supervision. Once allowing for differences in the research productivity of the supervisors, these researchers found no difference in publication between cross-sex and same-sex supervisors. The study does not exclude the possibility of other benefits in same-sex supervision. Conrad (1994) focuses more on the perceptions held by female postgraduate students and on the common communication patterns of women, recommending a number of issues that need to be considered when supervising female students. She notes that female postgraduate students are generally less satisfied with their supervisory experience than male postgraduate students and attributes this both to the qualities that women bring to supervision and to the context in which supervision takes place. Female postgraduate students are more likely to have male supervisors merely because there are fewer senior women academics to take on the supervisory role. Conrad and Phillips (1995) argue that women may find the isolation characteristic of postgraduate study a particular problem because of their preference for group work and collaboration. They make a case for structuring more group work into the experience of postgraduate students and highlight some strategies for ensuring more inclusive management of these groups.

Aspland and O'Donoghue (1994) have drawn attention to the increasing numbers of international students who are enrolling for postgraduate studies in Australian universities. They use case studies of international students in a masters programs in education to highlight some of the particular difficulties experienced by these students. The problems faced by Asian students, highlighted by Ballard and Clanchy (1984), include relations with supervisors, selection of a research topic, participation in discussions and writing the thesis in English.

Yeatman (1995) has questioned how appropriate traditional models of postgraduate supervision are for the more diverse student population now undertaking postgraduate research. She suggests that the traditional model of master and apprentice, based on a charismatic supervisor working with motivated, well prepared students, originates from 'universities in their elite and masculinist phases of history when PhD candidates were a tiny few and represented a select elite of aspirant academics' (p. 9).

The examination process

Given the importance of the examination process in postgraduate study, it is surprising how few studies have focused on this process. Johnston (1997) analysed examiners' reports of doctoral theses across a number of disciplines, highlighting issues of inconsistency in format of the reports and, more importantly, in the interpretation of the criteria. Conclusions about the focus of examiners' comments in this study were similar to those of Hansford and Maxwell (1993) who found that examiners most frequently commented on the presentation and writing features of a thesis. Ballard's (1996) analysis of the examiners' reports for successful doctoral theses focused on examiners' attitudes to the candidate, their expectations of supervisors, the basis for awarding unconditional admission to the PhD and the various audiences to which the reports are directed. Simpkins (1987) studied theses in the field of educational administration in an attempt to understand the way in which examiners assessed critical thinking. The study suggested that examiners in this field were looking for evidence of a style of reasoning which included informed understanding, objectivity, originality, intelligent mastery of objective argument, and knowledgable handling of discussion processes. Nelson's (1991) analysis of one research school in a university is critical of a number of aspects of the examination process including the workload it places on academics. In the same light, Crittenden (1997) has called for reconsideration of the current examination processes used for doctoral theses, highlighting the excessive resources and time each examination requires. The political and ethical issues associated with thesis examination are raised by Kamler and Threadgold (1996) who use a dramatised case study approach to highlight problematic issues.

Departmental organisation and environment

The emphasis on the departmental conditions for effective postgraduate research arise from a recognition that supervisors are but one of the factors influencing the postgraduate experience. Postgraduate students need a lively and supportive intellectual milieu and research environment and these cannot be provided by a supervisor alone (Powles 1992). As Elton and Pope (1992) argue, postgraduate students should not only be paired with a supervisor, 'but join a research community which, at its best, provides collegial stimulus and support throughout a student's research training' (p. 75). Studies by Parry and Hayden (1994) and Jones (1995) highlight variations in the organisation and environment of postgraduate supervision in different departments, while also suggesting examples of good practice. Specific examples include induction programs for postgraduate students, regular research-in-progress seminars, encouragement and support to attend conferences, informal gatherings of students and staff, inclusion in departmental activities and physical arrangements which allow postgraduate students to meet and work on their research within the department.

Johnston and Broda (1996) mention the difficulties in implementing some of these initiatives in education faculties which are relatively inexperienced in and under-resourced for research. Marsh (1997) outlines the initiatives undertaken within a faculty of education of a more recently established institution in which the skills of supervisors need to be built and a research culture for supervisors and students established. One issue of increasing concern is that of quality assurance in postgraduate supervision. Although processes for gathering student feedback on classroom-based teaching are widely used in universities, these standard processes do not translate readily to the context of postgraduate supervision. Because of the longer-term, more personal relationship between supervisor and student, it is much more difficult (if not impossible) for students to provide anonymous feedback on their supervisors' practices. As a result, postgraduate students are less likely to give critical feedback on the grounds that it may jeopardise their relationship with their supervisor. Some universities have developed schemes which attempt to overcome these shortcomings, relying on a third party to collect the data and on a profile of student responses to be collected over a period of time (Mullins & Hejka 1994). There is a need for more work in this area.

In recognition of the special needs of postgraduate students, several universities have established graduate schools which bring postgraduate students from across the university into one organisational unit. In other universities, graduate schools have been established at the faculty level. Holdaway (1996) supports the establishment of graduate schools or faculties with an argument based on the importance of postgraduate research to the research quantum of universities. Graduate schools specifically focus resources and support towards initiatives aimed at improving the quality of postgraduate supervision and the experience of postgraduate students.

Concluding comments

Much of the literature on postgraduate supervision assumes a traditional model of one postgraduate student working primarily with one supervisor over an extended period of time. Given the increasing numbers of postgraduate students in education and their widening diversity, there are grounds for questioning the efficacy of this traditional model of postgraduate supervision. There is some evidence that the traditional approaches are already being broadened through efforts by individual students to seek increased assistance and through arrangements which are put in place informally to cater more flexibly for part-time and distance students.

Approaches which are designed to provide a broader support and resource base for students should be trialed and evaluated, not only as supplements to traditional forms of supervision but as alternatives.

There appears to be value in the moves to conceptualise postgraduate supervision as a form of teaching and learning so that pedagogical principles can be used to explore ways of improving the experience for postgraduate students. While locked into traditional models, there is limited scope for experimentation and for overcoming many of the difficulties which students have raised over a number of years. In a context of accountability, there will be more pressure to listen carefully to issues raised by students.

With an understanding of the particular context of postgraduate research in the field of education, there is scope to argue the limited value of comparisons among disciplines based on performance indicators such as completion times and attrition rates. Although fields such as education have some lessons to learn from other disciplines, particularly the very differently organised sciences, there is also a need to highlight more clearly the specific student profiles within education and the specific nature of educational research which make comparisons across disciplines problematic. To this end, more effort should be directed to exploring the specific context of postgraduate research and postgraduate supervision in faculties of education.

References

Acker, S., Hill, T. & Black, E. 1994, 'Thesis supervision in the social sciences: Managed or Negotiated', *Higher Education,* 28, pp. 483-498.

Acker, S., Transken, S., Hill, T. & Black, E. 1994, 'Research students in Education and Psychology - diversity and empowerment', *International Studies in Sociology of Education,* 4 (2), pp. 229-251.

Aguinis, H., Nesler, M., Quigley, B., Suk-Jae-Lee, & Tedeschi, J. 1996, 'Power bases of faculty supervisors and educational outcomes for graduate students', *Journal of Higher Education,* 67 (3), pp. 267-297.

Aspland, T. & O'Donoghue, T. 1994, 'Quality in supervising overseas students', in O. Zuber-Skerritt & Y. Ryan (eds), *Quality in Postgraduate Education,* London, Kogan Page.

Ballard, B. 1996, 'Contexts of judgement: An analysis of some assumptions identified in examiners' reports on 62 Successful PhD Theses', Paper presented at the 1996 Conference on Quality in Postgraduate Research, Adelaide, 18-19 April.

Ballard, B. & Clanchy, J. 1984, *Study Abroad: A Manual for Asian Students,* Kuala Lumpur, Longman.

Becher, T. 1989, *Academic Tribes and Territories: Intellectual Inquiry and the Culture of the Disciplines,* Milton Keynes, SRHE/Open University Press.

Booth, A. & Satchell, S. 1996, 'British PhD completion rates: Some evidence from the 1980s', *Higher Education Review,* 28 (2), pp. 48-46.

Brown, G. & Atkins, M. 1988, *Effective Teaching in Higher Education,* London, Methuen.

Burgess, R. 1994, *Postgraduate Education and Training in the Social Sciences: Processes and Product,* London, Jessica Kingsley.

Connell, R. 1985, 'How to Supervise a PhD', *Vestes,* (2), pp. 38-41.

Conrad, L. 1994, 'Gender and postgraduate supervision', in O. Zuber-Skerritt & Y. Ryan (eds), *Quality in Postgraduate Education,* London, Kogan Page.

Conrad, L. & Phillips, E. 1995, 'From isolation to collaboration - A positive change for postgraduate women', *Higher Education,* 30, pp. 313-322.

Conrad, L., Perry, C. & Zuber-Skerritt, O. 1992, 'Alternatives to traditional postgraduate supervision in the social sciences', in O. Zuber-Skerritt (ed.), *Starting Research-Supervision and Training,* Brisbane, The Tertiary Education Institute, University of Queensland.

Cornwell, T. 1997, 'Disclosure plea on PhDs', *The Times Higher Education Supplement,* 25, p. 8.

Crittenden, B. 1997, 'A new theory for doctoral examination', *Campus Review,* August 6-12, p. 18.

Cullen, D., Pearson, M., Saha, L. & Spear, R. 1994, *Establishing Effective PhD Supervision,* Canberra, Australian Government Publishing Service.

Dunkerley, D. & Weeks, J. 1994, 'Social Science Research Degrees, Completion Times and Rates', in R. Burgess (ed.), *Postgraduate Education and Training in the Social Sciences: Processes and Products,* London, Jessica Kingsley, pp. 149-166.

Eggleston, J. & Delamont, S. 1983, *Supervision of Students in Research Degrees With Special Reference to Education Studies,* Birmingham, British Educational Research Association.

Elton, L. & Pope, M. 1989, 'Research Supervision: The value of collegiality', *Cambridge Journal of Education,* 19 (3), pp. 267-276.

Elton, L. & Pope, M. 1992, 'Research supervision - the value of collegiality', in O. Zuber-Skerritt (ed.), *Starting Research - Supervision and Training,* Brisbane-The Tertiary Education Institute, University of Queensland.

Evans, T. & Green, B. 1995, 'Dancing at a distance? Postgraduate students, supervision, and distance education', Paper presented at the 25th Annual Conference of the Australian Association of Research in Education, Hobart, November 26-30.

Grant, B. & Graham, A. 1994, ' "Guidelines for discussion": A tool for managing postgraduate supervision', in O. Zuber-Skerritt & Y. Ryan (eds), *Quality in Postgraduate Education,* London, Kogan Page.

Green, B. & Lee, A. 1995, 'Theorising postgraduate pedagogy', *Australian Universities' Review,* 38 (2), pp. 40-45.

Hansford, B. & Maxwell, T. 1993, 'A Masters degree program: Structural components and examiners' comments', *Higher Education Research and Development,* 12 (2), pp. 171-187.

Harman, G. 1966, 'Which way now for postgraduate education?' *Campus Review July 31-August 6.*

Hockey, J. 1994, 'New territory: Problems of adjusting to the first year of a social science PhD', *Studies in Higher Education,* 19 (2), pp. 177-190.

Hockey, J. 1995, 'Change and the social science PhD: Supervisors' responses', *Oxford Review of Education,* 21 (2), pp. 195-206.

Hockey, J. 1996, 'Motives and meaning amongst PhD supervisors in the social sciences', *British Journal of Sociology of Education,* 17 (4), pp. 489-506.

Holdaway, E. 1996, 'Current issues in graduate education', *Journal of Higher Education Policy and Management,* 18 (1), pp. 59 -74.

Johnston, S. 1995, 'Building a sense of community in a research Master's course', *Studies in Higher Education,* 20 (3), pp. 279-291.

Johnston, S. 1997, 'Examining the examiners: An analysis of examiners' reports on doctoral theses', *Studies in Higher Education,* 22 (3), pp. 333-347.

Johnston, S. & Broda, J. 1996, 'Supporting educational researchers of the future', *Educational Review,* 48 (1), pp. 269-281.

Jones, G. 1995, *Enhancing Postgraduate Supervision at UNE,* Armidale, The University of New England.

Kamler, B. & Threadgold, T. 1996, 'Which thesis did you read?', in Z. Golebiowski (ed.), *Selected Proceedings of the First National Conference on Tertiary Literacy: Research and Practice Vol 1,* Melbourne, VUT, pp. 42-58.

Kennedy, K. (ed.) 1994, *Reshaping Teacher Education: Faculty Renewal or Organisational Downsizing?,* Canberra, Australian Curriculum Studies Association.

King, M. 1997, 'Quality improvement through a university-wide survey of PhD students', *The Teaching Review,* 5 (1), pp. 18-25.

Knight, N. & Zuber-Skerritt, O. 1992, ' "Problems and methods in research" - A course for the beginning researcher in the social sciences', in O. Zuber-Skerritt (ed.), *Starting Research - Supervision and Training.* Brisbane, The Tertiary Education Institute, University of Queensland.

Kyvik, S. & Smeby, J.C. 1994, 'Teaching and research. The relationship between the supervision of graduate students and faculty research performance', *Higher Education,* 28, pp. 227-239.

Lee, A. & Green, B. 1995, 'Introduction: Postgraduate studies/ postgraduate pedagogy?', *Australian Universities' Review,* 38 (2), pp. 2-4.

Marsh, H. 1997, 'An institutional perspective on quality supervision', *The Teaching Review,* 5 (1), pp. 12-17.

McMichael, P. 1993, 'Starting up as supervisors: the perceptions of newcomers in postgraduate supervision in Australia and Sri Lanka', *Studies in Higher Education,* 18 (1), pp. 15-26.

Moses, I. 1988, 'Efficiency and effectiveness in postgraduate studies', in Department of Employment, Education and Training (DEET), *Assistance for Postgraduate Students: Achieving Better Outcomes,* Canberra, Australian Government Publishing Service.

Moses, I. 1992, 'Research training in Australian universities - undergraduate and graduates studies', in O. Zuber-Skerritt (ed.), *Starting Research - Supervision and Training* Brisbane, The Tertiary Education Institute, University of Queensland.

Mullins, G. & Hejka, E. 1994, 'The evaluation of postgraduate supervision', Paper presented at the Annual HERDSA Conference, Canberra, July.

NBEET 1989, *Review of Australian Graduate Studies, Initial Report by the Higher Education Council,* Canberra, AGPS.

Nelson, H. 1991, 'The gatekeepers: Examining the examiners', *Australian Historical Association Bulletin,* 68, pp. 12-27.

Over, R., Over, J., Meuwissen, I., & Lancaster, S. 1990, 'Publication by men and women with same-sex and cross-sex PhD supervision', *Higher Education,* 20, pp. 381-391.

Parry, S. & Hayden, M. 1994, *Supervising Higher Degree Research Students: An Investigation of Practices Across a Range of Academic Departments,* Canberra, Australian Government Publishing Service.

Parsloe, P. 1993, 'Supervising students for higher degrees by research in a social work department', *Journal of Further and Higher Education,* 17 (3), pp. 49-60.

Pearson, M. 1996, 'Professionalising PhD education to enhance the quality of student experience', *Higher Education,* 32, pp. 303 -320.

Phillips, E. & Pugh, D. 1994, *How to Get a PhD: A Handbook for Students and Their Supervisors,* Buckingham, Open University Press.

Powles, M. 1988, *Know Your PhD Students and How to Help Them,* Centre for the Study of Higher Education, University of Melbourne.

Powles, M. 1992, 'Policy and program issues in research recruitment and training', in O. Zuber-Skerritt (ed.), *Starting Research - Supervision and Training,* Brisbane, The Tertiary Education Institute, University of Queensland.

Ryan, Y. 1994, 'Contracts and checklists: Practical propositions for postgraduate supervision', in O. Zuber-Skerritt & Y. Ryan (eds), *Quality in Postgraduate Education,* London, Kogan Page.

Simpkins, W. 1987, 'The way examiners assess critical thinking in Educational Administration theses', *Journal of Educational Administration,* 25 (2), pp. 248-268.

University of Newcastle 1995, *Postgraduate Life: What the Students Say,* Newcastle University Postgraduate Students' Association.

Whittle, J. 1992, 'Research culture, supervision practices and postgraduate performance', in O. Zuber-Skerritt (ed.), *Starting Research - Supervision and Training,* Brisbane, The Tertiary Education Institute, University of Queensland.

Yeatman, A. 1995, 'Making supervision relationships accountable: Graduate student logs', *Australian Universities' Review,* 38 (1), pp. 9-11.

Zuber-Skerritt, O. 1987, 'Helping postgraduate research students learn', *Higher Education,* 16, pp. 75-94.

PART II:
The Experience of Supervision

Experiences of Supervisors in Facilitating the Induction of Research Higher Degree Students to Fields of Education

Sharon Parry
Southern Cross University

Martin Hayden
Southern Cross University

Introduction

What distinguishes effective higher degree supervision in research fields of education? What are the strategies commonly employed by higher degree supervisors in these fields? Which strategies best meet the needs of education students during candidature? These questions are important because they concern the special features of higher degree study in the diverse and dynamic research fields of education. In this chapter, we address these questions by drawing upon the views of experienced supervisors in education and by framing these views within the context of disciplinary diversity. A key argument in the chapter is that higher degree supervision is a process that supports the induction of individuals to particular academic disciplines. We first examine what students need in order to master disciplinary conventions and norms necessary for successful completion of higher degree studies in the social sciences, including education. We then provide evidence of the strategies used by supervisors in education to meet these needs.

The chapter is based upon an investigation of higher degree study and supervisory practices conducted across three Australian universities over the period from 1992 to 1996. A theme in the chapter is the importance of the epistemological and cultural characteristics of disciplinary settings in defining effective supervisory strategies. This theme is not sufficiently evident in the Australian literature on higher degree supervision. As a result, advice about effective supervision is often much too general to apply to specific settings. The chapter seeks deliberately to give expression to the views of supervisors. To this end it makes liberal use of quotes from interviews to give voice to the supervisors and to illustrate major themes in the findings. The supervisors quoted are drawn from a range of education fields, and in a few cases the views of doctoral students in education and of supervisors from fields located in the broader social sciences are also reported because they crystallise key themes appropriately. Research in education commonly exhibits characteristics of social science research and in the literature on academic disciplines it is usually categorised as part of the research base of the social sciences (see, for example, Burgess 1994). Two characteristic features of social science research, eclecticism and diversity, are frequently observed in the research fields of education (see, for example, Walker and Evers 1988, Becher 1989, Becher, Henkel and Kogan 1994). Recognition of these features is essential to an understanding of the nature of higher degree students' requirements of research supervision in fields of education.

The chapter begins with a conceptual perspective on higher degree supervision. There follows a brief outline of the data sources and data-collection procedures. Key aspects and important requirements of the research higher degree experience for students in social science fields, including education, are then described, and supervisory strategies reported by education supervisors to be effective in that context are reported. The chapter concludes with a review of the main themes from the data, and it recommends generally that higher degree supervisory practices should always take account of the need for students to learn the discipline-specific rules of the knowledge-making game.

A conceptual perspective

Underpinning the chapter is a conceptual perspective based upon an extensive literature on academic cultures and their organisation (see, for example, Clark 1963, King and Brownell 1966, Becher 1981, 1989, Harman 1988). In this perspective, higher education is viewed as comprising a diverse collection of disciplinary areas, each with its own sense of community, characteristic mode of inquiry, network of communications, body of scholarly traditions, and set of values, beliefs and conceptual structures. Within these disciplinary areas, sub-disciplinary areas and, within the sub-disciplinary areas, specialisms tend to evolve.

In most universities disciplinary areas are firmly but not restrictively bounded by academic departments, each with its own disciplinary and organisational culture. A department's disciplinary culture derives from membership by the staff of specialised academic communities that are national and international in their spheres of influence and through which knowledge in the disciplinary area is pursued and progressed. Its organisational culture derives from its leadership and management, its history and maturity, its resource base in the university, the personalities of its staff and the overlay of institutional imperatives on its management.

The *disciplinary culture* of a department ideally supports the *induction* of higher degree students to the specialised academic communities to which they aspire. The disciplinary context for the process of induction is neatly described by Clark (1983, p.34, p.76):

> The [academic] profession has long been a holding company of sorts, a secondary framework composed of persons who are objectively located in diverse fields, and who develop beliefs accordingly ... Around distinctive intellectual tasks, each discipline has a knowledge tradition - categories of thought - and related codes of conduct ... there is in each field a way of life into which new members are gradually inducted. (cited in Becher 1987a)

In the induction process each student learns how to make an acceptable contribution to a scholarly field. The process is completed when the student's thesis attains approval by experts in the field as representing an acceptable, original or substantial contribution at the Masters or PhD level.

The *organisational culture* of a department ideally supports *supervision*, that is, the process of guiding or directing a student through the induction process. Supervision is the mainstay of teaching at the level of research higher degrees. It involves the supervisor acting as a mentor, guide or adviser to an individual seeking to be inducted to a specialised academic community.

This conceptual perspective emphasises the importance of the process of induction to a disciplinary culture as the objective of higher degree supervision. Successful induction to a disciplinary culture is seen as being the product of a great many socialising opportunities organised within an academic department and by the student's supervisor. Not all of these will involve or require interaction with the supervisor. The notion of an effective supervisory strategy needs, therefore, to be defined far more broadly than simply a strategy involving one-to-one interaction between a supervisor and a student.

Sources of data

The chapter draws upon in-depth ethnographic interviews with higher degree supervisors at three Australian universities over the period from 1992 to 1996 (Parry and Hayden 1994, Parry 1997). The primary site for the interviews was a large research university in Melbourne. Interviews were subsequently conducted at two secondary sites, one a large research university in Queensland and the other a recently-established regional university in New South Wales. The data sets, which are principally concerned with doctoral study and supervision, were analysed within the broad categories of the sciences, the social sciences and the humanities. Fields of education were consistently located within the disciplinary grouping of the social sciences, though in some fields there were strong epistemological and cultural links with either the sciences or the humanities (for example, a tendency towards quantitative methods in science education, and a tendency towards documentary analysis in areas of educational theory).

In the initial survey at the primary site, three stages of data collection were implemented: first, interviews were conducted with postgraduate coordinators or heads of departments across 41 academic departments (including education) for the purposes of mapping the range and nature of the supervisory practices employed in particular disciplinary settings; second, interviews were conducted with groups of supervisors from five disciplinary areas (history, physics, economics, psychology and geology) with a view to identifying ways in which doctoral students are assisted to learn appropriate disciplinary conventions, traditions and values; and third, groups of higher degree students from the same five disciplinary areas were interviewed about their experience of supervisory practices.

In the follow-up survey, involving staff and students at the secondary sites, individual interviews were conducted with a large group of additional supervisors and students. Of these, fifteen supervisors and five doctoral students were drawn from fields of expertise spanning primary, secondary and higher education.

The methodology of naturalistic inquiry (Lincoln and Guba 1985) provided a framework for the collection of interview data. Particular emphasis was given to meeting the trustworthiness criteria specific to this methodology. The main themes from the findings emerged as a result of progressive focusing during the three stages of data collection. The first stage permitted a classification of supervisory practices by disciplinary grouping according to the beginning, middle and final stages of candidature. The follow-up stages enabled an exploration in depth of the nature of the disciplinary norms and conventions that were learned, how they were learned, and what supervisors did to provide opportunities for their students to learn them. The findings fell into two categories: first, the needs that supervisors and their students saw were critical to the successful completion of a higher degree, and second, the strategies adopted by supervisors to meet these needs. These categories, which are reported in the following two sections, are summarised in Figure 1.

Requirements of the research higher degree experience for students

Research in the eclectic and highly diversified fields of the social sciences, including education, deals largely with the nature of human experience, and knowledge is accumulated through the development of individualistic interpretations of particular phenomena. Overall, scholars do not share a common research paradigm or framework of thought, and it is therefore not unusual for there to be different theoretical perspectives, including interdisciplinary perspectives, on particular phenomena. In communicating knowledge, scholars must establish common ground with an intended audience by developing a theoretical position which is believable and based on a sound interpretation of relevant disciplinary traditions (see Bazerman 1981). Further, because knowledge is individualistic and interpretive, it is also critically important that scholars adhere to accepted methodological frameworks to justify their analysis and interpretation.

Figure 1

What Students Need to Learn	Supervisory Strategies to Facilitate Student Learning
• Mastery of theoretical developments relevant to their area of investigation • Adequate knowledge of a range of relevant methodologies • Knowledge of epistemologically - based conventions and cultural traditions specific to their field • How to succeed in a research environment that is largely individualistic in nature and where students must work independently • How to gain access to sources of empirical data	• Assess skills and capacities early in candidature • Make expectations explicit • Assist students to develop and maintain focus • Ensure productive supervisory meetings • Provide opportunities for learning from scholarly networks • Establish support structures within the Department or Faculty • Assist students with thesis writing

Hence, students undertaking research higher degrees in education are inducted into research cultures characterised by eclecticism, diversity, dynamism and intellectual divides. Five important requirements of this experience were reported by supervisors.

First, students need to develop mastery of theoretical developments relevant to their proposed areas of investigation. Many students begin higher degree study in education by intending to investigate a problem derived from their field of educational practice. Others have a broad area of interest which needs to be narrowed to a particular topic. For all students it is imperative to develop an individual theoretical position based on a sound knowledge of theoretical developments in the field. This invariably means having to examine in depth relatively new areas of literature, and it also means having to evaluate the relevance of existing theory to a research problem. The confidence of students is challenged by this process and reassurance is critical - as illustrated by the following remarks by a doctoral student in education:

I knew what I wanted to research but I didn't know what the theoretical developments were in the field. Actually the field is very broad, so I had to find ways to narrow it down. I did that by honing in on the work of a few key people and by getting to know some of them, and eventually, getting feedback from some of them.

A supervisor reiterated the difficulties for students:

> Even when you think you're shooting perfectly at the bullseye, you're relying on other people to actually keep you informed, guide you and tell you whether you've hit the bullseye ... So we have to help them to become skilled craftsmen who can do different things, and we send them to conferences as well.

Of interest here is the role of scholarly networks as a prime source of reassurance.

In developing a theoretical position, the identification of a primary discipline whose theoretical traditions will inform the student's work is of fundamental importance. Parry, Atkinson and Delamont (1994, p. 40), writing about the experience of higher degree students in the social sciences in Britain, argued that identification with a primary discipline (or 'discipline of origin') is 'important in providing a research framework from within which the student could develop his/her work'. They also observed that research frameworks and orientations in the social sciences differ markedly: some are more technically oriented, while others are oriented more towards the tacit knowledge of the practitioner. Differences such as these are not immediately obvious to the novice student and may need to be explained. An experienced supervisor in a more technically-oriented field of science education remarked, for example:

> It tends to be a thing I find with some students ... they don't realise all of the things they've got to justify in a particular research question ... they have to think out how they're going to analyse a [particular] question, for example, even before they've finished the survey ... I've got to constantly remind them of these kinds of orientations before they begin the study proper. It's kind of the way it's done.

Second, students need to develop an adequate knowledge of a range of methodologies from which they can select an approach for their own research. This is important because educational research requires scholars to justify their analysis and interpretation by employing appropriate and well-accepted research methods. It is also important for students to demonstrate the coherence between their theoretical framework and their methods of analysis because this coherence signifies a clear understanding of the research problem to an intended scholarly audience. In many settings, therefore, students are only admitted to higher degree candidature if they have completed methodology coursework. One supervisor reported: 'Our students can't move into a research project in our School unless they have completed research methodology either here or elsewhere'. Part of developing adequate methodological knowledge is the acquisition of appropriate technical and analytic skills. A difficulty for students here is that there may be limited opportunities for training in these skills. Becher (1993, p.120), drawing upon data collected in Britain, noted in relation to the social sciences that: 'There are seldom enough takers in any given specialism ... to allow a close focus on particular training needs ... nor is there usually a critical mass of doctoral students to make such programs viable'. Many supervisors in education recognise the limitations of a lack of critical mass. They also recognise that their students have technical and analytic training needs and so they encourage informal opportunities for skill-sharing:

> We know they have to pick up skills ... like word processing or using a statistical package during their candidature, and all of these are things that you'd love them to have when they came in, but they don't have them ... and sometimes we have to send them to enrol in special courses.

Providing opportunities for training is not always sufficient in itself, however, because many higher degree students in education are already experienced professionals who are reluctant to seek advice or learn from their peers. One supervisor explained:

> It isn't just as simple as giving them advice about what to do. A lot of them think they know it all already. In fact, sometimes we have students whose professional records are quite outstanding, and it is very hard on the supervisor who has to be critical of them. It is a very threatening situation for all concerned.

Third, students need to learn a wide range of epistemologically-based conventions and cultural traditions that are specific to their fields. While these may be well understood by experienced scholars, students must learn them by tacit means in the research environment. Students need to learn, for example, how to negotiate the sometimes conflicting theoretical perspectives and intellectual fashions that characterise research in fields of education. The extent of this conflict in one school of education was described as follows: ' ... there was a great article written by [a colleague] about certain education centres. One of the centres he called the Centre for Kicking, Biting and Scratching because the internal conflict at that centre was just remarkable'. Students also need to learn the ways in which knowledge is reported in particular scholarly fields. The 'rules of the game' for the expression of knowledge in academic specialisms are usually fairly widely understood by the practitioners, yet these rules are rarely made explicit and may be difficult for students to grasp. When asked to describe good thesis writing, for example, supervisors are usually unable to articulate the key features in their own fields, though they reportedly can recognise good thesis writing when they see it (Parry 1997).

Fourth, students need to learn how to succeed in a research environment that is largely individualistic in nature and where they have to work fairly independently without set work routines or close day-to-day supervision. Even in settings where there is a concentration of higher degree students undertaking research in related areas, the research endeavour is characteristically individualistic and is undertaken independently. Students can find the level of independence required difficult to manage, especially in fields where there are conflicting schools of thought or where research traditions may not be so well developed. An additional challenge is that research may have to be conducted in relative isolation because of the lack of a critical mass of scholars or students in a particular area. Yet another challenge is that, in the absence of close day-to-day supervision, students have to be well organised personally in order to make consistent progress, especially since many are juggling work, study and family responsibilities.

Finally, students need to learn how to gain access to sources of empirical data. Students may need assistance from administrators or executives in large organisations; they may need introductions to school principals or institutional data management personnel; they may need access to existing data sets; or they may need guidance from government bureaucracies about the implementation of large-scale public surveys. Increasingly, legal requirements constrain the collection of institutional data, and there are associated requirements such as those of informed consent. Supervisors widely reported that students in education fields were often naive about the costs and avenues for accessing data, and training in this area was regarded as an additional supervisory responsibility supporting an essential aspect of the higher degree experience.

Effective supervisory strategies

Education supervisors reported a wide range of strategies considered to be effective for enabling students to meet the requirements for success in completing a higher degree. The strategies are grouped and summarised in this section.

Assess skills and capacities early in candidature

Supervisors described how they provided a range of training opportunities in response to their students' needs, consistent with other studies (for example, Acker, Black and Hill 1994, p. 57). Supervisors also described a primary responsibility, given the level of diversity in fields of education, as being the early assessment of relevant skills and capacities. This process took a variety of forms. One supervisor characterised supervision in the early stages as follows:

> ... it's a definite difficulty with students ... often they don't come into [my] areas with a grounding from the undergraduate degree and what they have is a really strong interest in education generally ... So they don't really know where to start or much about the literature, if anything, and so in the first instance I point them to articles and establish what methods they are familiar with.

Another reported:

> It's really important to orient them towards certain articles and start them off so that they know that there is a focus. But I also make them find out for themselves what they are looking for, because there are different schools of thought, different research threads they've got to identify.

Another supervisor commented about early candidature:

> That's when I would step in and help a student to develop a background, maybe learn a new technique, read special books, write to somebody, meet a few people. You know, gradually to get some knowledge of an area.

The emphasis in the early stage of candidature was upon identifying the skills and capacities the student would need to complete the research envisaged. These skills and capacities ranged from a knowledge of theoretical and empirical developments to methodological, analytic and technical expertise, to identifying and understanding divergent schools of thought.

An issue for supervisors was that, owing to the diversity of research interests in a school or department, there were limited opportunities for short courses and group-based skills development. Consequently, individual supervisors frequently had to take responsibility for providing essential tuition: 'I might give them a particular reading from a methodology book, or the text from one of the [methodology] units, or things of that nature, and get them working on that'. Other supervisors reported taking some of the responsibility while at the same time encouraging students to learn from socialising opportunities within the department or school, or by taking short courses: 'I actually have to run little classes and teach people how to do things, and then graduate students can teach the new graduate students'.

Make expectations explicit

Experienced supervisors consistently emphasised the importance of making expectations about the role and responsibilities of both the student and the supervisor explicit at the beginning of candidature. A widespread practice concerned the provision of printed departmental guidelines, some of which were extremely comprehensive and addressed topics that included the resources available to students, the research interests of staff, responsibilities of students and supervisors, the department's thesis requirements and the university's regulations for candidature. Some supervisors considered, however, that printed guidelines could not adequately convey the roles or responsibilities of individual supervisors or students. Areas of responsibility which they preferred to discuss directly with their students included: avenues available for financial support, sources of technical and analytic support, the level of assistance which would be provided with the writing up of the research, ownership of data sets, ownership of intellectual property, the role of the supervisor in enforcing deadlines, and the role of the supervisor in providing scholarly contacts for the student, especially in ensuring well-informed advice and feedback on the theoretical, methodological and empirical aspects of the research.

In some cases, supervisors were committed to negotiating contracts with their students which made expectations, requirements and commitments during candidature explicit and clear. This reportedly was important because supervisors perceived the nature and extent of their responsibilities differently. One supervisor reported:

> There are things that I would actively want to see developed in a dissertation, concerning the critical, intellectual focus and cut. I would take responsibility for the approach being intellectually worthy and appropriate to the discipline.

In contrast, another supervisor reported:

> My view is that a student sets their own pace. You don't write a thesis for them. You can set ground rules such as 'I'd like to see you every two weeks', 'I wish to see a certain progress', 'you've got so many years to complete this in', and 'this is what the final thesis will be like'. But past that the student is very much on their own. I don't take a hands-on approach.

Another supervisor commented:

> I take fairly much a leading role in the beginning, but as time goes by, they will gradually cut loose ... I find I've got to push really hard before I've got students to the point where they're aware of the kinds of things they have to do, even with the literature search.

While establishing a contract of responsibilities was seen mainly as a means of clarifying expectations during candidature, contracts also made explicit the obligations which both supervisors and students often tacitly came to expect:

> ... there are situations where [students and supervisors] don't actually meet their institutional and professional obligations ... it really does come down then to quite difficult and indefinable matters of personal temperament and compatibility, which shouldn't come into it.

Establishing a contract of responsibilities could also clarify inexplicit and difficult-to-define aspects of the supervisory relationship, such as the level of independence expected at different stages of candidature and the level of input the supervisor might make to assisting the student to develop academic networks in the field of study. None of these would be covered by institutional requirements. Supervisors were agreed about the need to clarify expectations about the role and responsibilities of the student and the supervisor early in candidature. A small number went further, arguing that the processes of clarification need to be documented as a way of making explicit understandings that are otherwise tacit and open to interpretation.

Assist students to develop and maintain focus

Supervisors reported their strategies both for ensuring that students made steady progress and for checking on the disciplinary acceptability of the work in progress. Breaking up the research project into coherent but manageable sections was a widely reported strategy for assisting students to make progress. One supervisor reported: 'Well, I have them work out a table of contents as soon as the topic is decided. It might change as we go through, but it keeps them on track and we can set deadlines to it'. Another stated: 'I like to work with a time-frame. If you break the whole project up into do-able pieces, then the student isn't so threatened by the enormity of the task. And they can focus properly on one thing at a time'.

Supervisors generally agreed that once a thesis proposal was approved, some kind of scheduling was necessary to keep the momentum going. Some supervisors liked to set definite deadlines for completion of the literature survey, the data collection and analysis, and the writing up of the thesis. Depending upon the kind of research, some supervisors separated the data collection and analysis stages from the writing-up stage, while others did not. It is noteworthy that few supervisors in education encouraged students to write up their research in strict chronological order. Because the range of methodologies employed varied widely, with many students using designs which relied upon data collection and interpretation taking place simultaneously, and with some students making use of combined methodologies, writing up the research frequently was done most logically while data analysis was underway. One doctoral student in higher education described her supervisor's approach:

It was a nightmare. I never finished my literature chapter! Then I got a new supervisor who was very experienced. He just told me to forget the literature; I was wasting my time. He told me to write up the data chapters first, and then develop the literature according to what I had. And that's worked well for me.

An important theme concerned the benefits of being well organised for supervisory meetings and of keeping proper written records about the nature of discussions in them and the progress made between them. Records of supervisory discussions were seen to provide an ongoing map of progress as students developed their knowledge of the key theoretical developments in the field, and also to provide a concrete platform for possible directions to be debated and weighed up.

Supervisors reported using the notes as a springboard for suggestions about possible scholars who might be contacted, about potential contributions to conferences, about looking up new technical or analytic developments, and about related or very new research. Good organisation and keeping records of what was decided reportedly helped students to keep on track, or at least, to be clear about where they had taken a different course between supervisory meetings. Records of supervisory discussions were widely seen by supervisors as being a good basis for discussion about the focus of their students' work. Some supervisors recommended keeping a signed record of each supervisory meeting: 'It's really important to make things a bit formal. Then the students know they have to agree to complete certain tasks between meetings. And it keeps me on my toes, too. I can't be a week late with commenting on a draft'. In fields of education, where students typically have to juggle work and family responsibilities with higher degree study, supervisors reported losing contact with students from time to time: 'My memory just isn't good enough to remember what they are up to if I don't see them for a while. I have to have things written down'.

A majority of supervisors reported that they did not take responsibility for their students' progress, which they viewed as being their students' responsibility. A highly valued practice in this regard was to require students to keep progress logs. Some supervisors required students to keep logs of their developing literature bases, of their data collection and analysis, and of issues and concerns in relation to the development of conceptual and analytical frameworks. Others required only a reading log in the early stages of candidature. Others encouraged or required students to develop research diaries or journals that were used as the basis for discussion in supervisory meetings.

Other strategies for ensuring student progress were not concerned with particular practices, but instead were expressed as an attitude towards timing and focus which tacitly enforced certain goals. An experienced supervisor reported:

> I am always bringing the student back to 'why you're doing this?', 'how does it relate to the research question?', 'do we want to refine the research question again?', always coming back to what is likely to be appropriate or acceptable, but also to whether what we're doing is likely to be significant or acceptable.

Supervisors in education differed in their expectations about the pace at which students would resolve research topics and embark on the process of collecting data and developing a literature review, though their objectives were obviously made clear to students:

> Well, I would be getting worried if my [doctoral] students didn't have the topic worked out and a plan for the data collection after six months. But in that time, they would have had to submit a detailed research proposal and I would expect the literature, or most of it, anyway, to be reviewed, and I would have commented on that quite a few times along the way. And then

we would have worked out the methodology and made sure of any techniques or packages that had to be learned along the way. That sort of thing. You know, interview schedules sorted out, the survey designed and ethics approval done.

Another was more emphatic:

They really have to get it all worked out within three months or so. They've got a lot of work in resolving things, so the topic might change, but there's a lot of reading and preliminary work and the topic has to be resolved.

An interesting comment in this context made by one supervisor was:

In the old days, we might let a student work things around for quite a lot of the year. You hear all these stories! But I like to keep pushing the original research question. So even though it might change a lot, it is still something quite concrete that the student is working on, and usually there isn't too much wastage.

Ensure productive supervisory meetings

While wide variations are reported by supervisors in the frequency of supervisory meetings, their descriptions were fairly consistent when identifying the nature of meetings. Most supervisors used them as a means of checking progress and ensuring ongoing commitment to the completion of the higher degree research with the focus changing as the student progressed through the degree (see also Acker, Black and Hill 1994, p. 63). Describing variations in their frequency, one supervisor reported:

I like to see them once a fortnight, but I think that depends on where they are at in their work. If they are producing written work, we discuss it and they are going to need four weeks in between to piece it together.

Requiring students to provide written evidence of progress made between meetings was stressed by some supervisors. One commented:

... the most effective thing is if they've given you some written work ... where they actually put things down on paper ... And what you're basically doing is making some helpful suggestions on future research, giving them references ... generally just being supportive and trying to keep up the momentum. I think that's why regular contact is important.

Another explained:

Others simply refused to accept students who wanted to pursue topics not directly related to their own research interests:

> I refuse to take on students ... who are not ... in one of my two fields ... The pressure has been there on many instances ... I would feel I have to be on top of the literature and the principles of professional development and so on, and ... I would have to trust the students to do that for themselves. I wouldn't take the chance.

The relatively recent evolution of newer interdisciplinary areas for higher degree research in education has meant, however, that more supervisors have had to work jointly to provide appropriate supervision for students.

Because of the eclecticism and diversity of research in the various fields of education, many supervisors reported that they could not always confidently advise students on all aspects of proposed investigations. One of the strategies reported for overcoming the problem of students needing advice in a range of areas pertaining to a particular topic was to establish a postgraduate committee to review research proposals and receive work-in-progress reports:

> The supervisor and the student will work together in our school to draw up a proposal in writing that goes to the postgraduate committee seminar. It would [cover] the background, the problems, the sorts of questions, the literature that might be relevant or the way the research might be carried out, or the kind of analysis to be undertaken and so on. And [the students] would get a range of advice on that. It isn't always consistent, but you get a good picture of the state of play and the politics surrounding it, that's for sure.

Another supervisor reported a departmental strategy for supplementing supervision which was well received by supervisors and students:

> Our centre members will meet and arrange ... a higher degree day when the students present their programs. They are given constructive criticism and they are either ratified or sent back to do other work in developing the research, or it's just amended and sent on with more constructive criticism.

Assist students with thesis writing

Most of the supervisors interviewed expressed concern at the amount of work involved in assisting students to write well, largely because their students had not mastered discipline-specific conventions of writing at the level of the higher degree. One supervisor spoke for many when he commented:

> My first resort will be to tell the student what's bad about it. My second
> resort will be to go through it with a blue pencil and edit it. My third is to
> write the first section or the first two sections in a style that is appropriate,
> and then I'll say 'go away and follow this style for the rest of it .

This supervisor spoke for many when he expressed the frustration felt when students could not quite crack the code for thesis-writing in their fields. The supervisor in this case hoped that, by learning from example, the student would learn the style and the techniques, and might eventually be able to correct the suggestions written in by the supervisor. An especially important strategy reported by some supervisors was to clarify early in candidature the nature and extent of assistance with writing that would be provided later on. Some supervisors showed examples of comments on chapter drafts from successful theses to new students.

How discipline-specific writing conventions are assimilated and mastered is not yet well understood (Bazerman 1981, Becher 1987b), though the role of the supervisor and of broader socialisation processes in the discipline clearly play an important part (Parry 1997). What is clear at present is that supervisors largely expect students to learn conventions that are passed on by tacit means within the field. One said:

> I would always direct students to some theses in the library, and I would
> discuss the style in some articles. I also refer them to [a general writing
> manual]. I'll make comments on their work, and some small corrections,
> but I set limits to that.

Because supervisors may not be well versed in the linguistic principles and social traditions underpinning the conventions for writing in the field, it is worth examining models of good thesis writing with students and attempting to explicate some of the conventions and traditions of writing in the field. Recent research (Parry 1998) strongly suggests that the principal areas for discussion and explication with students concern the structure of argument, the conventions for citation and acknowledgment and the ways in which universally accepted knowledge in the field is expressed. Regarding structure, for example, there are field-specific norms for the structure of a thesis as well as for the development of argument through internal logic and the linking of ideas in paragraphs. In interpretive fields a 'narrative technique' may be employed, whereas in positivist fields the reporting of information using the 'topic and new' information technique is more usual. Typical conventions and traditions for reporting new knowledge need to be identified and discussed where possible. Each field of education has its own etiquette and conventions for citing previous authors and for forging new arguments from existing views in the literature. Appropriate as well as inappropriate techniques may well need to be discussed openly with students. Additionally, within each field of education, there is a body of universally known and accepted knowledge which does not have to be explained to members of the field. Terms such as 'Marxism', the 'signifier' and the 'signified' are simple examples of this

Orientations to Higher Degree Supervision: A Study of Supervisors and Students in Education

Robin Burns
La Trobe University

Rolene Lamm
La Trobe University

Ramon Lewis
La Trobe University

Research into the processes and experiences involved in supervision of postgraduate students is meagre. Issues canvassed include supervisor accountability to students (Chapman 1974, Welsh 1978) and the identification of student problems (Moses 1984, 1985, Powles 1989, Simpson 1970), and there is a small literature on student and supervisor issues (Bargar & Mayo-Chamberlain 1983, Candy 1988, SERC 1983). The notion of 'disciplinary cultures' has been invoked to examine the diversity of approaches both to specialised knowledge (Becher 1989, Parry 1997), and Parry and Hayden (1994) have looked at aspects of supervision in a variety of disciplines.

The research reported here is based on education, which is characterised by students who are mature professionals, mainly studying part-time. The field is further marked by a disparate range of discipline backgrounds, research experiences, and intellectual traditions amongst both staff and graduate students. Such multidisciplinarity, as well as the professional base, can present problems for students, and student-staff relations in the development of the research agenda (Parry, Atkinson & Delamont 1994).

The present research charts both student and supervisor expectations and experiences of higher degree work in education, to see if there are common elements of concern and of practice which could be the basis for improvement of the process of higher degree supervision. There were three research phases: the first part took place within a project which looked at the higher degree experience in three professional fields: social work, health sciences (non-medical) and education. The main aim was to find out how higher degree students and their supervisors conceptualise and experience the process of doing a higher degree and their respective roles in that. In the second phase education students and supervisors were interviewed. The third phase canvassed those who had recently graduated with a higher degree in Education, in order to see how successful graduates viewed their higher degree studies. Data from these phases will be presented, which will allow a comparison of current and completed students, as well as supervisors.

Research design and method

A questionnaire was used to identify the characteristics of the graduate population, their rationale for further study and a self-evaluation of their studies in terms of their coping, pressures and satisfaction. The survey was developed and trialled by researchers from three professional areas at the university. It was adapted for use with the graduates. Follow-up semi-structured interviews were conducted individually with a sample of students, both current and completed, and with supervisors, in order to elucidate the perspectives and experiences of each in the student-supervisor interaction.

The first phase involved sending the questionnaire to all students (N=370) enrolled in Masters and Doctoral programs in education in first semester, 1993. There were 314 replies, a response rate of 85% which indicates the high interest in the investigation. In the third phase, those students who had completed in the previous 5 years (N=140) were mailed a questionnaire in semester 2, 1994, and 104 returned them, a response rate of 74% which is again high and indicative of continued interest in their experience.

Coursework students (MEd and EdD) were not included in the second interview phase. This enables more ready comparison with the experiences of students in other fields where research higher degrees are the norm, and where most of the research on supervision has been undertaken. In order to identify both 'best practice' and more problematic aspects of supervision, as seen from the students' perspective, those who indicated they were 'satisfied' or 'very satisfied' with their current higher degree studies constituted one group, and those who were 'not so satisfied' or 'not at all satisfied', another. Degree, gender and age were also incorporated into the sampling frame. Eight students were interviewed in each of the groups, present and completed candidature.

Fourteen staff were interviewed, approximately one-third of the staff in 1993 and 1993-4 who undertook research supervision. The supervisors of the sixteen students were included though two later withdrew. Staff were included from different research areas within the School, all of whom supervised at least 10 research students. The gender proportions were close to that of the tenured staff

(3:7, F:M respectively). The findings were offered for discussion at postgraduate workshops in the School, and at a staff seminar.

The student experience

(i) *Who are the students?* A demographic profile of the students is found in Table 1. The students in both groups are very similar. They are mature aged, with considerable professional and life experience at the start of their higher degree work. Most entered via a postgraduate bachelors degree or diploma rather than the honours degree that is more usual in non-professional disciplines. The students have come from increasingly diverse professional fields and employment experiences, while the staff are almost all from teaching, which may impact on student-supervisor satisfaction.

Table 1: Demographic Profile of Higher Degree Students

	Current students	Completed students
No. and % of respondents	314 (85%)	104 (74%)
Percentage female	68%	68%
Average age	40	43
% doing coursework degree	62%	42%
% doing research degree	38%	58% (PhD:60%; MEd/MA: 40%)
% part-time	83%	84%
% on scholarship or grant / leave from employment	10%/16%	-
% employed full-time	63%	-
% grads employed full-time	-	78% (15% P/T)
Average work experience	15 years	19 years
% with honours degree	14%	12%
Employment sector	58% teaching, 9.5% tertiary educ. 5% nursing	50% teaching 23.5% tertiary educ. 2% nursing

The higher degree students in the Graduate School of Education have grounds to view themselves as competent professionals with heavily committed work lives. Their age and life stage suggest that they have substantial competing demands of work, family and other commitments. The issue of the older professional is itself complex in terms of how the student views her or himself as a competent professional on the one hand, and as a naive student on the other. Such awkwardness in self perception can mean that students may be embarrassed to request help from the supervisor because there is a strong sense that they should know such things. This tendency was highlighted in the interviews, and was particularly evident with students who are also members of university staff. A second factor affecting the complexity of the older student relationship with a supervisor is navigating the change from the clearer teacher-student relationship of their undergraduate days to the present more unstructured staff-student relationships. Assumptions are made about the relationship but may not be articulated between student and supervisor. The optimal relationship would seem to be one of collegiality, while recognising students' need for support and affirmation.

(ii)   *Why do a higher degree?* The rationale for postgraduate enrolment in education seems to be intrinsic, although some students expect career advancement with the additional degree. The primary reasons provided by respondents, both current and completed, for their candidature were the anticipated intellectual stimulation and interest in the research topic, enhanced career prospects, and the expected personal satisfaction.

(iii)   *How prepared do students feel?* Given that few of the students have undertaken the traditional university route to a higher degree, the first degree with honours, they could be expected to feel unsure of some aspects of undertaking a higher degree. While there was some ambiguity about interpretation of the responses to the question, only 12% of the current students, and 9% of the completed ones, considered they were 'not so well prepared' or 'not at all well prepared', the fact of successful completion probably contributing to the smaller percentage feeling this way in the second group.

(iv) *How satisfied are students with their candidature?* Students were asked to report on the extent to which they feel satisfied with their studies. The language used in the response options for this item may lead to different interpretations. However, as indicated in Table 2, the results appear to reflect a reasonable level of satisfaction. Not surprisingly, the successful students were more satisfied than the current ones.

Table 2: Level of satisfaction with higher degree candidature

Very satisfied	Fairly satisfied	Not so satisfied	Not at all satisfied
32% (59%)*	51% (38%)	13% (3%)	4% (0)

* the figures in brackets are the results for the completed students' responses

(v) *How pressured do students feel?* The questionnaire asked students to indicate the degree of pressure they were experiencing or had experienced with their studies, acknowledging different potential sources of pressure. Table 3 reflects substantial levels of perceived pressure.

Table 3: Pressure experienced with higher degree candidature

Very much adversely pressured	Somewhat pressured	Not so pressured	No pressure reported
23% (21%)*	51% (51%)	17%	9%

* the figures in brackets are the results for the completed students' responses

A significant source of pressure was balancing the competing demands of home, job and study. The complexity of the material being dealt with was seen as a moderate source of pressure. Neither finances nor difficulties with supervision was considered an important source of pressure. The relief of finishing hardly affected the perception of pressures experienced during candidature.

(vi) *What predicts satisfaction?* Each of the variables was correlated with students' reported level of satisfaction. Of the 13 measures available, seven correlated significantly with being satisfied ($p<.01$). Table 4 records the significant correlates of satisfaction and the respective correlation coefficient for each.

The major correlates of satisfaction were effective staff contact, motivation, level of support from work and feeling prepared. Being a teacher also correlated significantly with satisfaction. Despite the substantial levels of pressure reported by candidates, which is primarily associated with balancing the competing demands of home and university, the levels of pressure experienced were not ($p<.05$)

producing environment' working so independently; another noted this independence as a reason for choosing the particular supervisor. And most received at least some written feedback from their supervisor(s), though as discussed below, this was not always considered helpful or even adequate, and long delays in returning work were also noted adversely.

None felt that they were too dependent on their supervisors, one noting that her supervisor needed 'to learn to let go'. Few said that they received input from other staff or students at the university. For those on campus, moral support from others was considered important, and the overseas student had organised a regular seminar with fellow students from their country to check cultural interpretations. Students felt they needed more encouragement to participate in things on campus, and although several favourably mentioned general briefings about postgraduate work, most complained about lack of information about procedures and facilities. They felt that supervisors should take the initiative to tell them things they ought to know.

A number commented that their supervisor was committed to their research topic, but lacked detailed knowledge, especially knowledge of their professional field and experience. Given the large range of professions from which the students come, this is hardly surprising. It would appear that a number of professionals are finding it convenient and congenial to undertake a higher degree in education, but there are negative consequences of this in terms of matching their experience and interests with appropriate staff expertise. Only one, an academic, mentioned that he would 'have to get over my embarrassment' in order to ask for advice, and to admit that he 'actually need[s] a supervisor'.

(ii) *Successful candidates' perspectives.* These people were able to identify both positive and negative features, unclouded by the immediacy of a particular event associated with identifiable sentiments, as happened with some of the current students. The inherent anxiety in higher degree work was also over. They were able to evaluate their degree experience in the light of their career, professional life, personal development, interest and fulfilment, with the disadvantage from the current research perspective that the salience of some of the negative or difficult experiences had faded.

The comments on the positive features of higher degree study fell into three broad areas - those for whom the experience was one of induction into an academic culture, those whose professional status and confidence increased, and those where the personal gains were most notable. The academic gains included maturing as a critical reader; further:

> What I've got out of it is really the satisfaction of feeling on top of the field and contributing to the literature.

> It was about moving into a research culture and really having the satisfaction of knowing something very well in a way that a lot of people don't in the area. Being in a way an expert, that's what I like, I just like that feeling.

For those where professional gains were uppermost, comments focussed on the extra status that having a higher credential gave. A sense of greater job security was also mentioned.

More common were comments on personal satisfaction: at meeting the challenge, gaining personal confidence, and personal fulfilment:

I think I got a lot more out of the PhD than I had imagined.

I was taken seriously, it was a chance to reinvent myself in a different environment.

The nature of the supervisory relationship was mentioned as a source of satisfaction, e.g. for the critical discussions that took place between them.

Supervisor strengths and helpful behaviours were considered. Academic and personal aspects again featured in the comments. Students respected the experience and knowledge that supervisors had, their rigorous critique, their reputation as active researchers, and their communication skills, both oral and written. They also appreciated the inter-personal relationship: 'He was always very sincere and open in our relationship', said one; another noted 'He was a mentor - I respected him'. Patience, helpful direction and even the fact that 'He was there and he was consistent' counted with students. Practical help in tackling problems, positive feedback and encouragement were highlighted amongst the helpful behaviours of supervisors.

The successful students were articulate about the role of student-supervisor interaction: 'The personal contact is really crucial'. It appeared that a positive, relaxed, collegial relationship often eased the student acceptance of criticism and negative feedback. However the factor that was seen as helpful to a number, the informality and growing friendship, could also lead to awkwardness when students simultaneously wanted the supervisor to step into the disciplinary role.

The graduates recognised the need for students to take responsibility for their own progress, to have a sense of perseverance, to take criticism in a positive way rather than being too sensitive and feeling vulnerable, and generally stressed the need for independence, though one stated that the ideal was to be given unobtrusive direction. Given their concerns about support, discussed below, these judgements seem to be influenced by reflection after completion, rather than how they felt at the time. As another stated:

The ideal is a supervisor who supports what you do, is familiar with your topic, can advise you to read certain things ... can assist when you're stuck in a trough, not push too hard, be aware of your limitations ...

(iii) *Supervisor perspectives.* Staff in general believed themselves to be competent, very adequate supervisors, albeit some admitted to small areas of their practice that were 'less than perfect'! They generally considered that they had good relationships with their students, as defined in their terms.

All said that their major priority was to ensure that students 'get through'; several also mentioned induction into scholarly culture. They considered that supervision is 'part of the job', but that they also got satisfaction from it, though one stridently dissented. One regarded it as an ideological commitment, seeing his students as his potential change agents in schools. All were vague about the School expectations regarding supervision, where there appeared to be positive regard for supervisors with large numbers of candidates. However there is no direct form of acknowledgment for additional effort or lack thereof, and there was an enormous disparity between supervisors regarding supervisory and other teaching loads. None thought the teaching profession had any expectations from higher degree work.

The supervisors all said that supervision was probably deleterious for their own careers; each had at least 12 postgraduate students, and they spent their time reading other people's writing, not doing their own. Supervision required reading drafts and other work to discuss with students, which was often not sufficiently relevant to their own areas of interest. However, they all said they gained job satisfaction from supervising, except when students 'can't write', or appear to have low motivation. They varied on how much practical help they thought they should give. They also varied in the patterns of interaction with their students and their concept of supervision.

All but one expressed some reservations about the preparedness of some students to undertake higher degree work: poor writing skills were most often noted, but lack of methodological preparation, lack of substantive content knowledge, lack of theoretical knowledge and lack of conceptual clarity were also mentioned. They acknowledged that some of these were barriers to successful student completion, and added low motivation, part-time student status, and work and family obligations, as further barriers. One mentioned that poor supervision also contributed in some cases, and one said lack of support for higher degree work by the teaching profession was a problem.

Staff expectations differed regarding the nature of meetings, who should initiate, how often they should be conducted, whether or not written work should be presented and if so, whether or not in advance. There were differences in whether or not they would notice a lack of student contact, and if so, what they would do about that. None had published jointly with their students, and only one had encouraged students to attend and give papers at relevant professional conferences. Joint publications were seen to be unacceptable by peers in the School. It is believed that students at that academic level should produce their work alone, part of the strong sense that students should have total ownership over their material, including topic choice.

Supervisors differed in how they handled concerns about non-intellectual aspects of their students' difficulties, though most were prepared to listen but reluctant to encourage them to talk about personal issues. All considered that they would deal openly with any interpersonal conflict that arose with a student, and that the issue of having both to support a student and criticise the work did not lead to any major conflict of interest, even if they had to tell a student his or her progress was unsatisfactory. However, the latter did appear to be problematic for at least some supervisors who felt extremely reluctant to confront a student about poor progress or perceived lack of ability, choosing rather to 'string them along'.

Two sources of induction into the nature of supervision were discussed by supervisors: formal guidelines and their own experience as a student and on the task. Supervisors indicated an awareness of University regulations and School guidelines about supervision though not all were familiar with the latter. Some used the School manual with their students initially, to establish mutual roles and responsibilities. There is no procedure in the School for briefing supervisors or discussing supervision.

Those who enjoyed positive, worthwhile graduate experiences have a model whereby they appear to measure their own behaviours. Those who did not value their own experiences know what to avoid but have to formulate their own practices. Many supervisors simply learn on the job. Some joint supervision experiences helped beginning supervisors, as did general discussion with more senior staff.

Major student concerns

The most commonly articulated student issues were collegiality, isolation and loneliness, the need for support and validation, and for structure and direction. These themes came up strongly for both current and completed students.

(i) *Collegiality*. Students considered it preferable and pleasant when they felt a sense of collegiality with their supervisor. Students who reported this friendly collaborative situation, mentioned a sense of partnership and mutual respect, a facility of interchange of ideas and reading materials, and they were generally much happier with the nature of their studies and their relationship with their supervisor(s). Similarly supervisors who experienced this collegial relationship reported a greater degree of satisfaction with the supervisory task. To some extent this kind of collegiality is more likely to occur when student and supervisor share a similar area of interest. As one graduate put it, 'My supervisor made me feel as though I was a co-worker, that we were two equals in a sense, involved in an academic challenge, and academic endeavour ...'.

Students appreciated supervisors who made themselves available to meet or contact when deemed necessary. Meetings after hours, perhaps at home, a cafe or place of student's work, to facilitate requirements of part-time students and to provide less formality, were positively regarded by students. The creation of an environment most conducive to an easy exchange of ideas seems to be highly advisable.

(ii) *Isolation*. This is perceived as a serious problem by the students in this sample. In most interviews it was mentioned by students and also by supervisors. Acker et al. (1994) refer to this as detachment, which they found to be particularly prevalent among education students. In the present study, students pointed out that there is a difficulty which appears to be specific to education owing to the lack of commonality and the varied academic backgrounds, so that it is hard to find shared common knowledge.

Thesis writing in the humanities and social sciences is a solitary experience. Students work long hours alone and frequently have little contact with anyone other than their supervisor(s). There is both personal psychological isolation and loneliness that they experience, and intellectual loneliness through not having adequate contact even with other research students. Some supervisors attempt to combat this problem in a number of ways. Examples include introducing their graduate students to one another, arranging social functions or seminars so that students can enjoy an intellectual environment in general, and encouraging them to present papers at in-house seminars and conferences. Group meetings with the supervisor are only possible for supervisors who have large numbers of students working on related topics. Supervisors who facilitate introductions to others are valued. School conferences for higher degree candidates have been attended by fewer than ten per cent of students, mostly full-time ones. Those who have attended rate them as positive, helpful experiences.

Facilitating the interchange of ideas was deemed by many students and supervisors to be important in the systematic induction of students into the graduate world of ideas. Students who also happen to be members of staff reported how helpful their university milieu is in providing an academic and intellectual environment which is constantly positively reinforcing.

(iii) *Validation and support.* Students need validation and support for their ideas and for their work. They would like encouragement for doing something worthwhile. Students express a need for recognition of their ideas, they want to know that their supervisor acknowledges their efforts and places value on their work. Many students remarked that written work was returned with numerous errors highlighted, but where any aspect was good or acceptable, no mention was made. A common refrain was:

I need someone to tell me it is worth it.

Candidates want to know and be reassured periodically that their project has value. Most comments seemed to be predominantly negative which students experienced as not getting anything 'right'. Supervisors feel that they need to correct and refine, but they *assume* that no comment means that the work is satisfactory. They may even say that orally, but the effect of multiple corrections, especially in red ink, is negative, as one student exclaimed:

Supervisors need to tread softly, and use a green pen!

Closely related to the notion of validation and support for ideas is the issue of support for the individual.

In the middle darkness you need support. I got very depressed.

Students generally felt a need for more pastoral care, more nurturing. Even students who were essentially satisfied with their supervision reported comments such as:

I missed some mothering really!

There was a lack of the 'feminine'.

I needed more moral support; just basic caring.

Students wanted to be seen as people and they perceive the supervisory task as more encompassing than simply dealing with a thesis. Students believed they themselves are being supervised. These issues came through with the successful students, too. They were able to put the experience in a broader perspective, some recognising that:

How can one supervisor meet all your needs?

On the whole, they particularly valued supervisors who recognised the different stages of higher degree work, especially the intellectually 'horrible', 'stuck' times. One commented that 'the rest of my life was for me to sort out'. Others indicated that they wanted more encouragement, and appreciation was expressed for those supervisors who provided both practical and emotional assistance during the low periods. Variations in response indicated individual difference in need, as well as variation in the extent to which they believe they can impose upon the supervisor for help. This in turn may relate to the nature of the supervisory interactions, especially where supervisors were perceived to signal a lack of time and energy and students felt intimidated about approaching them. On the other hand, one of those who considered the encouragement had been generous, said:

Sometimes when you're working alone you go through stages where you feel flat, and you think why am I doing it, does anybody really care, well they seemed to show a great deal of genuine interest and that was always a source of inspiration for me.

Equally, one was acutely aware of a lack of both interest and support. On the whole, the completed students felt adequately supported, though some would have liked more recognition:

I think when you're doing a research thesis, you're so alone that you really look for someone to ... I don't know, gear you up or pat you on the back or something when you're feeling down.

There was a sense that they wanted someone 'above and beyond the sort of written guidelines of what a supervisor must do in order to be a really good supervisor'.

(iv) *Structure and direction.* A number of students who enjoy and feel capable of independent work and are self motivated and directed still feel the need for structure and direction from the supervisor and frequently remarked that what was provided was inadequate. In particular, a number felt that they wanted more guidance at the beginning of their work, and that part of the problem of not knowing how the process of allocation to supervisors worked was also not knowing where to start and what was expected of them especially regarding the production of written work and initiating meetings. Some also looked for suggested readings in the early stages, and several spoke almost resentfully of having to go to professional colleagues for contacts in their research area. One overseas student set up a small, regular support group of fellow countrymen from other fields to check interpretations of some of his material. Students also felt that supervisors should take the initiative to tell them administrative matters, including information about facilities and prerogatives (most of these are in the higher degree manual). Too much independence was seen as anxiety provoking. They considered it important to achieve a balance between dependence and independence.

Completed students showed most concern about evaluation of and assistance with writing. While several commented positively on the supervisor's ability to provide affirmation of the work and 'a sense of encouragement and direction', and others acknowledged the need for that encouragement but considered that it was 'not their job to be a counsellor', the need for positive 'genuine interest' seemed to be satisfactory. They needed validation of their ideas and their output:

It's pretty hard when you don't know whether you've reached the standard.

They frequently expressed a need for support with the development of writing skills and more guidance in this area. Some felt their supervisors simply assumed they had the skills and experience.

(v)   *Communication.* It seemed that there was a very definite additional issue though not articulated overtly, namely communication between supervisor and student. The interviews revealed such situations as a supervisor who put in inordinate amounts of time with detailed editing of written work paying the finest attention to language and spelling, while a student's lack of appreciation was evident in return. The student noted that the supervisor had only been given a first draft and she would have liked general overall comments relating to content and not to English expression which she would have got round to editing at a later date. This is clearly a case where articulating the issue would have been helpful. If a plea could be made on behalf of supervisors at this stage, it would involve concern at the multiple drafts which are now being produced thanks to word processors. The status of a particular draft, and what sort of feedback the student would like at each stage, would be helpful: if one finds errors of content and expression, one has no basis on which to assume that they will automatically be corrected by the student.

The converse was seen too - students who would have liked more clarification of errors and expectations of written work and actually felt that they had been given inadequate guidelines for improving their work. Supervisors in those instances often felt they had provided clear indications of problems and deficiencies.

It would appear to be helpful to both parties if a contract were formalised at the beginning of supervision whereby both supervisor and student can feel comfortable with a mutual arrangement setting out in unambiguous terms personal goals, expectations, roles and responsibilities as well as time lines. At this early time the supervisor would need to disclose a personal style of supervising and critiquing.

Communication about roles and expectations also includes the supervisory relationship. It may need to be reassessed or re-negotiated at various times during supervision, not just at the start (Candy 1988). The importance of clarifying all these and other pertinent issues regularly to avert misunderstanding and time waste is crucial. Clearly the responsibility for adequate communication is both on the supervisor and the student. This is delineated in the literature by Phillips and Pugh (1987).

Main concerns of supervisors

These revolved around questions of time, matching of student and supervisor, and the examination process.

(i) *Time*. There was a generalised feeling of time pressure. For some the time constraints related to the number of students being supervised as well as a heavy lecture load. Others considered that they agreed to supervise too many students and the sheer quantity of reading and marking material was overwhelming. Frustration was evidenced in some cases at not being able to spend enough time reading around their students' main fields. Time was mainly problematic in terms of reading and commenting on drafts rather than finding the time to meet with students, although the latter caused some difficulty in relation with part-time students who were only available after hours. In general supervisors were sympathetic to these practical requirements and were adaptable in terms of time and place of meeting. A number of staff lamented the time needed for editing, especially when it related to poor quality of writing. In general this was felt to be a greater concern with MEd coursework theses than with PhDs. The role of editing was not uniformly adopted as part of the supervisory task. The academic pressure for publication seemed to some to be in conflict with the supervisory role. Those who extensively edited sometimes felt they were helping to write the thesis they would have liked to have written themselves.

Discussion of findings with colleagues and students

Preliminary results of this study were presented to a group of education staff and at two postgraduate student conferences in the School. Issues raised included student complaints about the nature of their contact with supervisors and the School in general, staff expertise in the area of a student's topic, dual supervision, and better matching of supervisor and supervisee. Contact proved difficult to discuss among staff and the issue was deflected onto practices and workloads in the School in general. The creation of a School 'culture' was seen to be hampered by the different disciplinary, theoretical and methodological backgrounds and interests of staff. There was also a perception of lack of student interest. Other difficulties canvassed were the ways of allocating responsibility and initiative within the supervisory relationship, and the different expectations arising out of the fact that students are mature professionals.

Students seemed reluctant to say much in the group setting, even when facilitated by a fellow student. However, the discussions point to the reality of different perceptions and expectations. How to find the right supervisor, and the possibilities of changing ones were more readily discussed.

Conclusions

The study highlighted what had been found in earlier research, especially by Moses (1984, 1985), that personality, professional and organisational factors can be distinguished, and that any or all of them can be problematic for students.

The most important finding is that student satisfaction is most associated with the nature of student contact with the supervisor(s). The level of supervisor interest in a student's topic, and the degree of supervisor commitment to the individual and to the research, is perceived by many students as very important to their higher degree experience. And as the completed students indicated, collegial contact in particular was significant and satisfying. Even acute personal issues were experienced as less of a pressure when relationships with supervisors were satisfactory. These results point to validation as a person as a significant aspect of student satisfaction with the higher degree process.

Supervisor and student perspectives are clearly different. Even if supervisors tend to smooth over difficulties, and students to focus on them, students consider it difficult to find a supervisor, and are unclear about the protocol for establishing and maintaining a satisfactory relationship with that person. A number felt that too much onus was placed on the student in the whole process, even in finding their way administratively.

There was some agreement between staff and students in this study on recommendations for improvement. This revolved around two issues: how students establish a topic and find appropriate supervisors, and how to negotiate a supervisory contract, with an emphasis on better communication, clearer delineation of responsibilities, and the possible need for change at different stages of the higher degree process. Both finding an appropriate supervisor, and developing a mutually suitable process, could be enhanced by greater compatibility between supervisor and candidate. The three orientations delineated here suggest possibilities for better staff-student matching, or at least for student-supervisor negotiation, in order to reduced frustration and unproductive use of time and energy. Greater knowledge of the process of supervision, and the characteristics, orientations and issues that supervisors and students bring to it at different stages, can surely promote more satisfactory experience and outcomes, whether those are framed in terms of quality control, cost-effectiveness or personal fulfilment.

References

Acker, S., Black, E. & Hill, T. 1994, 'Research students and their supervisors in Education and Psychology', in R. G. Burgess (ed.), *Postgraduate Education and Training in the Social Sciences: Processes and Products*, London & Bristol Penn., Jessica Kingsley, pp. 53-74.

Bargar, R. R. & Mayo-Chamberlain, J. 1983, 'Adviser and advisee issues in doctoral education', *Journal of Higher Education*, 45 (4), pp. 407-432.

Becher, T. 1989, *Academic Tribes and Territories: Intellectual Enquiry and the Cultures of the Disciplines*, Milton Keynes, Open University Press.

Candy, P. C. 1988, A dozen dilemmas: Tensions implicit in supervising graduate research students, Paper delivered at the annual conference, Higher Education Research and Development Society of Australasia (HERDSA), University of Melbourne (mimeo).

Chapman, P. 1974, 'On academics and student supervision', *ANZ Journal of Sociology*, 10 (2), pp. 147-149.

Elton, L. & Pope, M. 1989, 'Research supervision: The value of collegiality', *Cambridge Journal of Education*, 19 (3), pp. 267-276.

Moses, I. 1984, *Supervision of Higher Degree Students - Problem Areas and Possible Solutions*, St Lucia, Queensland, Tertiary Education Institute, University of Queensland.

Moses, I. 1985, *Supervising Postgraduates*, Kensington NSW, HERDSA Green Guide No.3.

Parry, O., Atkinson, P. & Delamont, S. 1994, 'Disciplinary identities and doctoral work', in R. G. Burgess (ed.), *Postgraduate Education and Training in the Social Sciences: Processes and Products*, London & Bristol Penn., Jessica Kingsley, pp. 34-52.

Parry, S. 1997, Doctoral Study in its Disciplinary Context, PhD Thesis, La Trobe University.

Parry, S. & Hayden, M. 1994, '*Supervising Higher Degree Research Students: An Investigation of Practices Across a Range of Academic Departments*, Canberra, Australian Government Publishing Service.

not only idiosyncratic attributes but are embedded in relationships of class, gender, ethnicity, age and similar social divisions, as well as claims to power and knowledge that are negotiated and re-negotiated throughout the relationship. Importantly, supervision takes place in an institutional setting and usually within a particular discipline. The institution itself can also be located within broader frames of research policy, state funding, national culture and so forth. The shadow nature of these contextual considerations in the literature is probably due both to the paucity of sociological attention to the supervision process and to the difficulty of actually studying such factors, especially in combination.

In this chapter I argue that we have been underestimating the complexity and ambiguity of supervisory relationships. My sources will be somewhat eclectic: the research literature; my own experience as a university teacher working in graduate departments of education since 1972 in Britain and Canada; a research project on supervision in education and psychology carried out with colleagues in England in 1989-1991; and a taped focus group discussion with a group of eight graduate students and ex-students and two faculty members in education in a Canadian university in 1997. These sources are mostly from departments and faculties of education, although the supervision research project also studied psychology departments, and it should be noted that generalizations might well need to be modified for other fields. A limitation is that there is insufficient space to develop a discussion of the impact of contexts such as the departmental culture in which the relationship takes place and the wider features such as the policies on research degrees and academic work that shape what is done in the institution, although I will allude to such matters briefly.

Negotiating supervision

There are some explicit and implicit models for the supervisor-supervisee relationship contained in the literature. Some are 'pair' models like parent and child, expert and novice, guru and disciple (Brown & Atkins 1988). More helpful are arguments that flesh out what the responsibilities of each individual might be. To oversimplify a bit, the supervisor's role could be characterized as falling into two main conceptions: 1) manager or director; 2) facilitator. In the first conception, the supervisor's main task is to keep the student moving along the stages of dissertation research by telling him/her what to do; in the second, the role is less overt and the supervisor tries to respond more to what the student wants and 'needs'. (There is probably a third point on a continuum at which the supervisor is almost entirely laissez-faire, there only in spirit.) The two main conceptions match respectively what could be seen as a technical-rational view of the process (it can be predicted, understood, controlled, improved) and a negotiated-order view (what happens is emergent and depends on interpretations and strategic responses). This argument is developed further in Acker, Hill & Black (1994a).

The research project on higher degree supervision in education and psychology in Britain provided many insights on the supervisor-student relationship. This study, conducted by Sandra Acker, Tim Hill, and Edie Black, was a funded, two-year project which involved qualitative interviews conducted in 1990 and 1991, producing usable transcripts from 67 students, 56 supervisors and 14 'others' such as heads of department or administrators. Three departments in each discipline participated. Results of this research suggested that supervisors and students could be regarded as having preferences for particular styles of working, although supervisors stressed that they made adjustments according to situational factors and what they thought students wanted or needed. Students seemed to develop one of several orientations which we called individualistic, academic, taking charge, supported, and 'buffeted about' (Acker, Transken, Hill & Black 1994b). Although most published advice to students follows the technical-rational line, the negotiated order model is a better description of much that happens in practice.

What is it that is being negotiated? We can consider, for example, negotiations over procedural issues such as how often supervisors and students will meet, what the typical content of a meeting is, how much work the student will be expected to do in what time frame and to what standard; how much direction the supervisor should provide and how much further input such as reading and editing chapters s/he should give. Like many situations in everyday life, what I am calling negotiation is usually done quietly and not often called to conscious attention or reflection, although there are cases (such as when students and supervisors come from different cultures) where the players may be advised to bring expectations into the open and make limits very explicit (Aspland & O'Donoghue 1994, Channell 1990, p. 80). Examples of different expectations, negotiated more or less well, can be found in the British research. Here is a case where a student wanted the supervisor to be more focused in their meetings:

> Sometimes they [meetings] haven't worked because I've got eight things to talk about and we talk about the first one and the hour has gone and he's got another student waiting outside. So I sometimes say, 'Before you say anything, Bill, there are eight things I was hoping to cover in this session'. So in a sense I've been more formal than he has, and that's something I've learned to do. (Male student)

In contrast to 'Bill', (all names are pseudonyms), this supervisor tries to control everything that happens:

> That's the way I handle all my meetings: what's our agenda, what are we trying to achieve, what's our time line? And I would say, 'Okay, I would like to get this on the agenda' and then we would go through whatever it was and then I would say at the end something like, 'Are we okay now?' or I might say, 'Look I think we're pressed for time, I think we ought to wrap this up. Given what we said at the outset is there anything we need

to get done before you leave? Would you please make a note of what we've agreed and send me a copy'. (Male supervisor)

Another student is clearly unhappy with the meetings with her supervisor but can't work out how to change the situation:

> There's a feeling that I need to perhaps have some set time where I could say, you know, or she could say to me 'You have three quarters of an hour of my time' ... I'm feeling for an almost a clue for her to say, you know, 'I've had enough of you now' or 'That's the end of the session' and there isn't any. (Female student)

The negotiated order model has its shortcomings, however. Further complexities stem from the ambiguity of the relationship. Procedures for conduct of meetings seem straightforward compared to some of the other questions that arise (or lurk, unaddressed) during the process of supervision, such as how much should be expected from a supervisor or how close the relationship should be between student and supervisor. Complications also arise from the social location of the main players - in terms of their identification as 'students' or 'supervisors' and also in terms of differential resources and perspectives related to gender, class, race and other such attributes.

Differential locations

The purpose of guidelines, advice manuals, and other technical-rational solutions is to reduce ambiguity, and they are welcome to the extent they contribute to this outcome. Nevertheless, even the wording in such guidelines can leave matters open to interpretation, as Barbara Grant (1996) has shown for one university. Students are constructed as powerless and compliant (arrangements are made for them) but as ultimately responsible for their own fate (where problems arise, they are to take the initiative in discussing them with the supervisor, and where an effective relationship is not forthcoming, to discuss the matter 'promptly' with the Head of Department (HOD) or Dean. If they try to work through problems in the relationship first, they may not then be 'prompt' enough, not to mention the assumption that the HOD will be an independent thinker in the matter. The document includes the phrase 'the responsibilities of the student include...' which leaves open the possibility that the student responsibilities extend into uncharted territory. It is likely that because students are unsure what is open to negotiation, and which of their desires are appropriate to voice, dissatisfaction can linger, even reaching the extreme Kathleen Heinrich (1995) calls 'silent betrayal'.

Schneider (1987) reminds us that the parties are not equally powerful in the university social order:

> [T]he female graduate student is dependent on professors for admissions, grades, recommendations, committee memberships, and financial and research opportunities. This dependency is greater for graduate students than it is for undergraduates; careers are often determined by the association and contact with one or very few faculty members ... graduate students may not be able to drop courses or change committee members without major repercussions, especially after years of data collection ... the option of leaving when partially through a graduate program is bureaucratically, academically, and economically problematic. (pp. 48-49).

Although Schneider's analysis is about women students, much of it applies to all graduate students. Grant and Graham (1994) refer to 'unequal underpinnings' of the supervisory relationship, given that the dissertation is 'likely to be the student's major work focus while it is one small aspect of the supervisor's current workload' (p. 165). Being in such a structurally disadvantaged position may lead to a certain amount of resentment, perhaps covered up by impression management or 'fronting' (McGregor 1996, Olesen & Whittaker 1968). Faculty members, especially those who do not exercise power in the university hierarchy and whose work lives may seem to be spiralling out of their control, find it bewildering to be regarded as such powerful figures and wonder why students seem at one moment obsequious and at another resentful. The implicit model here is one of class conflict or domination, with the supervisor exercising 'sovereign power' (Grant and Graham 1994, p. 167). Like Grant and Graham, I think this model contains important insights but is also problematic - the supervisors themselves are embedded in work relations that do not necessarily empower them, and many of the students themselves have an expectation of 'upward mobility' into an academic position in time. Also, the students and supervisors are in most respects united in their wish for a successful outcome. Where the model is helpful is to remind us that different parties are differently located in the structures that make up graduate education, and that their perceptions, and indeed their interests-at-hand (Pollard 1985), will inevitably be correspondingly different.

An example will help develop the notion of different locations. It concerns finding a supervisor and is drawn from the Canadian focus group. In the institution where this discussion was taped, the norm is for students to do a year or more of course work, and then have to persuade a faculty member to act as dissertation supervisor. MA students will need an additional faculty member and doctoral students two others to make up the thesis committee. For wholly or partly part-time students, it may be several years before this moment arrives. Students are assigned to advisors on arrival, but these advisors are not expected to supervise (although in some departments there is a suggestion that, indeed, that person may become the supervisor), a situation which caused some confusion in a few cases. Some, usually full-time, students in the focus group had been given the advice that course selection would be important in terms of sizing up and establishing rapport with potential supervisors; others did not know this or figure it out until it was too late. Several then had the task of trawling through faculty members in their own and

scepticism and suspicion. In contrast, supervisors in my experience regularly trade anecdotes about students' demands knowing no bounds and about what they believe are their own self-sacrificing, altruistic, unrewarded responses (see also Acker & Feuerverger 1996, 1997, Park 1996). There seems no easy negotiated solution to such differently situated ways of seeing.

A student is a student is ...

While acknowledging the importance of locating perspectives in 'supervisor' and 'student' frames, we must move beyond seeing all supervisors, or all students, as interchangeable. This conceptualization is a major flaw in the supervision literature. Diversity among students can stem from idiosyncratic characteristics or ways of interpreting their situation (Acker et al. 1994b). It can also stem from what I will call 'registration status' - essentially whether they are full or part-time students. It can stem from the myriad of other features of people's lives related to the operation of gender, race, class, age and other attributes.

   Below I expand first on the importance of registration status, mainly as it emerged in the British research project but with some support from the Canadian focus group discussion. Then I look at some of the complications that emerge when we take into account relations of gender and other positions and resources. In the process, we will see that 'power' no longer seems simply vested in the supervisor - a more flexible approach is called for.

   In the British research, what stood out in shaping student perspectives, rather to our surprise, was whether the student was registered full time or part time, and if the latter, on what basis (Hill, Acker & Black 1994). Part-time students might be either 'detached' - usually working full time outside the university and whose contacts apart from the supervisor were minimal - or 'semi-detached' - in the university working full time, usually on a faculty member's research project, and simultaneously registered as a part-time student. Of course the variables were not independent; for example, full-time students were more likely than the others to be young, in psychology rather than education, and to have funding for their studies. But there was far from a perfect correspondence between registration status and other characteristics. The importance of registration status was that it stood as a representation of where the student was vis-a-vis the academic world. It strongly shaped expectations for supervision and how students coped with indifferent supervision if they encountered it. Full-time and part-time 'semi-detached' students were more likely to voice dissatisfaction than detached part-time students, even though the latter got little by way of material benefits from the university (they were rarely given desks, lockers, or access to other facilities; they knew few other students or faculty members). Detached students usually had other sources of self-esteem and support, however, and they were not so dependent on supervisors and the graduate student experience for validation. Some who were making little progress blamed themselves or stressed how little the degree mattered as they were so enjoying their research experience. Full-time students complained more about not getting sufficient supervisor time and they often had financial worries. Semi-detached students were characterized by their marginality in both the student world and the faculty one. Their progress on dissertations was impeded by their work responsibilities; yet they were not accepted as equals to faculty members and many expressed discontent with their ambiguous situations.

I had not expected similar issues to arise in the Canadian focus group. Nevertheless, there were parallels. Some students in the focus group talked about how difficult it was for them to find a supervisor or know the ropes when they lived at a distance or could not 'be around' for other reasons. One student commented:

> When I look back there was a real difficulty, and I think it's common to students that do their work here on a part-time basis, and that is that there isn't a relationship building among students and among faculty. So you don't know faculty that well and they don't know you that well in terms of developing bonds and knowing where your different interests and faculty interests are.

Another student explained that because she lived in another province, she took courses for two consecutive summers before she was able to do her residence year. She stressed how difficult it was to meet people and 'it's really just by luck that you happen to encounter a course where people are instrumental in furthering you along your way'. She gave more detail:

> The problem when you come as a summer student is that often the advisor that you have been assigned isn't there in the summer. That was the case with me. I came for two summers, but my advisor was never present in the summer. And he doesn't answer e-mails, so when I e-mailed him from [her home] I never got any response. So I just said well, maybe he's not interested. I found out subsequently that he just is not a good e-mailer, he doesn't like to read it. Anyway, once I did meet him in the fall after that second summer of work, he was very helpful.

A third student added to the discussion:

> I think we undervalue the [effects of] being outside, like living in [suburb], for other people too who are outside of [city where the university is], you can't underestimate the value of just being on the premises, being seen, being able to be on these committees and whatever else, and getting to know people not just through courses but through a number of things.

Again, it would seem that negotiation is not enough.

Gender, intimacy and power

If we return to our identification of ambiguity as characterizing the student-supervisor relationship, we note that a particularly difficult question is how close the personal relationship between the student and the supervisor should be. In general, both the faculty and the students in the British research said they preferred a professional relationship, with some distance, but in practice some relationships were close and some were almost non-existent. Some staff tried consciously to keep students at a distance, employing strategies such as not giving them their home telephone numbers and not asking them about their personal lives. One male supervisor told us: 'I don't actually see it as my function to be their support and soulmate and someone who will get them through the next five years of general living. I don't think that's my job', while another male supervisor went to the opposite extreme: 'They've all got my home telephone number. They come and visit me ... some stay with me ... I get very close with them'.

It is difficult for students (or supervisors) to gauge the appropriate degree of intimacy. One woman student had hoped for a closer relationship with her female supervisor, saying sadly, 'There was a time when we were quite close, but then she really clouted me away'. Another woman student expressed similar hopes:

> [In the meeting] we talked about Melanie [the supervisor] because she's been going through a bad patch, so I think, but that felt good because it felt like somehow I was getting a bit closer to her, that she was opening up a little bit to me, and that was like a kind of little self-disclosure that made her seem ... a bit more human as it were. I felt much better.

Another female student had a number of problems with her male supervisor, who seemed to be indifferent, distracted, and inaccessible. The alternative to indifference seemed to be harassment:

> Fiona [another student] is a bit different because she, I think they get on very well because she's superbly beautiful and she's very charming and I think when she arrived Simon [the supervisor] was very interested in her, and so he got her a research assistantship and she's designed a program and he's been working very closely with her. I think she has different problems with him in that he will be calling her up at all times of the day and even when she's at home, and wanting her to work, you know, all hours of the day and night.

Several commentators point to the difficulty managing the degree of potential intimacy in the supervisor-student relationship, especially when there is a hint or more of sexuality. Colin Evans, in a study of university foreign language departments in Britain, speculates on the parameters of the gender imbalances common in universities. In modern language departments, the students are mostly young women and the faculty middle aged men, but 'the sexual elements of this relation are almost never acknowledged ... The whole gender question is an emotional and intellectual no-go area' (pp. 134-5). Participants retreat, he suggests, into a father-daughter role relationship. Calls to incorporate 'caring' more centrally into teaching (Noddings 1988), easily extended to supervision, require some attention to 'the delicate balance between too much and too little loving care' (Booth 1994, p. 36). In a small study of women doctoral students in education with male supervisors, Heinrich (1991) found that 'androgynous' rather than traditionally masculine or traditionally feminine approaches to advising were more productive. When the relationship was collegial, sexual attraction could be transformed into a caring friendship.

Hulbert (1994) also tries to identify problems and possibilities that are likely to surface with each potential gender combination. She believes that male-male relationships will be task and achievement oriented. Female-female pairs will focus both on achievement and nurturance; there is an early empathy and identification and the student will want to know how the advisor has dealt with role and personal issues in her own life; also the student may need help with confidence raising. The danger, Hulbert believes, is that the nurturing side may outweigh the academic one. Male supervision of females is a common situation and these relationships tend to have a distant quality, perhaps in order to avoid the dangers of intimacy. Hulbert is more hesitant to characterise female supervisors of males, as this combination is relatively rare.

There were a few cases of female supervisors and male students in the British data. One was particularly interesting as it seemed to embody the potential difficulties and contradictions inherent in this pairing. The participants seemed unsure of whether they should be acting as man and woman or supervisor and student, as these alternatives (if followed stereotypically) would lead to different results in dominance terms. Similar reversals have been reported by Walkerdine (1981) and Gallop (1995). As Gallop points out, it is all very well for a feminist teacher to give up her authority in the interests of her female students coming to voice, but confronted with a male student she will want to take it back again. In our case, the male psychology student, John, was unhappy that another prospective supervisor had left the university, and Catherine, the substitute, was clearly second best in his eyes. His interview was full of contradictions. He praised Catherine's intelligence and gave her credit for solving major problems with his work. Then he compared her to the supervisor who got away, and said Catherine didn't really come up to that sort of standard: 'It's hard to describe, you know, but in times of real anger, I've sort of like, really felt down and you think oh god, she's just so bloody stupid'. He also had other criticisms of her: she lacks humour and 'is a very nervous character ... smoking cigarettes, drinking cans of coke, god knows how much ... there's always a can of coke there, she must get through more caffeine, god knows'.

John sees Catherine virtually every day: 'I never let it go for more than, say, a couple of days really. I mean I always see her, even socially, you know, go for a drink or something'. He says he's been away for weekends with various people in the department and she is included in the group. He discusses 'a weekend by the sea, and we hired a car and I drove up with Catherine, and we just had a weekend there ... we used to go for a drink occasionally ... never just me and her, it was usually a group of people, say, from the department ... there's certainly no distance socially. I mean, I feel completely relaxed with her'. Nevertheless, John asserts that Catherine is too busy and not available enough: 'Like I say, she's a workaholic, and like a lot of the time I have to go through and explain things to her which I've already explained and like she's forgotten about or at least forgotten the gist of it'. He even complains about her reluctance to come to his office:

> I'm on this floor, I'm on the third floor and she's on the second ... And you know, it's a case of, I've only seen her in my office twice or something like that. And it would be nice, once in a while, if she just popped in and just said 'how's it going, what are you doing?'

In trying to make sense of this supervisory relationship, the gender dynamics are hard to ignore. Age may also play a part. John is 27, while Catherine is about six years older. Had she been still older and a more commanding figure in her field, some of the ambiguity in the relationship might have been reduced. As it is, John does not seem quite sure whether Catherine should be regarded as an authority figure, a girlfriend, a friend, or a mother. Discussion of women supervisors tend to suggest that relationships of daughters (students or junior faculty) and mothers (supervisors or senior faculty) will be tense and unresolved, much like the two quotations earlier from women students who wanted closer relationships with their women supervisors. Heinrich (1995), in an article on female doctoral students and supervisors, finds some cases where advisors and advisees managed a warm collegiality, a sharing of power. But others turned into 'iron maidens' supervising their 'handmaidens' or took the stance 'power disowned', whereby the supervisor, by not using her power, betrayed the student; or the student, by keeping silent and not making her needs known, betrayed herself. Both Heinrich (1995) and Keller & Moglen (1987) in their stories of competition among women in the academy make extensive use of maternal analogies such as inadequate mothers and ungrateful daughters. Heinrich (1995) refers to 'powerful psychological forces' (p. 447) and while these may well be at play, I would argue that it is more promising to regard gender (like power) as a resource that can be inserted into situations with not entirely predictable consequences. We need to pay more attention to the situations themselves, with their contradictory norms and negotiations around power, gender, reciprocity, and intimacy. We could ask, for example, what were the circumstances under which John and Catherine's uneasy relationship could continue without some clarification or intervention from more senior faculty? If (some) women advisors are overly concerned with the personal, what social expectations bring that about and what leads to change? In Canadian interviews conducted for another project, women faculty frequently complain that they are virtually forced into nurturing (female) students as the men avoid it and the students expect it (Acker &

Feuerverger 1996). If they stop, they will be presumably labelled iron maidens and criticized for being unwomanly!

Beyond gender

In fact, the concentration on gender in some of these studies may have served to distract attention from some pressing questions about where students and supervisors are located on other dimensions and in other ways. The literature on graduate student supervision has been remiss in not looking at race, class, and age, for example, and almost as unlikely to notice whether students are fully engaged in their study or are part of what Baird (1990) calls 'the forgotten minority', studying part-time (the detached and semi-detached students in the British supervision research). In writings by black feminists, there are certainly indications that they survived graduate school despite, rather than because of, the response they found there (Bannerji 1991, Carty 1991, hooks 1988). A study of a large US Midwestern university concluded that minority women had fewer professional socialization experiences than majority women; that is, they were less likely to report being mentored, holding research and teaching assistantships, co-authoring papers with faculty or being introduced to wider academic networks by the faculty (Turner & Thompson 1993).

An American study of graduate students in engineering, history and economics, found that students from the United States, with their more fluent English, were more likely than international students to be teaching assistants, which gave them helpful experience for the future as well as office space (Friedman 1987). In engineering departments, research associateships were more likely to go to the students from abroad, but advantages were not always apparent because they worked in groups where the professors did not give much individual assistance. American students had more outside sources of support and were better integrated with student peers. Friedman's study as well as Channell's (1990) research in Britain found that faculty saw overseas students as highly problematic, mainly because their greater needs and expectations for close supervision resulted in extra work for the supervisor. Similar sentiments were expressed in our British supervision project interviews. Aspland & O'Donoghue's (1994) interviews with five overseas students in Australia found that these students were disappointed and disillusioned about what they saw as inadequate supervision. Overseas students paid much higher fees than did home students (also the case in other countries) and some of these students believed they were not getting 'value for money'.

Age and class feature less often in the literature. Because many of the students interviewed in the British study were 'older' - for example former or current school teachers studying for a higher degree - they were aware that academic careers might not be open to them, even when they desired them. It was curious to find individuals in their forties refer to themselves as 'geriatric' or 'oldsters' (Acker et al. 1994b). Most, although not all, of the interviewees who made such references

National and funding body policies on research and higher education will also be influential. For example, in the late 1980s, in an effort to increase the proportion of students with fellowships that actually finished doctorates, the British Economic and Social Research Council instituted a policy of sanctioning departments (and at one time whole universities) which had submission rates below a certain threshold by not allowing fellowship holders to enrol in those institutions. Even though only a minority of students held such fellowships, the policy had a major impact on social science departments, with practices and procedures that had been unchanged or unnoticed for years receiving discussion and review. Submission rates rose in many institutions. Research into the graduate student experience (such as our project; see also Becher, Henkel & Kogan 1994, Burgess 1994) was also stimulated.

The relationship between student and supervisor is also affected by the current state of academic work, and the academic labour market, again in a particular national context. In many countries, academic work has become intensified and a combination of demographic changes and expansions and contractions of opportunity for higher education have produced a situation where today's doctoral students will need to fight for a place in academe, if that is their goal. The student now has to publish and gain teaching experience while still in graduate school to stand a chance of gaining an academic job (Hulbert 1994). So the student needs more help from the supervisor, just at the time when the supervisor is experiencing work intensification and rising expectations for academic productivity.

Departmental cultures are likely to shape student-supervisor relationships. Departmental cultures reflect both institutional cultures and disciplinary ones (Becher 1989, Evans 1988) as well as developing along their own more idiosyncratic lines over time. They are also the main sites in which particular practices are developed and policies are mediated. Thus, for example, departments have procedures for admissions, for following up student progress, for coordinating student activities, for student participation in departmental committees, and so forth. In theory at least, the difficulties experienced by students in the focus group in finding supervisors might be mitigated by a different department practice. Also relevant is the ratio of students to supervisors in a department: where each supervisor has many students, the ability of that supervisor to provide a nurturing, mentoring environment for all of those students may be correspondingly limited. In the British research, departments, even within the same discipline, varied considerably in their practices and policies, the typical mix of students, and the prevailing ethos or climate of the department. In four cases where we had collected supervisors' descriptions of ethos systematically, the departments could be described in one-word phrases: for one psychology department, 'friendly', for the other, 'thrusting'; for one education department, 'changing', for the other, 'individualistic'. The relationship between the supervisory process and its departmental context certainly deserves more attention than I can give it here, or than it has been given in the past.

Conclusion

One theme in this chapter has been that the student experience is far from homogenous, depending as it does on what the student brings with her or him, the particular match with a supervisor, the discipline, the institution, research policy and the academic labour market, and the culture of a department. Attempts to systematize the process have increased in recent years and are welcome. Yet there is a sense in which the relationship at the core of supervision, including aspects of both power and pedagogy, cannot be made entirely predictable or homogenized. Students and supervisors should understand that they may operate from very different perspectives that are rooted in their structural location within the academy. Moreover, these perspectives are further influenced, although by no means in simple fashion, by attributes such as gender and class origin. Further influences such as those of departmental culture are not well understood, either. The supervisory process is certainly complex, subtle, pivotal, crucial, responsible and important - but it remains elusive, mysterious and ambiguous as well.

References

Acker, S. & Feuerverger, G. 1996, 'Doing good and feeling bad: The work of women university teachers', *Cambridge Journal of Education,* 26 (3), pp. 401-422.

Acker, S. & Feuerverger, G. 1997, 'Enough is never enough: Women's work in academe', in C. Marshall (ed.), *Feminist Critical Policy Analysis*, Vol. 2, London, Falmer Press. pp. 120-140.

Acker, S., Hill, T., & Black, E. 1994a, 'Thesis supervision in the social sciences: Managed or negotiated?', *Higher Education*, 28, pp. 483-98.

Acker, S., Transken, S., Hill, T., & Black, E. 1994b, 'Research students in education and psychology: Diversity and empowerment', *International Studies in Sociology of Education*, 4 (2), pp. 229-251.

Aspland, T. & O'Donoghue, T. 1994, 'Quality in supervising overseas students?', in O. Zuber-Skeritt & Y. Ryan, (eds), *Quality in Postgraduate Education*, London, Kogan Page, pp. 59-76.

Baird, L. 1990, 'The melancholy of anatomy: The personal and professional development of graduate and professional school students', in J. C. Smart, (ed.), *Higher Education: Handbook of Theory and Research*, Vol. 6, New York, Agathon Press, pp. 361-392.

Bannerji, H. 1991, 'But who speaks for us? Experience and agency in conventional feminist paradigms' in H. Bannerji, L. Carty, K. Dehli, S. Heald, & K. McKenna, *Unsettling Relations*, Toronto, Women's Press, pp. 67-107.

Bannerji, H. 1995, 'Re: turning the gaze', in S. Richer & L. Weir, (eds), *Beyond Political Correctness*, Toronto, University of Toronto Press, pp. 220-236.

Becher, T. 1989, *Academic Tribes and Territories: Intellectual Enquiry and the Culture of Disciplines*, Milton Keynes, Open University Press.

Becher, T., Henkel, M. & Kogan, M. 1994, *Graduate Education in Britain*, London, Jessica Kingsley.

Booth, W. 1994, 'Beyond knowledge and inquiry to love', or 'Who mentors the mentors?', *Academe*, 80 (6), pp. 29-36.

Brown, G. & Atkins, M. 1988, *Effective Teaching in Higher Education*, London, Methuen.

Bowen, W. G. & Rudenstine, N. 1992, *In Pursuit of the PhD*, Princeton, Princeton University Press.

Burgess, R. (ed.) 1994, *Postgraduate Education and Training in the Social Sciences: Processes and Products*, London, Jessica Kingsley.

Carpenter, M. 1995, 'Female grotesques in academe: Ageism, antifeminism, and feminists on the faculty', in V. Clark, S. Nelson Garner, M. Higonnet, & K. Katrak (eds), *Antifeminism in the Academy*, New York, Routledge, pp.141-165.

Carty, L. 1991, 'Black women in academia: A statement from the periphery', in H. Bannerji, L. Carty, K. Dehli, S. Heald, & K. McKenna, *Unsettling Relations*, Toronto, Women's Press, pp. 13-44.

Channell, J. 1990, 'The student-tutor relationship', in M. Kinnell (ed.), *The Learning Experiences of Overseas Students,* Milton Keynes, Open University Press, pp. 63-81.

Clark, B. R. (ed.) 1993, *The Research Foundations of Graduate Education*, Berkeley, University of California Press.

Clark, B. R. 1995, *Places of Inquiry: Research and Advanced Education in Modern Universities*, Berkeley, University of California Press.

Connell, R. W. 1985, 'How To Supervise a PhD', *Vestes*, (2), pp. 38-41.

Conrad, L. & Phillips, E. 1995, 'From isolation to collaboration: A positive change for postgraduate women?' *Higher Education*, 30 (3), pp. 313-322.

Council of Graduate Schools 1991, *The Role and Nature of the Doctoral Dissertation,* Washington, D.C., CGS.

Evans, C. 1988, *Language People*, Milton Keynes, Open University Press.

Friedman, N. 1987, *Mentors and Supervisors*, IIE Research Report Number 14, New York, Institute for International Education.

Gallop, J. 1995, 'The teacher's breasts', in J. Gallop, (ed.), *Pedagogy: The Question of Impersonation*, Bloomington, Indiana University Press, pp. 79-89.

Grant, B. 1996, Unreasonable practices: Reading a code for supervision against the grain, Unpublished paper, Centre for Professional Development, University of Auckland.

Grant, B. & Graham, A. 1994, ' "Guidelines for discussion": A tool for managing postgraduate supervision', in O. Zuber-Skeritt & Y. Ryan, (eds), *Quality in Postgraduate Education*, London, Kogan Page, pp. 165-177.

Heinrich, K. 1991, 'Loving Partnerships: Dealing with sexual attraction and power in doctoral advisement relationships', *Journal of Higher Education,* 62, pp. 514-538.

Heinrich, K. 1995, 'Doctoral advisement relationships between women', *Journal of Higher Education,* 66, pp. 447-469.

Hill, T., Acker, S., & Black, E. 1994, 'Research students and their supervisors in education and psychology', in R. Burgess (ed.), *Postgraduate Education and Training in the Social Sciences: Processes and Products,* London, Jessica Kingsley, pp. 53-72.

Hockey, J. 1991, 'The social science PhD: A literature review', *Studies in Higher Education,* 16, pp. 319-332.

hooks, b. 1988, *Talking Back,* Toronto, Between the Lines.

Hulbert, K. D. 1994, 'Gender patterns in faculty-student mentoring relationships', in S. Deats & L. Lenker (eds), *Gender and Academe: Feminist Pedagogy and Politics*, Lanham Md, Rowman & Littlefield, pp. 247-263.

Karamcheti, I. 1995, 'Caliban in the classroom', in J. Gallop (ed.), *Pedagogy: The Question of Impersonation*, Bloomington, Indiana University Press, pp. 138-146.

Keller, E.F. & Moglen, H. 1987, 'Competition: A problem for academic women', in V. Miner & H. Longino, (eds), *Competition: A Feminist Taboo?*, New York, The Feminist Press at the City University of New York, pp. 21-37.

McGregor, A. 1996, The professional socialization of nursing students: Failure as a social construction, Unpublished EdD Dissertation, University of Toronto.

Moses, I. 1985, *Supervising Postgraduates, Higher Education Research and Development Society of Australasia Green Guide No. 3.* Sydney, HERSDA.

Ng, R. 1993, ' "A woman out of control" : Deconstructing sexism and racism in the university', *Canadian Journal of Education,* 18 (3), pp. 189-205.

Noddings, N. 1988, 'An ethic of care and its implications for instructional arrangements', *American Journal of Education*, 96 (2), pp. 215-230.

Olesen, V. & Whittaker, E. 1968, *The Silent Dialogue: A Study in the Social Psychology of Professional Socialization*, San Francisco, Jossey-Bass.

Park, S. 1996, 'Research, teaching and service: Why shouldn't women's work count?', *Journal of Higher Education*, 67, pp. 47-84.

Pearson, M. 1996, 'Professionalising PhD education to enhance the quality of the student experience', *Higher Education,* 32 (3), pp. 303-320.

Phillips, E. & Pugh, D. 1987, *How To Get A PhD*, Milton Keynes, Open University Press.

Pollard, A. 1985, *The Social World of the Primary School,* London, Holt, Rinehart & Winston.

Richey, C., Gambrill, E. & Blythe, B. 1988, 'Mentor relationships among women in academe', *Affilia*, 3 (1), pp. 34-47.

Schneider, B. 1987, 'Graduate women, sexual harassment, and university policy', *Journal of Higher Education,* 58, pp. 46-65.

Smith, P. C. 1993, 'Grandma went to Smith, all right, but she went from nine to five: A memoir', in M. Tokarczyk & E. Fay (eds), *Working-class Women in the Academy,* Amherst, University of Massachusetts Press, pp. 126-139.

Tierney, W. & Bensimon, E. M. 1996, *Promotion And Tenure: Community and Socialization in Academe*, Albany, NY, SUNY Press.

Rosie argued that her supervisor did not understand because he failed to take the time to listen, and that, because she was an overseas student, 'he expected problems'. Based on this assumption, Rosie believed he used a range of avoidance strategies that effectively allowed him to talk at her, but he failed to engage in a meaningful dialogue with her. For example, he avoided any sort of in-depth meeting in preference to brief telephone conversations. In face to face dialogue, he would answer her questions with a brief response and if more information was required by Rosie he would refer her to another agency. These agencies included editing officers within the Guild, staff within the international students office or other lecturers of Chinese origin.

> I went to his office many times, and he was unwilling to give me time. You know I was waiting for him, he was on the phone 10, 15 minutes and I think it's not the way he should do this when we have made a time to meet. He's not helpful at all, he is not considering that you are [a] student from another country ... and that's very personal you know ... he is not willing to help or understand your situation. No wonder he does not understand me. He does not try.

Rosie believed that he was more comfortable communicating with her in the small postgraduate meetings that the Department organised on a monthly basis. She found the meetings 'generally useful' but argued that they were less than helpful in contributing to her personal project. 'We will talk about it later' he would often respond to Rosie's request for a one-on-one meeting, implying that she should hold her question over until the next postgraduate meeting. When she raised issues at such meetings, he would answer her indirectly by addressing the whole group and making the assumption that her problem was also a concern for the whole group. As Rosie so perceptively noted, 'most of the time this was not the case and students become irritable with me for speaking up'.

However, what was really demeaning for Rosie in this context was not simply his inability to personally address her concerns. On the rare occasion that he did address her, he would often pose questions to which 'he already knows the answer', yet would engage in a public scrutinising, seemingly to humiliate her in front of her peers.

> Once I was talking about my dissertation in this group and he asked me what is the meaning of a word that I used - like qualitative. He asked me right after I had just explained it and somebody said 'oh yes I understand that'. He went on and said 'but how come you used that word - do you really know what it means ?' I was asking myself 'why is he asking me this because he knows I know its meaning because it is in my work and he has never asked me this before?' I am very embarrassed about this because everybody is here and he asked me the meaning of the word when he knows what it means and so do the others. Does he think that because I am a foreign student that I cannot understand it?

This type of incident occurred regularly at postgraduate meetings causing Rosie to experience high anxiety levels and feelings of decreasing confidence. Further, during or following these awkward discussions, her supervisor would commonly make a number of asides to other staff members or students that would result in laughter.

> After I explain these things to him and he said OK, he turned to the other side, to the one sitting next to him and they say something and they, laugh. Maybe not at the same thing, but at the time, I think so.

In pondering the reasoning underpinning her supervisor's lack of commitment to talk and engage in dialogical supervisory relations, Rosie contended that, like many Australians that she had met, there was a lack of willingness to be accepting of her difference.

> I think it is not so easy to find somebody in Australia who is really open or treat you the same as the local people ... he is not willing to open up or try to have an effective relationship, with foreign students ... I don't think he is keen on helping students from other countries. You know he just sits ... all he will do for you is just tell. He is not giving any extra time to discuss with you. What I need is some kind of support, you know, spiritual support ... to build up your confidence in doing things.

Rosie's response to her supervisor's failure to recognise and value her presence within the relationship was contradictory in many ways. During our interviews and conversations, she expressed bitter feelings towards him and was often in a high state of anxiety and emotional instability. Yet when we discussed possible ways of dealing with his lack of recognition, and confronting what was problematic for her, she preferred to accept that 'this is how he feels about me as a foreign student'. She continued:

> Basically, I don't think you can do anything, you know just to tell him that you know that you don't like how you're being treated, you cannot say it right, you cannot do anything like this ...

and later,

> I just tell myself I've tried, that's all. So what can I do? I mean that's all I can really do. If you want to have a good relationship of course both parties have to try but if I try, you know he just ignores it, so (there's) nothing you can do ... You cannot do anything really ... I accept that's the way they do it here. So that's why I don't feel angry. I think that's the way they want to, so, of course, it up to them.

he should realise by now that I do not need to see him each week. Maybe I know more than him and do not want to see him. But he still likes to see me each week. It is like he is checking up on me all the time still.

Referring to an earlier period of her candidature Mi Ra conveyed her relationship with her supervisor in the following way:

You feel relaxed with him and even if you ask some stupid question, he won't laugh at you. He treats you like a friend and most of the time like a father to a daughter.

Issues such as the desirable distance established between student and supervisor, the place of deference in student-supervisor relationships and rules of protocol between a teacher and a learner do reflect many of the qualities of a father-daughter relationship when considering the context of learning in Asian countries. So it is not surprising that this type of relationship emerged early in the candidature. However, as the three years drew to close she felt that his image as a father had become more remote. By the end of third year she expressed the concern that she had lost respect for her supervisor who seemed to be losing interest in her work. In the late stages of her enrolment the father-daughter relationship was characterised by 'disinterest' and other feelings that 'I am unsure of how to describe'. Specifically, Mi Ra believed his disinterest was in response to her decreasing dependence on him. She was particularly offended by his lack of contact in her final year:

The first two years were just fine but this year he just keep[s] asking me why I haven't been to see him, why haven't I finished and all that and he stopped meeting me. I just don't know.

Mi Ra, like Deli, was offended by a man who proclaimed such commitment earlier on, yet, late in the project, was perceived as 'desert[ing] us when we probably need him the most'. They rationalised that it was their increased expertise in the field and the resultant lack of dependence on their respective supervisors that resulted in the changing relationship:

[That] because we know more than our supervisors they no longer want to know us like their daughters - they have forgotten us.

The continuing dilemma for both Mi Ra and Deli was whether to confront this distancing from their supervisors at the time when they most needed support for the final submission. They did not do so. It is argued here that the women experienced the ambivalence of being both daughter and scholar within a supervisory relationship that kept them repressed as daughters, while at the same time liberated them as scholars. The ambivalence of whether to resist or whether to comply was overwhelmed by a deep seated loyalty they felt to their respective father-figures; a loyalty fraught with feelings of compliance that were integral to obeying their wishes as 'good' daughters do.

The experiences described by these women and the ambivalence implicit in their 'bifurcated consciousness' as both scholar and daughter are embedded in a 'ruling elite' of supervisors whose conceptual apparatus (Smith 1987, 1990) determine a complex set of objectified, gendered and racist supervisory practices, and a generalised social consciousness that is constructed from a patriarchal standpoint. This collective have created modes of supervision that lose sight of and devalue the day to day experiences of students' work through the control and regulation of supervision from normative and paternalistic perspectives. Such regulation maintains women's silence as does the law of fathers over their daughters. This is not simply a race or gender bias within supervision but a partial and limiting hegemonic set of practices that manufacture particular supervisory relations that foster women's consent to patriarchal values and ethos.

As a result, women like Deli and Mi Ra become deeply immersed in supervisory relations in which they have little authority. They lack any proper title to patriarchal modes of supervision, positioning themselves outside that membership as subservient daughters struggling to make sense of these ambiguities. At the same time, they appear to be complicit in their silencing through consent. Consequently, Mi Ra and Deli became partners in trivialising their own subjectivity and their research. They adapted their supervisory relations to live inside a discourse as daughters within their fathers' predetermined space. The supervisory discourse was not theirs, but one that 'expresses and describes a landscape' in which they were 'alienated' and which 'preserves that alienation as integral to its practice' (Smith 1987, p. 36). They became complicit in the perpetuation of the father-daughter relationship that significantly reshaped their emerging subjectivities early in the candidature. They were initially quite comfortable within the cultural, pedagogical and material relations of supervision that were characterised by a childlike dependence on a father figure. However, it was in their final year that the rupturing of these relations occurred. It has not been identified as to when this rupturing took place exactly, but both students agree that this seems to have occurred as a result of both supervisors taking them for granted as the thesis came to its final stages. The supervisors were not prepared to support their daughters as a father should. The ambiguities that arose for both Mi Ra and Deli suggested that we needed to 'examine who produces what for whom' (Smith 1987, p. 54).

Why was it that Mi Ra and Deli chose not to overtly disrupt the undesirable supervisory relations with their father figures? Was it due to a cultural subservience that was deeply rooted in a traditional deference to authority figures such as their fathers or their supervisors? Was it that they were not prepared to reveal their inner subjectivities as daughters to their father's critical gaze? (Gal 1991). Was it that they felt so devalued as women that their status failed to empower them to speak? Was it simply that they did not have access to the cultural language necessary for critical engagement of this nature? (Tannen 1992).

that addressed certain questions that he put to her at the outset. Willie became incensed and argued:

> He requires me to study another MBA program. I do not think this is necessary but I feel that because he is my professor that I must oblige him. It is not our way to challenge the professor about these things so I must do so. Huh! But, I feel very angry deep inside me because of the expense but more than that. I know what he is talking about but he does not recognise this in me. I feel I am having my project taken away from me I feel very removed from what I am expecting to do.

As time unfolded, and with the arrival of the next semester and the same requirements being made of Willie by her supervisor, she had reached a point of extreme frustration, was experiencing increasing levels of anxiety and had requested her husband to come to Australia to care for her. She had reached a point of vulnerability that seemed impossible to address.

> This man is driving me crazy. He does not allow me to do a PhD. He is putting up a fence that is keeping me away from it. I am wasting my time here. I cannot think like a business woman anymore ... I feel like a little girl and he is my emperor but not an emperor that I respect.

The nature of the ongoing problems were threefold. Firstly Willie was being kept within her institutional place by a supervisor who claimed that she was not ready to write a PhD due to her lack of 'appropriate knowledge'. Willie argued that this was an incorrect position that he was taking. She continued to argue that her knowledge of international marketing was far greater than his. Further, she claimed that his lack of examples from the international context ratified that this assertion was correct.

> He keeps me out of things by always using Australian examples. He talks about MIM and National Mutual and other Australian companies that I do not know. When I say is this like KFC or McDonalds or Coca-Cola he says he does not think so. How can I understand him if he does not refer to the international trends and issues. It is not that Australia is bad but it is not helpful to use these examples about international marketing.

The second issue that challenged Willie was the supervisor's response to her written work. She acknowledged that her writing was 'needing a lot of work', so she approached the challenge of writing English seriously.

> I find it difficult and wasting of my time to write all of these papers that he wants. What is it giving to my PhD? Nothing. So I say to myself, well, this will help you with your writing. I know all the content. I have known it for many years even though he tells me I know nothing. So I write for many

hours. I read all of his textbooks and I go and listen to him talking. I know it all so I practise my writing. But what I am feeling sick about is that he gives me no feedback. He marks my work like a MBA student, saying your writing is weak, but that is all.

Throughout this twelve month period Willie received little constructive feedback from her supervisor. She reported that the feedback that she was receiving was posed predominantly as a series of rhetorical questions throughout her writing that in effect, contributed little to her development. Questions such as 'What does this mean?' or 'How does this influence the outcomes?' or 'Is this referenced correctly?'; and most commonly, 'What are you really saying here?', reoccur throughout his written comments. There was little evidence of strategically relevant feedback that assisted Willie in refining her writing. As a consequence she spent a great deal of time and a great deal of her own resources financing extra tuition from a range of external agencies.

I am very dissatisfied with his feedback about my writing. It offends me that he does not think I am worthy of more extensive comments that will help me improve my work. I told him I need his help. I want to learn from him, but it seem as if he does not want to give his knowledge to me. What I try to talk to him about this, it is no better. If my work is so bad, how is it that I passed the university's English test? I passed the examination in English and my English is good enough for an MBA. Is this not true?

The trauma of this dislocation from her work and from a productive supervisory relationship was further exacerbated when Willie met privately with her supervisor to engage in talk about her project and the problems that she was experiencing. This is the third factor that finally led her to withdraw from her PhD program.

I have a lot of trouble even talking to my supervisor. First of all, I have difficult in saying what I think. I am nervous because we are taught at home as students to sit quietly and do not interrupt because it is offensive. I try to talk to him only about the PhD business, but this too is not always successful. I ask the question but most of the time I do not understand his answer. Now, not like the local people, I do not ask the next question because I do not have the confidence with my supervisor to do this. If he was my client I would certainly ask the question, but I am his client and it is not my place to ask the question when I do not understand. But it is more than this. Inside I am feeling he has no confidence in me. He thinks I am not worthy of his time. I think most of the time he does not want me for a client. He wants to pass by me because I am a problem client. We do not make the right connections.

She argued further that their communication attempts were further constrained by the way in which her supervisor 'spoke too fast'.

> He speaks quick and I don't understand. I can't catch up and I think he sees this. I am writing my notes very fast and I say, 'Excuse me?' but he continues on just the same. But it makes no difference. He just keeps going ... When I want to use the tape recorder he just says, 'No it is not necessary - you must get used to Australian accents'.

Willie continually referred to the nature of this type of dialogue and content of these sorts of interactions, discursively constructed to place her outside the supervisory relations in ways that she felt he 'could not be bothered with me' or that 'he is not motivated by my project'. While she was not prepared to ascertain the reasons for this dislocation, she inferred that it was related to his lack of respect for her expertise in international marketing. Whether this lack of respect was related to his feeling threatened by her expertise or due to cultural insensitivities, we were never able to ascertain because of her sudden withdrawal from her candidature at the close of the first year.

With the support of her husband who remained in Australia for the latter half of the year, Willie decide to withdraw from her PhD program and return to her position in China. She argued that she did not have the confidence to approach the Departmental Head about her unsatisfactory situation, and that it would 'be better for everyone to leave it all behind'. While she and her husband acknowledged that it would be difficult to explain to her employing authorities the difficulties that she had faced, she felt that

> my successful past will protect me. I have done many good things for my company. This is my only failure. Deep in my heart I know it is not all my fault but they will not believe me. I will have to work very hard to overcome this shame and this terrible waste of company money. I feel sad that I will be disappointing them and I am disappointing myself. I have never failed before. It will be difficult but my husband will support me also. We just want to leave it all behind us here in Australia.

With the analysis of this situation came the realisation that the supervisor held a different orientation to supervision than Willie. The supervisor and Willie came together in a supervisory partnership from differing speaking positions, that were culturally embedded and failed to make connections within the process of supervision. No reconciliation seemed possible due to a fundamental incommensurability (Ang 1995, p. 64) that existed regarding each partner's positioning concerning the cultural relativity of knowledge, modes of supervisory interaction and aspirations for Willie's doctoral work. The marginal situatedness of Willie's experiences within supervision in this context impacted upon her reshaping identity. She experienced ongoing feelings of failure and a lack of confidence, unable to find a shared vision with her supervisor.

The ambiguities that arose as a result of Willie's supervisor's attempts to 'normalise' her thinking in the field, made her 'feel like a foreigner in her own world' (Ang 1995, p. 65) to the point that she felt it was impossible to relocate herself within a culturally and materially meaningful doctoral project. It is argued here that the ethnocentric demands of her supervisor bifurcated her supervisory world to the point that she had no place in it either conceptually or materially. The cultural disrespect that he held for her knowledge and experiences is a result of white/Western hegemonic thinking that assumes a particular cultural orientation to knowledge and learning is far more significant than any other. He displayed complete disregard for forms of knowledge that are constructed elsewhere, particularly in the East. His actions implied that if a subject such as Willie does not have, or does not 'receive' the culturally specific knowledge of the dominant group, despite her status in the global business community, she will not have the appropriate knowledge to move forward into higher degree study in Australia. Once again, we witness the assertion of power - pedagogically, culturally and materially- within supervisory relations from the 'privileged positioning' of the supervisor. In this case the normalising techniques pursued by the supervisor dislocated Willie from a relevant knowledge base by asserting that certain forms of knowledge and marketing practices (white/Western) were more culturally significant than others (Asian/Eastern). In repositioning herself within the politics of supervision, Willie internalised what was problematic as her own failing. Despite the ambiguities inherent in the relationship, Willie felt 'trivialised' and expressed deep-seated dissatisfaction with her supervisory experiences in Australia.

These stories offer insights into the feelings of powerlessness and inadequacy experienced by each of the women. Despite this, the women argued that it was not appropriate to 'speak out against' their supervisors. Supervision had been a demeaning experience for each of these women, causing her amongst other things to question her identity as a scholar. These feelings of failure perpetuated a continuing silence for some of the women at the close of their candidature (Luke 1994). This silence will no doubt be continually misread by the broader community. The supervisors, for instance, may, based on hegemonic thinking, interpret this silence as symptomatic of the subjugated status of 'Asian' students within the Western university community (Luke 1994). Such misconceptions must be addressed, for in many ways the silences reported in this study were indicative of an inner assertiveness and confidence that emerged with the closure of the candidature. Supervisors may well be unaware of the complex meanings underpinning such silences and thus may need to develop a better understanding of how silences such as these are used by students. As has become evident here, the use of silence, the experiencing of ambiguity and the invisible presence that some students experience as central to supervision , can reveal mixed messages. It is arguable that supervisors should not read these silences/ambiguities/invisible presences incorrectly as 'indexical of passivity and powerlessness in social encounters' (Luke 1994, p. 214). This simply endorses the perceptions of Asian learners as othered and gendered students who remain on the margins of supervisory relations. If supervisors are sincere in engaging in and problematising cross-cultural supervision, they must more fully examine and come to understand the voices that they so often mute within supervisory relations.

Feedback on Writing in Postgraduate Supervision: Echoes in Response - Context, Continuity and Resonance

Sally Knowles
Murdoch University

Introduction

This chapter explores what is known about the written feedback postgraduate students receive on their thesis drafts. It is surprising that such an important and routine exchange of information has received so little consideration, and yet it may be the main gauge by which both parties measure whether the supervision as a whole is successful or not. Providing feedback which combines thoroughness and sensitivity, and which is necessarily critical, analytical and evaluative, is a difficult balancing act. That gratitude for the supervisor's feedback frequently features in the acknowledgement sections of theses is perhaps an indication of the importance postgraduates place on it, and just how valuable (albeit undervalued) it is in helping student writers learn to exercise autonomous judgement in evaluating their own work (Yeatman 1995).

Given that feedback is one of the most critical components in the labour of producing a thesis, it is important to consider the specific institutionalised practices which produce it. What is/are the supervisor's role or roles? How do students make the transition to evaluating their own writing, and how are the tensions between doing independent work, yet needing to work with a supervisor resolved? How do students deal with their own subjectivities and supervisors' expectations and experiences, and what sort of inner dialogue and negotiation do they use to deal with them? Greenhalgh (1992) points out that in principle, a supervisor's 'response to a draft not only delivers a message at the semantic level but also plays out the social relationship between reader and writer, teacher and student' (p. 402). A problem, however, is that the relationship may be played out in feedback that is invasive and damaging rather than constructive and reaffirming. Grant (1996) encountered students who believed their work was excellent but 'received a less than excellent result' and when they told 'the tale of their supervision' it was 'sometimes apparent that the guidance and feedback they were given was inadequate, thoughtless, contradictory, or even punishing' (p. 10). From this it follows that issues that need to be explored in supervision include ethical considerations (such as rights and responsibilities and how these are negotiated to establish the appropriate amount and kind of assistance), and attitudes to writing development and productivity (the efficacy of the feedback and its effects on subsequent student writing).

Theorising about feedback to take account of social relationships requires an understanding of context. It is the aim of this chapter to examine 'context' and the pedagogic practices which support the process of feedback, including the formation of subjectivities imbued in such practices. In what follows, I outline some of the context-specific aspects of feedback which are a feature of thesis writing and which require explicit negotiation between both parties, especially when cross-cultural dimensions are involved.

Because of the paucity of studies on feedback in general and on postgraduate supervision in education faculties in particular, it is necessary to draw on the broader literature on thesis supervision in this article and extract those elements which do refer directly to feedback. The specific implications for education students will be discussed throughout the chapter.

The pedagogical context of feedback

Feedback provides students with 'echoes' in response to their work in progress, with important implications for their sense of being heard. Virginia Woolf wrote of 'echoes' being synonymous with 'resonance, context or continuity' (three themes that will be taken up later in the chapter). Echoes are reliant on people and places. They serve as reflections of oneself 'filtered through intelligences and feelings of others' (McNaron 1983, p. 502). All writers depend on echoes from readers to feed back critical responses to validate, support and enhance the qualities of their creative endeavours. However, due to the ambiguity in institutional discourses and the complex and idiosyncratic nature of supervision the echoes may be distorted. The central question of this chapter therefore is: how do students and supervisors negotiate textual exchanges in the production of a thesis?

Recently, universities have been urged to rethink and reevaluate postgraduate pedagogy and to regard supervision as a 'co-productive' relationship (Lee 1996) where the student and supervisor 'engage in thinking, theory and reflective doing, making their academic theories impact on practice in significant ways' (Kamler & Threadgold 1996, p. 57). How then can feedback practices be most usefully conceptualised? One way to begin is to see them as 'critical conversations' during which the student's writing is intimately scrutinised. Given that social relations play a part in such conversations, there are possibilities for miscommunication in the giving and reading of explicit advice about conventions and cultural values.

In the writing relationship between supervisors and students, supervisors are positioned as universal readers who are able to speak on behalf of all readers. In dispensing this authority, the students' writing may be treated differently over the period of candidature: it may be allowed to proceed, or be given provisional approval, or interrupted and halted and future directions negotiated. Receiving and responding to written feedback is part of the process of making a thesis text. This feedback is 'the raw material' (Torrance & Thomas 1994, p. 116), which supplements and fortifies the writing in the working draft, and enables the student to construct a more refined version. Because the process of writing is integral to the research process as a whole, feedback triggers revision and thus textual production is interwoven in a recursive process which involves drafting and revising.

According to Bargar and Duncan (1982), providing feedback is 'the most complex function the [supervisor] must perform and the most difficult function to perform well' (p. 28). It is a cause for concern, therefore, that the 'role of supervision as teaching remains profoundly ambiguous' (Green & Lee 1995, p. 43). Supervision is 'a far more private and less observed form of teaching than other classroom-based forms of teaching in which academics are engaged' (Johnston 1995, p. 18). Because most postgraduate teaching is focused on mentoring as opposed to instructing (Taylor 1995) it is seen as something 'other than teaching' and is conventionally understood by the academy more in terms of research rather than as teaching (Green & Lee 1995, p. 40). It is this understanding which Connell (1985) contends impacts significantly on the nature of postgraduate education because it perpetuates attitudes to learning and teaching which are not always conducive to good supervisory practices. Connell argues that supervision 'has to be seen as a form of teaching', raising 'questions about curriculum, method, teacher/student interaction, and educational environment' (1985, p. 38). Because the relationship in postgraduate supervision is constituted in terms of *research,* some supervisors may construe that their responsibilities are limited to assisting with their student's research needs alone.

In this latter sense, the authority of the feedback given is based on 'knowledgeability' and the supervisor's 'capacity to be properly, scientifically critical' (Salmon 1992, p. 21). However, feedback is not a neutral act of reading. The supervisor's feedback on thesis drafts is as much shaped by cultural and social values and disciplinary norms as is the writing of the thesis. Therefore, both parties must explicitly negotiate their conceptual biases and orthodoxies and recognise that feedback and the responses it elicits will reflect such belief systems, values and practices. This is not to say that 'institutional expectations [and] academic canons are homogenous or static', for as Harris (1997, p. 2) points out, they are 'games of truth' which 'are contested, changeable and indeterminate'. Supervisors can and do reflect on their experiences and change or modify their work practices, and challenge academic norms by adopting alternative practices (within reason); and students are not merely 'passive recipients of academic norms', they can and do 'actively participate in fashioning their own projects and academic subjectivity' (1997, p. 2).

A number of researchers have begun to examine various aspects of the supervisory relationship (Moses 1992, Powles 1988, Acker, Black & Hill 1994). What emerges from these studies is a picture of the vastly different perceptions (and some uncertainty) regarding these relationships, concerning appropriate roles and responsibilities and the most appropriate strategies to use to encourage writing. A study by Cullen et al. (1994) found that writing assistance was a distinct task of

The disciplinary setting

A supervisor's responses to student writing arise from a combination of their pedagogical and disciplinary background, ideological standpoint and their expectations of the roles of supervision. Their responsibilities include ensuring students learn the disciplinary conventions, values and traditions for the advancement of knowledge. Their feedback provides the means for ensuring that the quality of the student's writing meets the standards of the examining institution and of the discipline. Interestingly, this is usually the only context in which 'academics do provide written advice about the cultural rules and conventions by which they expect their students to behave' (Ballard & Clanchy 1988, p. 8). The feedback given on drafts will reflect attitudes (formed by their own disciplinary enculturation) towards the degree of familiarity the student is expected to have acquired of the writing conventions pertaining to that discipline. So, some do not see that teaching the language of disciplined inquiry is their role. Students in turn will behave in characteristically different ways as they receive feedback at different stages of progress. For example, if a student is not aware of the necessary stylistic and other conventions for the display of disciplinary knowledge, they may regard feedback which identifies the characteristics of writing valued by the discipline as merely conforming to a set of arbitrary (and incomprehensible) conventions.

A major strand of interest in disciplinarity studies is to understand how patterns of postgraduate education are influenced by the epistemological characteristics of a particular discipline. Differences in methods of inquiry, their criteria for evaluation, ways of reporting knowledge, and ways in which writing is used to establish and produce new knowledge shape disciplinary practices (Joliffe 1988, p. viii) and the 'efficiency with which, and even the degree to which, novices can come to understand and use writers' knowledge in the field' (Joliffe & Brier 1988, p. 54). Students in education would seem to be at a particular disadvantage with respect to expectations about conventions because education is built on a multi-disciplinary base. The thesis they write may well be in a different disciplinary area to that of their undergraduate degree. In all disciplines supervisors need to provide opportunities to discuss the implicit assumptions about disciplinary practices that they convey in feedback.

The dominant liberal discourse of postgraduate education is predicated on the notion of the active involvement of students in organisational/institutional practices; the possibility for them to act in their own interests as autonomous individuals, and their equal status with their supervisors (Grant 1996). This construction influences views and practices such as how the development of writing abilities can best occur. The danger here is that only those student needs that are known or assumed will be translated and negotiated into supervision practices. An important project for further research will be to provide a clearer idea of disciplinary differences and in particular how disciplinary (and multi-disciplinary) discourses affect the feedback provided by supervisors, given the 'different assumptions about the nature of written discourse' including 'assumptions about audience, purpose, conventions of style and format' (Anson 1988, p. 3).

Dealing with different needs

What of the supervisor's appreciation of different needs, such as those pertaining to gender? The literature and institutional discourse is relatively silent on such issues, just as it is on culture and the experiences of students from equity groups. With reference to Non-English Speaking Background (NESB) students Grant (1996) points out that difference 'is safely contained' by means of focussing on 'the clean difference of language' (p. 5). There is clearly a need for research to extend knowledge of the needs of these particular groups, while at the same time acknowledging the idiosyncracies of difference.

There is literature emerging which pinpoints difference as a key contextual element. Conrad's (1994) research, for example, highlights the different communication styles which may be present when women students work with male supervisors and how these exchanges may lead to the perception that women are seen as less 'intellectually solid' than men. The study suggests the perception may be a reflection of 'differences in communication styles rather than differences in a student's grasp of the field' (p. 54).

Parry and Hayden (1994) found that the matter of helping students write, particularly NESB students, proved a contentious issue, with some supervisors expending large amounts of time assisting students and worrying over how much of a contribution the supervisor should make. Nonetheless, supervisors need to be sensitive to cultural influences on their student's writing in order to provide appropriate feedback. Because expectations of how ideas are presented vary across cultures, the qualities that constitute 'good' writing are not universal, and students from different backgrounds will write in characteristically different ways. This makes it imperative to offer clear guidelines and informative feedback so that students can successfully meet their supervisors' expectations and observe conventions established by Western cultural writing traditions as well as challenge them. Biggs (1997) writes that 'conceptual colonialism' involves 'imposing the concepts of one's own culture on another culture, as *if* they were universals' (p. 3). On the issue of voicing educational discourse, Keech (1996) reports that when supervisor feedback concentrates on grammatical errors alone 'the rhetoric of a culturally inclusive curriculum is disguised as a pedagogy which maintains privilege and limits possession of 'proper' literacy to those who share a common cultural knowledge and history' (p. 127). In a case study of international Masters students, Aspland and O'Donoghue (1994) identified some students who experienced difficulties due to the supervisor's 'cultural understandings' (p. 64). As an example of this they cite a Melanesian student who was offended by 'culturally insensitive ... impersonal written comments' which conveyed 'personal inadequacies' (p. 72).

Continuity

The literature reports that most supervisors do adopt different strategies to suit different students and different phases of the research (Acker, Black & Hill 1994, Hockey 1991). Over the period of candidature students become 'their own independent critics, well able to evaluate their own efforts and to set their own standards both of quality and of productivity' (Salmon 1992, p. 23). The facilitation of this development calls on the supervisor's skills and experience in giving constructive criticism, especially at times where students feel unsure of their new status when new and unfamiliar tasks and responsibilities unfurl before them. Thus, the relationship may be seen as developmental and dynamic in nature. During meetings there is a need to establish the appropriate amount and kind of assistance with writing, while also acknowledging that, with regard to feedback, flexible boundaries are needed because feedback should change over time. There needs to be understanding on the part of both parties that conditions will alter as candidature (and personal development of the student/supervisor relationship) progresses.

A difficulty for some students initially will be their inexperience in discussing their needs as to the kind of guidance they may need, 'with many students err[ing] on the safe side by making too few demands with unfortunate implications for the effectiveness of their working arrangements' (Grant 1996, p. 11). Supervisors need to be aware that students will gain confidence in articulating their needs at different rates. As they gain more independence there is a change in the relationship with the supervisor and some may question or resist the feedback provided. Difficulties for supervisors with respect to giving feedback include:

- the amount of input they should provide as regards drafting, writing, and correcting the thesis (Parry & Hayden 1994);
- how much rewriting can they do before it impinges on the student's claim to originality and independent achievement (Moses 1985);
- dominating or destroying the writer's voice through extensive polishing by the supervisor of the student's writing (Moses 1985);
- losing the thread of the work due to intermittent readings;
- giving realistic feedback without discouraging the student (Wajnryb 1993);
- not having time to check whether comments on previous drafts were understood, and
- ensuring consistency in feedback where there are two supervisors.

Resonance

To provide feedback which 'resonates' with the student writer the supervisor needs to make an effort to interpret what the student had in mind to open up possibilities for intellectual growth and creative expression. Thus, feedback in effective working partnerships needs to involve responses to the text which are not just confined to engendering institutional standards, but which also create opportunities for students to question academic norms and régimes of truth. These responses would be long-sighted in nature – able to look beyond form so as not to highlight problems and deficits and encourage compliance to disciplinary conventions. By sending back more useful echoes we can 'interrupt our own and also our students' standard ways of thinking and talking about the conversations we conduct in writing' (Greenhalgh 1992, p. 409). Explaining why the stance of the supervisor and the provision of emotional support is important, Salmon (1992) adds that the 'apparently most helpful interventions by the apparently most well qualified supervisors can, quite inadvertently, act to undermine rather than enhance the personal confidence which is so fundamental to the carrying through of original research' (p. 88).

These observations attest to the complex and delicate nature of supervision and the possibility that pedagogic practices may be at variance despite the supervisor's and student's common goals. Thus, in effective relationships there need to be opportunities to discuss the feedback, either to understand it or to identify how to improve it. The following points, drawn from the combined experiences of students and supervisors, summarise the general characteristics of collaborative relationships:

- the supervisor is accessible and the student is able to rely on the continuation of feedback and support through a process of ongoing dialogue and direct involvement as they strive to integrate the thesis into a coherent document;
- the supervisor assesses the adequacy of the student's writing skills, encourages the student to start writing and keeps her/him writing, negotiates a suitable structure for the thesis, explains genre conventions, and clarifies details regarding standards of the required final format through guidance on research procedures, on literature in the area, and on thesis writing (Moses 1992);
- the supervisor reads, comments and returns all work quickly (one to two weeks) so the responses can connect with the student's thinking while it is current (Lever-Tracy 1993);
- that feedback is critical, sufficiently detailed and specific with examples given so that it is evident that the supervisor has actually done a detailed reading;
- comments are well-structured and followed-up by a meeting to discuss them and/or suggestions for further reading;
- explanations are provided if sections are struck out by the supervisor;
- feedback is legible and comprehensible and students are able to understand the comments (e.g. the handwriting, or the reason for a particular word choice or comment, or the editing symbols used), and
- the supervisor demonstrates an understanding of the creative process through sharing their own insights of writing which enhance the student's appreciation of the learning processes they are experiencing.

The importance of the match between the student and the supervisor and the quality of the supervisory relationship are brought into focus during the finishing stages of the thesis, during what is described as the most difficult phase of the process. This is the point at which difficulties may arise within some student-supervisor relationships (some relationships do not survive) or at which students may give up (Rudd 1985). The student is also dependent on the supervisor's informed criticism before submission can be approved (the supervisor possesses institutional power to sanction the thesis text).

Common areas of concern raised by supervisors and students at this crucial stage are summarised below:

- Suggestions for reformulations and amendments made by the supervisor may be met with anger and frustration as the student may be willing to expedite thesis submission due to diminishing motivation and impatience to finish.
- The time needed to produce the final thesis is most often underestimated by students (Parry & Hayden 1994), just as the demands on the supervisor may be.
- There is sometimes disagreement over the readiness of the thesis due to 'problems with expression in final drafts, editorial omissions and failure by the student or the department to comply with administrative arrangements' (Parry & Hayden 1994, p. 111).
- Students regard the revisions as merely conforming to arbitrary conventions and 'maybe also an expression of power' (Clanchy, in Cullen 1993, p. 40) so there may be a struggle between both parties.

Discussion and conclusion

There have been no attempts to date to document the diverse and productive approaches supervisors use in their feedback practices, nor of supervisors' metacognitive awareness of their strategies. The tendency to disregard this aspect of supervision reflects the general lack of consideration given to supervisory meetings (Brown & Atkins, 1988). The tacit, special knowledge of the supervisor needs to be better understood. At present it is essentially 'a mysterious and intimate phenomenon' (McWilliam & Palmer 1995, p. 32) or 'well-kept secret' (Bargar & Mayo-Chamberlain 1983, p. 423). Given the mystique surrounding supervision, Johnston (1995, p. 18) suggests that 'for this reason alone it is imperative for supervisors to come together in some way on a regular basis, sharing their experiences, problems and successes of their supervisory roles'.

What is known about feedback mostly focuses on quantity (amount of assistance) and on the construction of the product of research and the supervision of the student's intellectual work. Little attention has been given to the co-learning which develops in a co-productive relationship between the student and supervisor, or on the role of feedback on writing in constructing the student's emerging identity as a researcher.

The literature so far may not even begin to reflect the position in the area of education research theses, an area characterised by intakes of experienced professionals. In education, although students' professional interests usually determine their choice of topic, they may nonetheless feel insecure about their topic and the thesis genre, especially if they have experienced a long separation from study. A further issue for supervisors and students is that of diversity, given that supervisors in education are usually not specialists in the student's particular research topic, unlike supervisors in other disciplines. Therefore, giving feedback which is able to appraise the student's scholarly contribution while respecting their professional insights, status and individual needs for encouragement constitutes a challenge.

The argument of this chapter is that if supervision problems are to be avoided, expectations must be clarified between both parties. When students are encouraged to express their needs regarding the kind of guidance most needed, strategies are grounded in the needs and the perceptions of the student him or herself *(context)*. In addition, both parties need to decide how feedback should proceed and change over time *(continuity)*. The supervision process needs to facilitate an experience where writing is a co-operative exercise in which mutual learning occurs and opens up possibilities for intellectual growth and creative expression *(resonance)*. Thus, feedback in effective working partnerships involves responses which are long-sighted in nature. In a co-productive relationship, feedback fosters the student's capacity for autonomous judgement and encourages the student to obtain feedback from many other readers, such as peer writing groups and thesis advisory panels.

Symmetrical and supportive partnerships that provide multiple opportunities for feedback produce a resonant 'web of echoes' (McNaron 1983, p. 505) for the postgraduate student writer. When these contributions to a student's creative efforts provide 'reliable and familiar echoes' (McNaron 1983, p. 505), the quality of such efforts can be validated, supported and enhanced. Such a stance on feedback implies that the student, as the author of the research, must ultimately define and refine their thinking and decision-making processes so that the final thesis is personally crafted within the researcher's individual philosophy. Validation of the student's emerging identity as a writer can be achieved by delivering messages which are aligned to the student's personal concerns and vulnerabilities. At the same time, it is important for both parties to recognise the way in which language is implicated in construction of social relations and is mediated through these processes of production and interpretation.

References

Acker, S., Black, E. & Hill, T. 1994, 'Research students and their supervisors in Education and Psychology' in R. Burgess (ed.), *Postgraduate Education and*

Training in the Social Sciences: Processes and Products, London, Jessica Kingsley, pp. 53-72.

Anson, C. M. 1988, 'Toward a multicultural model of writing in academic disciplines', in D. A. Joliffe (ed.), *Advances in Writing Research, Vol. 2: Writing in Academic Disciplines*, Norwood, N.J., Ablex, pp. 1-33.

Anson, C. M. (ed.), 1989, *Writing and Response: Theory, Practice, and Research*, Urbana, Illinois, NCTE.

Aspland, T. & O'Donoghue, T. 1994, 'Quality in supervising overseas students?', in O. Zuber-Skerritt & Y. Ryan (eds), *Quality in Postgraduate Education*, London, Kogan Page, pp. 59-76.

Ballard, B. & Clanchy, J. 1988, 'Literacy in the university: An anthropological approach', in G. Taylor, B. Ballard, V. Beasley, H. Bock, J. Clanchy, & P. Nightingale (eds), *Literacy by Degrees*, Milton Keynes, SRHE & The Open University Press, pp. 7-23.

Bargar, R. R. & Duncan, J. K. 1982, 'Cultivating creative endeavor in doctoral research', *Journal of Higher Education*, 53 (1), pp. 1-31.

Bargar, R. R. & Mayo-Chamberlain, J. 1983, 'Advisor and advisee issues in doctoral research', *Journal of Higher Education*, 54 (4), July/August, pp. 407-432.

Biggs, J. 1997, 'Teaching across and within cultures: The issue of international students', in R. Murray-Harvey & H. C. Silins (eds), Proceedings of the HERDSA conference *Learning and Teaching in Higher Education: Advancing International Perspectives*, Adelaide, Flinders Press, pp. 1-22.

Brown, G. & Atkins, M. (1988), *Effective Teaching in Higher Education*, London, Methuen.

Connell, R. W. 1985, 'How to supervise a PhD', *Vestes*, (2), pp. 38-41.

Conrad, L. 1994, 'Gender and postgraduate supervision', in O. Zuber-Skerritt, & Y. Ryan (eds), *Quality in Postgraduate Education*, London, Kogan Page, pp. 50-58.

Cullen, D. J. (ed.) 1993, *Quality in PhD education*, Proceedings of the 1 July 1992 Symposium Panel Discussion, CEDAM, Canberra, ANU, pp. 33-47.

Cullen, D. J., Pearson, M., Saha, L. J. & Spear, R. H. 1994, *Establishing Effective PhD Supervision*, Australian Government Publishing Service, Canberra, Commonwealth of Australia.

Dudley-Evans, A. 1988, 'One-to-one supervision for students writing MSc or PhD Theses', in A. Brookes & P. Grundy (eds), *Individualisation and Autonomy in Language Learning*, ELT Documents 131, The British Council, pp. 136-141.

Grant, B. & Graham, A. 1994, ' "Guidelines for discussion": A tool for managing postgraduate supervision', in O. Zuber-Skerritt & Y. Ryan (eds), *Quality in Postgraduate Education*, Kogan Page, London, pp. 165-177.

Grant, B. 1996, 'Unreasonable practices: Reading a code for supervision against the grain', in *Proceedings of the quality in postgraduate research: Is it happening? Conference*, University of Adelaide, Flinders, University & University of South Australia, electronic format, pp. 1-12.

Green, B. & Lee, A. 1995, 'Theorising postgraduate pedagogy', *The Australian Universities' Review, Feature Issue Postgraduate Studies/ Postgraduate Pedagogy*, 38 (2), pp. 40-45.

Greenhalgh, A. M. 1992, 'Voices in response: A postmodem reading of teacher response', *College Composition and Communication*, 43, October, pp. 401-410.

Harris, P. 1997, 'Postgraduate labour: Questions of independence and self-discipline', unpublished paper SSHE, Murdoch University, WA, pp. 1-11.

Hockey, J. 1991, 'The Social Science PhD: A literature review', *Studies in Higher Education*, 16 (3), pp. 319-332.

Johnston, S. 1995, 'Professional development for postgraduate supervision', *The Australian Universities' Review, Feature Issue Postgraduate Studies /Postgraduate Pedagogy*, 38 (2), pp. 16-19.

Joliffe, D. A. (ed.), 1988, *Advances in Writing Research, Volume Two: Writing in Academic Disciplines*, Norwood, Ablex, New Jersey.

Joliffe, D. A. & Brier, E. M., 1988, 'Studying writers' knowledge in academic disciplines', in David A. J. (ed.) *Advances in Writing Research, Volume Two: Writing in Academic Disciplines*, Norwood, New Jersey, Ablex, pp. 35-87.

Kamler, B. & Threadgold, T. 1996, 'Which thesis did you read?', in Sofia Golebiowski & Helen Borland (eds), *Selected Proceedings of the First National Conference on Tertiary Literacy: Research and Practice, Academic Communication Across Disciplines and Cultures*, Melbourne, VUT, pp. 42-58.

Keech, M. 1996, 'Literacy, culture and difference: Feedback on student writing as discursive practice', in Z. Golebiowski & H. Borland (eds), *Selected Proceedings of the First National Conference on Tertiary Literacy: Research and Practice, Academic Communication Across Disciplines and Cultures*, VUT, Melbourne, pp. 127-139.

Lee, A. 1996, 'Working together? Academic literacies, co-production and professional partnerships', Plenary address to the First National Conference on *Tertiary Literacy: Research and Practice*, Melbourne, VUT, 14-16 March.

Lever-Tracy, C. 1993, *Outpost*, (4), Newsletter of the Flinders University PGSA.

McNaron, Toni, A. 1983, 'Echoes of Virginia Woolf', *Women's Studies International Forum*, 6 (5), pp. 501-507.

McWilliam, E. & Palmer, P.1995, 'Teaching tech(no)bodies: Open learning and postgraduate pedagogy', *The Australian Universities' Review, Feature Issue Postgraduate Studies/Postgraduate Pedagogy*, 38 (2) pp. 32-34.

Moses, I. 1985, *Supervising Postgraduates*, HERDSA Green Guide No. 3, Higher Education Research and Development Society of Australasia, Kensington.

Moses, I. 1992, 'Departmental and institutional facilities and processes', in Ingrid Moses (ed.), *Research Training and Supervision*, Proceedings from the ARC & AVCC sponsored conference, May, Canberra, AVCC, pp. 54-59.

Parry, S. & Hayden, M. 1994, *Supervising Higher Degree Students: An Investigation of Practices Across a Range of Academic Departments*, Canberra, Australian Government Publishing Service.

Powles, M. 1988, 'The problem of lengthy candidature', in *Assistance For Postgraduate Students: Achieving Better Outcomes,* Canberra, Australian Government Publishing Service, pp. 26-44.

Radecki, P. M. & Swales, J. M. 1988, 'ESL student reaction to written comments on their written work', *System*, 16 (3), pp. 355-365.

Rudd, E. 1985, *A New Look at Postgraduate Failure,* Surrey, UK, SRHE, University of Guildford.

Salmon, P. 1992, *Achieving A PhD - Ten Students' Experience,* London, Trentham Books.

Taylor, P. 1995, 'Postgraduate education and open learning: Anticipating a new order?', *The Australian Universities Review, Feature Issue Postgraduate Studies/Postgraduate Pedagogy,* 38 (2), pp. 28-31.

Torrance, M. S., Thomas, G. V. & Robinson, E. J. 1992, 'The writing experiences of social science research students', *Studies in Higher Education,* 17 (2), pp. 155-167.

Torrance, M. S., Thomas, G. V. 1994, 'The development of writing skills in doctoral research students', in R. Burgess (ed.), *Postgraduate Education and Training in the Social Sciences: Processes and Products*, London, Jessica Kingsley, pp. 105-123.

Wajnryb, R. 1993, 'Strategies for the management and delivery of criticism', *EA Journal*, 11 (2), pp. 74-84.

Yeatman, A. 1995, 'Making supervision relationships accountable: Graduate student logs', *The Australian Universities' Review, Feature Issue Postgraduate Studies/ Postgraduate Pedagogy*, 38 (2), pp. 9-11.

Acknowledgements

Barbara Grant, Centre for Professional Development, University of Auckland
Shirley Grundy, School of Education, Murdoch University
Allyson Holbrook, Faculty of Education, University of Newcastle

PART III:
Personal Accounts Of, and Reflections On, Doctoral Supervision

Shifting Gears: Learning to Work the Discourses of Academic Research[*]

*Barbara Comber***
University of South Australia

Shifting gears: Learning to work the discourses of academic research

I had already done research. I had written and published. However, when the Dawkins era of tertiary education reform brought about the metamorphosis of the former colleges of advanced education, like many educators in colleges of advanced education in the early nineties I was without a PhD, without the credential that not only counted, but was becoming essential. Along with many colleagues in the teachers college sector I had been teaching and conducting small scale research projects for over a decade. Yet ARC (Australian Research Council) remained an alien acronym and people with PhDs were rare, especially but not exclusively, amongst female academic staff. The discourses of academic research – both the burgeoning theoretical fields informing literacy studies and the apparatus surrounding competitive research grants – represented new ground for me.

As a former school teacher, I had been recruited into the teachers college because my recent school teaching experience added credibility to inservice awards. While this practical knowledge was not discounted in the nineties, it became clear that new forms of intellectual capital were needed in the new universities. In many such institutions the need to develop a 'research culture' and to enhance the qualifications of the academics became an urgent priority. Some of the newer universities, such as the University of South Australia - my employer - made provision for the support of doctoral studies through Cathie scholarships and other forms of study leave. (I received two forms of support during my doctoral studies, a six-month Cathie Scholarship and Assisted Leave.) It was in this context that I commenced my doctoral studies late in 1991. I interrupt what seems a far too neat-clean-and-tidy account with some messier observations signalled in italics and indented.

---

[*]   Allan Luke has kindly given his permission to be named in this chapter.

^{**}   Barbara received the award of PhD from James Cook University in 1996.

The candidate, the research problem and the supervisor: A brief history

As a school-based classroom teacher and as a tertiary educator my focus in 1991 was language and literacy education and it remains so. I had already completed part-time graduate courses, including a Graduate Diploma in Reading Education and an MEd(Hons) with the goal of understanding better how to help children learn and teachers to teach reading and writing. In an era of educational reform characterised by optimism that there were indeed solutions out there just waiting to be found, I was an active contributor to progressive educational discourses and professional practices. However in the mid to late eighties a number of challenges to progressive literacy pedagogies were being made from an equity perspective.

It is unnecessary to revisit these debates here, however this brief history is relevant to my experience of doctoral supervision because researching and writing a thesis does not take place in an historical vacuum. Supervisory practices and pedagogical relationships are contingent upon the particular histories, circumstances and commitments of both supervisor and candidate. Partly I needed to pursue doctoral studies because of the changing nature of the institution where I was employed. My work was changing and I needed to change in order to be able to do it. However I also wanted the intensive and in-depth learning that such an educational opportunity presents and the pleasure of ideas and time to think sustained me through the hard work of the writing.

> *Despite these grand hopes, many times throughout I felt deskilled and overwhelmed and somewhat of a fraud. Who was I to think I could do this kind of scholarship, who was I trying to kid?*

Because the challenges of socially critical educators and my ongoing research and educational questions related to the relationships between literacy and social justice, I asked Allan Luke, who was at that time based at James Cook University Townsville, if he would supervise my doctoral research. He invited me to send him my recently completed Masters thesis and to write to him about my current research questions, interests and preoccupations. After an exchange of letters, Allan agreed to supervise my thesis. His letter of response recognised what I could already do as a writer, confirmed the importance of my research questions, encouraged my desire to do empirical research in schools and at the same time recognised what I would need to learn in order to do it. He told me what he thought was missing from my earlier work and I told him what I needed and wanted from the PhD and from him as a supervisor.

To sum up, we agreed that a high priority was the expansion of my theoretical knowledge and that Allan would provide specific and direct advice and alert me to the pros and cons of going in particular directions. We agreed that he would advise me of any problematic contradictions in the theoretical ensemble I assembled. We agreed that getting the writing to work would be my responsibility (though ultimately he gave really helpful advice here too). As I had done similar school-based case studies before, I needed less supervision with the design of the actual empirical project.

> *Sounds neat eh? My lurking fear was that my theoretical deprivation and what I saw as chasms in my knowledge [baggage from my teacher education history] would catch up with me; that my eventual examiners would find my readings of Foucault faulty; that their feedback would read, 'I'm surprised you didn't refer to'... Given these anxieties, Allan's promise of advice on theory was really helpful.*

As I produced the corpus of empirical data, I kept in e-mail contact with Allan and at the same time I made my way somewhat tentatively into and through the recommended new theoretical material. During this time I wrote exploratory letters testing out hunches about the 'data' through different theoretical lenses and in connection with other research. For me it was like shifting gears as I learnt to read and write in new ways.

> *This was painful as I often felt lost for words, as though my words were the wrong words, or as though my new words hung on me like someone else's clothes and I would be caught out wearing them. The paranoia of a PhD student knows no bounds.*

When I began to write chapters and bits of chapters, Allan responded to the deluge of e-mail; recommended other doctoral theses for me to read; made time for intensive meetings around my drafts; helped map out how the thesis might look; provided comprehensive reading lists and new leads to follow; disagreed with specific interpretations and lines of argument; and offered warnings about potential contradictions and dead-ends. I enjoyed, and my work benefited from, honest critical feedback that always left me with places to move to and action to take.

> *I also wrote e-mails to Alan about how I was going to write the chapters instead of the chapters themselves. The trick was to look as though and feel as though you were somehow making progress. My stalling tactics were more obvious than I thought.*

At the same time, I gradually established with my colleagues and peers a local collaborative network of research students who wrote and talked about our research – the reading, the data, the theory, the analysis, the writing, the confusion, the exhaustion, the excitement, the self-doubt, the pain etc. These were colleagues whose work I respected and who had themselves taken on the risks of mid-life doctoral studies. On bad days we pondered why we hadn't done this when we were younger and with more brain cells intact. Then we remembered other doctor 'so-and-sos', who were no smarter than we were and who had somehow managed to successfully complete their PhDs. On good days we celebrated each other's breakthroughs or simply the surprise of the day's word count. We fantasised about life after… the thesis. We planned writing weekends at beach houses where we could keep each other under surveillance, laugh about how seriously we took our work and then go back to work again. As far as was possible we avoided the isolation that such study often demands.

There is insufficient space in this short chapter to provide a detailed narrative of the thesis experience and such accounts tend to be far more interesting to the writer than the reader. I suspect also that the supervisor's story may well be different. However two circumstances impacted on my experience of supervision which are relevant here. Firstly, I sought out a particular supervisor on the basis of his scholarship and educational research. Secondly, the result of this decision meant that I functioned as an external student. Ultimately the distance had, I believe, a number of positive effects. It meant that I needed to commit my thoughts to text, rather than to conversation. The e-mailed letters became a way of thinking through what I was learning, confronting confusions and occasions for supervisory assistance that was targeted and focussed on specific problems. The distance meant also that the meetings that we did plan became goal-directed and intensive.

> *But this account edits out the agony that went with writing about other people's lives, people who had trusted me with access to their professional lives. What was I doing with them? Working through the guilt to an ethical position from which to write the research involved many tears. Supervisors witness a lot of crying!*

At the beginning of my doctoral thesis I had already benefited from thoughtful and encouraging supervision in my previous studies. I had already supervised research projects at these levels myself, so I was aware of what I needed as a learner and what I valued in my teachers. However writing the doctoral thesis required, what were for me, new forms of analytical and textual practices and I relied heavily on my supervisor to help me to learn how to do this. In practice, this meant that Allan provided me with very specific feedback and advice concerning problems in the thesis text such as over-claiming, speculation or the need to write more authoritatively.

> *This kind of feedback is not easy to give or receive. It is so much about authority and identity, about power and humility, about co-constructing a researcher subjectivity, but this kind of feedback I continue to find very helpful when I write research now and when I try to help colleagues and students.*

About advice and working out what works for you

Metaphors abound about the thesis experience. It is often compared with giving birth. At the other extreme, images of death prevail, such as 'the final throes'. My daughter, at various stages of her childhood, referred to my collected works variously as 'mummy's foetus', mummy's faeces' and finally as 'mummy's thesis'. I appreciate the idea of struggle, humorously invoked by her earlier mispronouncements. However, providing advice can be a cliché-ridden affair. My advice to students now is to treat all advice as problematic, but to keep listening on the chance that someone will trigger a strategy that works for you.

The danger with accounts such as this is that particular conditions which impact on the process of supervision and learning are insufficiently explained and that the tactics which work in one context are heard as universally the way to go. During the course of my study I developed many tricks for sustaining myself, including going away to write where I had a view of the sea, writing with friends, setting impossible deadlines and then working all out to come close to meeting them, checking my e-mail after every thousand words and so on. The fridge, the washing machine and the telephone each took on new and positive connotations in my life…. But jokes aside, the supervisor can only do so much. Finishing a PhD is very much about developing strategies for work and learning that you can sustain and which sustain you in your particular context.

My advice to students is:

- know why you are doing a PhD
- know your intended supervisor's research and publications
- work with a supervisor who does the kind of intellectual work you'd like to do
- work with a supervisor who is committed to similar educational goals
- negotiate at the outset what you need to learn from your supervisor
- establish peer networks to provide feedback, advice and collegial support.

Now, as a supervisor myself, I know that such ideals are not easy to achieve. As senior academics take up separation packages, research students are 'orphaned' in the process and it is no longer unusual to experience more than one supervisor during a candidature. The match between supervisor expertise and student needs becomes difficult to bring off. Perhaps in these times it is even more important to negotiate openly how you're going to work together, what you have to offer as a supervisor and what you don't, and how and where students might find other people to advise them in particular areas. As a supervisor, I try to replicate many of the practices which I enjoyed as a student, to:

- make my research and writing available
- link students to a wider community of scholarship

- recommend related research and theory
- closely listen to, read and respond to ideas in the making
- provide direct feedback on thesis drafts.

I learnt a great deal from my supervisor and as a result I very much believe that students should think long and hard about who they invite to supervise their research. This means having a critical analysis of one's own work and being informed about active researchers in the field you're intending to pursue. Taking the time to confront where you're going and why and what it means in the context of your professional and personal life is useful. For me, doing the doctorate was not only something I felt I needed to do for the piece of paper (though the credential was and is significant) but also something to sustain me as a teacher, a researcher and a learner.

Matters of Choice[*]

Garry Kidd[**]
Bond University

My Macquarie Dictionary reminds me that collaboration on the one hand is to work, one with another or, on the other, to cooperate treacherously! Having enjoyed a memorable period of PhD candidature it is very difficult to appreciate that the process could be construed in less than positive terms. Come to think of it though, personal accounts of higher degree supervision involving an unsatisfactory collaborative relationship occur with sufficient frequency such that I should have little need of a lexicographer's reminder. Thinking back to the time when I was preparing to commence my PhD candidature I am struck by the extent to which the notion of a collaborative association with my prospective supervisor seemed hardly to enter my mind. Given that I was scarcely cognisant of the matter, it now seems that my choice of a nurturing and generous supervisor was more likely a matter of serendipity than design. Notwithstanding that the matter of choice is a two-way street, there may be fewer less-than-memorable supervision partnerships were prospective candidates more mindful of the extent to which the process of supervision involves productive collaboration and sensitive recognition of each one's investment in the process. And, of course, the same must be said of supervisors. What then might personal reflections on my choice of supervisor contribute to prospective candidates and to the type of supervisor I hope I have become?

Choosing a supervisor

With the usual clarity of hindsight I now see how fortunate was my choice of supervisor. While there are those who would say 'damned lucky', I like to think that prospective PhD candidates really do have some room to manoeuvre and choices to make within the constraints of discipline area, preferred research focus and, of course, unearthing an academic who is prepared to supervise one more hapless candidate.

---

[*] Frank Naylor has given his kind permission to be named in this chapter.

[**] Garry received the award of PhD from The University of Melbourne in 1992

In the light of my experience, one of the strongest recommendations that I can make to others is to undergo a 'preliminary' period of candidature with a prospective PhD supervisor by beginning with a Masters degree by research. This type of approach requires more than a little forward planning, but it might pay dividends in the longer term. In my case, fellow tyre-kickers, Masters candidature was an admirable road test. Both supervisor and student have sufficient opportunity to establish an amicable, cooperative, and fulfilling academic association. The road test returned the award of The University of Melbourne Freda Cohen prize for outstanding Masters research in education, a Postgraduate Research Award for PhD studies followed, and at that point I suspect that both student and supervisor thought they had struck gold. Clearly, however, our academic accomplishments as students are not produced in a vacuum. These we either share with our supervisors or, in some cases, achieve in spite of them.

I had always thought that I worked best in relative isolation. And I recall, as I rode into my PhD candidature on the crest of a wave, I considered my ego not so fragile that I could neglect the courtesy and conventions of acknowledgment. Yet again, however, hindsight suggests that I had neither accurately estimated the magnitude of my supervisor's contributions nor appreciated the extent to which the process was collaborative. On reflection, my supervisor understood well that a candidature undertaken in total isolation may not be either a particularly desirable or sustainable learning experience. Regularly we enjoyed a meal or coffee at University House, colloquium presentations were organised, conference presentations were facilitated, lectures to graduate students were scheduled, and so on. As my former supervisor now tells me, the experience of candidature is also a process of socialisation. So much for 'learning in a vacuum'. But there were other incidents that appeared to ratify my choice of supervisor.

Prior to commencing PhD candidature I had observed the interactions of other PhD candidates with my prospective supervisor. While this was a salutary experience, the most compelling evidence was available from the University library - dissertations submitted for the PhD by my prospective supervisor's former students. Two theses, in particular, sanctioned my choice and remained in my mind for the duration of my candidature and beyond as exemplars of outstanding scholarship. It seems to me that this type of snooping is really worthwhile, even though there may be somewhat deleterious effects resulting from coming across a 'really hard act to follow'. Parenthetically, speaking of the authors of those theses my supervisor was fond of remarking the presence of 'a mind behind the pen'. I suppose I grew with each crisis of confidence, but always hoping that my pen would not be remembered as the one on autopilot.

Formative experiences

Beginning the process of writing the thesis was possibly the lowest point and the most daunting of my experience of candidature and I clearly recall the awesome power of a benign but stubbornly blank sheet of A4. My supervisor's notable contributions at that time included a fair measure of encouragement, resisting the student-inspired flourish of trenchant criticism, rapid turnaround of chapter drafts, and wise recommendations on thesis structure. Finding the structure of the thesis was, for me, the key.

Of a number of formative experiences associated with candidature, including my supervisor-choice behaviours, the most memorable was submission of jointly authored papers for publication, prior to surrendering my thesis for examination. This was, in retrospect, the pinnacle of a host of collegial and generous experiences, and one that I can strongly recommend. While the process was valuable, the critical comments of anonymous reviewers brought to light points that might otherwise have surfaced in an examiner's report.

As the process of sustaining the dissertation rolled on, I recall a short list of strategies and attributes that seem to have served me well. First, in terms of time and event management, I found it useful to contemplate personal choice from an either/or perspective - 'either you can watch "Home and Away" or you can have a PhD'. This one works well for simple and unequivocally minded souls like myself. Second, it is hard to imagine that the process can be sustained if we are not immersed in our research. I suggest that you should carefully consider the consequences of embarking on a doctoral research program in which you have marginal personal interest. Third, it is likely that curiosity sustains a great deal of intellectual endeavour. If you are not curious perhaps you should consider an alternative path to fame and fortune. And a final counsel of perfection: strive to achieve some sense of balance in terms of thesis, relationship, home, friends, and family.

Now as a supervisor of postgraduate and higher degree candidates I find myself trying to emulate the best features of my supervisor. It seems that my choice of supervisor has certainly determined far more than the immediate outcome of PhD candidature. And, yes, there is little doubt that the type of supervisor I hope I have become has been largely determined by the personal qualities and style of my supervisor (which he claims were formed in reaction to his own miserable experience as a PhD candidate!). While I have no difficulty acknowledging that a successful and fulfilling candidature depends on the confluence and unique qualities of both parties in a supervisory partnership, Associate Professor Frank Naylor's supervision has been, however, a really tough act to follow. I have to say that if you are in the market for an inspirational, generous, and scholarly supervisor, perhaps you might be the one to draw him out of retirement and persuade him to select just one more PhD candidate.

While the matter of who chooses whom might not attract a great deal of serious interest, clearly PhD candidature, both embarkation and passage, might best be seen as a special kind of reciprocal and collaborative partnership. That point may be well understood by supervisors. Perhaps, then, it would be wise if prospective candidates were to carefully consider questions of intellectual resourcing prior to committing themselves to either supervisor or project. After all, this too is really a matter of choice.

Coping with Change

Ilana Snyder[*]
Monash University

Multiple supervisors

Three supervisors in three years. With the first, I designed the study, produced a formal proposal and collected the data. She then moved from Monash to another university to take up a Chair. While I awaited the arrival of the new appointment in Language and Literacy Education, the Faculty's Research Adviser became my *de facto* supervisor. He helped me battle through the statistical analysis and provided solace when I despaired at the hiatus in supervision. In the final year of my candidature, the third supervisor took over. She responded swiftly and generatively to successive drafts in the period in which I did much of the hard thinking and writing. During those three years, I thought myself most unfortunate not to have had the consistency and stability of a single supervisor.

I have since learned that having more than one supervisor is not so unusual. The circumstances, however, may vary. They may be like mine - an academic leaves. It may be that a shift to a supervisor with different expertise is indicated by a change in the study's direction. Or the relationship may prove so unsatisfactory to one or both parties that ending it is the only solution. Whatever the situation, the point is that it is not necessarily a bad thing to have multiple supervisors. The departure of the first triggered anxiety, even a sense of betrayal, but, as a result, I gained confidence in my ability to be an independent researcher. Moreover, with hindsight, I was privileged to be exposed to three contrasting but equally enriching perspectives on my study.

Learning along the way

Before I began my PhD, I had some notional views of what supervision meant, but also two related educational experiences. The first was when I completed a Masters in Education at the University of Houston ten years earlier. In that program, I was

---

[*]   Ilana received the award of PhD from Monash University in 1990.

assigned a 'supervisor' who helped me map a course, provided counsel, and supported me when I prepared for the dreaded 'Comprehensives' (final examinations). Her role was predominantly nurturing, but she has remained a mentor and close friend. The second experience was when I completed an extended research project under the supervision of the professor who taught 'Writing and Computers', the subject I took in the Graduate School of Education, Harvard, and which provided the catalyst for my PhD research. We met on a number of occasions to discuss the design and implementation of the study, the analysis of the data and the interpretation of the findings, and finally, the write-up. We also communicated by e-mail when I had questions: to my bemusement, she was more helpful in that medium than face-to-face.

By the time I enrolled, I understood that supervision involved one-to-one discussion, guided decision-making, some emotional support, and the opportunity to be advised by someone with greater expertise in research and writing. And my experiences with all three supervisors at Monash supported these beliefs. But I also somewhat naively entertained broader expectations. I imagined that I would work with a single person who would be expert in all aspects of research processes and familiar with all the bodies of theory and research literature the study would embrace. I even hoped that my supervisor would become a close and trusted friend to whom I could openly reveal fears and frustrations related to the research. But it is like looking for the perfect partner in life: when you are suckled on Hollywood idealisations of the institution of marriage, the reality can be altogether different. Similarly with supervision: the person who embodies every desired characteristic simply does not exist. It did not take me long to learn that a supervisor meets certain requirements and needs but not all, and that this is fine. We live in the real world, not one governed by impossible fantasies and dreams.

By the end of my candidature, I knew that supervision is both an institutionally constructed arrangement at the same time as it is a profoundly personal relationship. It is both an enabling and constraining relationship which becomes somewhat of a balancing act by the participants. On the one hand, it is a period of apprenticeship and an opportunity to be guided by a role model. On the other, particularly in education faculties, when the student has been, and often still is, a teacher in her own right, it can be difficult adjusting to the role reversal. Perhaps there should be greater equality, but complete equality is neither possible nor warranted as the supervisor is by definition more expert and experienced. But the supervisor should also be an effective teacher and expert guide, capacities which cannot be assumed. Indeed, a training program should be required before academics take on their first doctoral students as well as regular opportunities for ongoing professional development in this important sphere of academic life.

Getting credentialed

A PhD offered me the possibility of working in a university, something I more or less always wanted. It also offered a personal, intellectual challenge. In an unreconstructed, younger self, I imagined that the only way I could be associated with the academy was to marry an academic. That coveted opportunity never presented itself. When I did my Masters in the mid-1970s, the desire to do a PhD had surfaced, but I succumbed to an even stronger desire - to have children. Combining the two endeavours did not seem feasible. However, I eventually took up the option almost a decade later after a taste of research at Harvard in a fascinating area which, I believed, had important implications for literacy education - literacy and the use of the new electronic communication and information technologies. It was probably the synergy between my enduring desire to do a PhD and the identification of an area in which to do it that finally propelled me to enrol.

And it was hard work. At one level a PhD is about original ideas and imagination but, more importantly, it is about good organisation, discipline, self-motivation, perseverance and, again, desire. Wanting it. Wanting it badly. Wanting it as quickly as possible. Desire was a most effective motivating and disciplining force.

Like all major endeavours, there were high points like the moment when I discovered the elegance of statistically significant differences between the two comparison groups; another, when I revealed the findings of the study to a surprisingly entranced audience at my first conference presentation ever. But there were also low points: I was devastated when I realised that the elaborate writing evaluation scales that I had painstakingly devised did not work; and when I wrote up the study - a year before I submitted - and sent the article off to a prestigious journal, I sustained my first rejection. These were all experiences that I shared with my supervisors, but ultimately, I was on my own both for the good times and the not so good.

There were also surprises associated with doing the PhD. I had never imagined it to be such a lonely pursuit. When I did my MEd in the States, friends doing their doctorates were part of an intellectual, collegial community. They did course work together, most were employed as teaching assistants within the Faculty, and even when they were doing the research component were in regular social contact with each other. They formed a cohort of students with similar goals and pressures. The closest thing we have in Australia is the professional doctorate. By contrast, I felt isolated and almost came to hate my study at home, even though it was the most aesthetically pleasing room in the house. When I began my first Outside Study Program, I felt loath to stay at home, fearing that I was returning to the silence which I thought I had left behind in my professional life. By the end, however, I realised that my sense of isolation was an almost inevitable rite of passage.

But I did have support networks beyond those provided by my supervisors at Monash. Two close friends were doing their PhDs at the same time as me at other institutions. Just as e-mail is now my connection to the rest of the world, during my candidature when I spent so much time at home in front of the computer screen, the phone became my lifeline. I spoke to these friends regularly, daily at particular stages. A favourite topic was our supervisors. What they said, how they said it, what they did not say. These two friends provided counsel, our conversations, a safe context in which to express concerns, anxieties, pressures, frustrations and above all to laugh.

My first supervisor published an ironic journal article that analysed the genre of Acknowledgements which frame most dissertations. The sentiments are often effusive: Many, many thanks to 'kind', 'positive' supervisors who are the source of 'sound advice' and 'generous encouragement'. Without their help, 'the PhD could never have been completed'. Then come the lists of supportive colleagues, friends and, usually in last place, the long suffering family members who have had to tolerate absence, obsession, take-away food and irritability. Even though such expressions of gratitude lend themselves to satire, they are probably often genuinely felt - they certainly were for me.

Assuming the role

As a supervisor, I have been shaped by my own experiences, those of my friends and what I have read in journals about the contractual arrangement. As a relatively recent graduate, I know that the experience of doing a PhD is both evolutionary and unstable for *both* parties - the supervisor as well as the candidate. I am aware of the importance students attach to these regular yet not frequent meetings. I respond to any writing a student gives me within a few days. I do not leave students waiting; I minimise interruptions. In our sessions together, I try to give the student my undivided attention. I am conscious that when I take a phone call or an inquiry at the door, I am interrupting the flow of the interaction. I remind myself of the significance of the meeting for the student and, as far as possible, make it the student's time. I encourage students to make contact with other students. If I had a bigger office, I would have two comfortable armchairs so that we could sit in a physical proximity that could sponsor more equal dialogue. I am always conscious of the power balance. However, being sensitive to the needs of students does not mean that, in practice, I am the model supervisor. I know that the ideal does not exist, but it is still a goal to strive towards.

Some suggestions for prospective PhD students

Choose your supervisor carefully. Ask other academics and students for recommendations. Also investigate the gossip about individual academics. Retain some scepticism, but what other students have to say can provide some very interesting insights. Decide what you want from a supervisor: someone who is going to be available regularly, who will read your drafts quickly and closely, and who will give you detailed feedback. However, at the same time, think carefully about what you expect from yourself. It is also important to develop independence and confidence as a researcher and writer. These qualities are unlikely to emerge if you are too dependent on the supervisor. Establish wider networks. Find other students with whom you can build a support network. Do not allow the supervisor relationship to become too important. Ultimately, the relationship is about your progression - from apprentice to authority - and you have a major role to play in that process.

Towards a Sustainable Relationship Between Supervisor and Student

*Ray Barker**

My general observations and impressions of the supervisor-student relationship operating in universities have come not so much from my own four experiences of supervision, but from third-party chats and shared confidences about the trials and tribulations of both supervisors and students. Establishing the parameters of a supervisor-student relationship is no different from many other human relationships. Both parties have to live with the numbers that fall, but given goodwill on both sides, improvement can be effected.

Accepting the experiences of others

Individuals differ and so do the paths travelled by supervisors and students, even though the end objective is common to both. Acceptance is essential by all stakeholders of the varying and variable backgrounds of the individuals involved. For example, one can predict that the number of postgraduate students in their chronological middle and senior years will increase as lifelong learning, self-paced learning, web-site usage, credits for work experience, multi-disciplinary studies and globalization attract more educational attention and options for further study multiply. A student can have a full lifetime of educational and work experiences when they enter into a research degree.

I started my first degree, aged twenty-five, after six and a half wartime years in the Royal Australian Navy. These years included survival of a sinking (HMAS Perth) and helping to build the Burma/Siam railway for the Japanese. The fourth year course in Psychology at Sydney included a piece of independent research work. My experience with my supervisor was to hand in my completed work. Such was the staff workload in 1949. Following graduation and having worked my way to England on a coal burning tramp steamer I worked under Hans Eysenck at Maudsley Institute on his attitude research project contacting and interviewing Oswald Mosley's Black Shirts in the East End of London, but also I was exposed

---

*   Ray received the award of PhD from the University of Newcastle in 1996.

to some teaching by Anna Freud and counselling by Cyril Burt. Marriage, money and desire to work in industry led to an appointment as Assistant Psychologist at Rowntrees of York. Research was actively encouraged by the company and Leeds University accepted a proposal for a study of 'Induction' for a Masters in Industrial Psychology. My supervision involved close monitoring of my work (chiefly the development of measuring instruments) at weekly meetings by a world authority on cheese tasting. The supervision was regular, targeted and formal. It was my research activities at Rowntrees into such factors as fatigue in the factory, development of simulators for psychological assessment, labour turnover at the school to work level, development of group selection techniques and analysis of lifting strains which attracted the attention of staff at Leeds. Subsequently I lectured on industrial psychology at universities such as Hull, Sheffield and Manchester.

On being approached by British Petroleum (at the end of my work at Leeds) to join a commissioning team for their new oil refinery at Kwinana, Western Australia, I entered a new phase of work experience and learning. One aspect of my responsibilities at Kwinana was training, but involved relationships with unions and industrial relations generally. Once again I was invited to lecture, this time at the University of Western Australia. I ran a section of the Economics course on 'Introduction to Industrial Relations', plus I conducted a weekly Saturday morning seminar for final year psychology students on 'psychology at work'. I left BP to enter the neophyte Australian consulting industry and from 1958-1985 worked as a consultant in various countries, including Australia, in various industries and companies, sometimes as manager of multidisciplinary projects and sometimes as an individual contributor.

Upon 'retirement' I enrolled at Sydney in an Australian History Masters course. My supervisor gave me extreme latitude in researching the history of Hydraulic Lifts in Sydney 1880-1920. That study led to my pursuing a PhD at Newcastle, attracted there because of a particular historian on the staff who worked in the area of youth and work in colonial Sydney which dovetailed with my findings about boys' accident rates working on hydraulic lifts. However, I was introduced to another staff member as my supervisor and I didn't even know, at that time, that this was a Faculty of Education. But I didn't care where I was. I wanted to press on with my new project which was beginning to take shape around the core issue of the impact of sectional interests (unions, employers, government) on industrial training of boys.

So closing the circle, here I was seventy-years-old with the abovementioned working history saying 'How do you do' to an obviously energetic young woman from the Faculty of Education half my age. We eyed each other and started work. Eight years later we have published and presented several joint papers even though our core academic interests differ. I feel sure such relationships are not uncommon and are increasing.

The uniqueness of the relationship

The assertion is made that despite marked differences in background which supervisor and student bring to the relationship there is a standard form to the process of establishing and maintaining an effective working relationship. Structured targeting and measurement of progress seem likely to feature more prominently in the future. Each supervisor/faculty/university has to establish what is considered to be a balance between more procedural structure and the independent uniqueness of each scholar. It is an age old problem - structure versus flexibility. I would not suggest a highly structured standardised process, but there is a need for heightened awareness of five sequential aspects of the relationship. These are the interview before acceptance, induction, settling in, middle period, and the end stretch.

(i)   Interview with student before acceptance by the supervisor

What is the objective of such an interview? Is it solely to check that the regulatory acceptance requirements are met or should it be deeper and more wide-ranging? I feel the process would be improved by probing the applicant's work habits, the assistance received during past academic work, assessment of their previous work and any impediments likely to impact on the smooth progression of the proposed research. The accumulated knowledge of supervisors about failures and successes among research students could be very useful at this stage, but appears to be under-utilised and inaccessible to students. Similarly the experience of the supervisor in relation to the proposed thesis should be discussed with the applicant and opportunity provided for the applicant to assess that experience. As an aspect of staff development a programme to develop skills to handle this first step in the relationship would be well considered.

In the draft of this article a further 1000 words were devoted to an enlargement of the five phases or aspects of the supervisory relationship. The editor decided such a detailed enlargement would end up on the cutting room floor. Operationally this provides a glimpse into the supervisory relationship at its very start. With reference to one of my initial thesis proposals my supervisor's first words were 'this needs a lot of work'. Remember the student is assessing the supervisor as well as the other way round. I knew the supervisor was establishing a power base and setting the on-going structure of the relationship, but other opening options may have improved my initial assessment of that supervisor.

(ii)   Induction

Certain things have to be cleared up during the induction phase by the supervisor. Such as, what can the student expect about such matters as time together, time keeping, presentation of papers, standards, turn around time for presented draft work, ethics and procedures? A written confirmation of agreed arrangements may prove worthwhile. Clarity about expectations and procedures at the beginning of a three to six year relationship should be axiomatic.

Supervisors should help the student to find out about type of, and access to, university and faculty facilities. Other things include communication of departmental organisation, introduction to staff, including librarians and non-academic staff, and to sources of in-house communication such as seminars and notice boards, and to useful information such as lists of conferences, social arrangements, names of union representatives etc. Students should be made aware of current research within the faculty and relevant PhD theses.

(iii) Settling in

Several potential friction points such as time spent with the student, change of supervisors, slow submission and/or return of drafts, should be discussed and resolved at an early stage rather than lingering on to be resolved throughout the candidature in a fumbling, frustrating manner. My experiences were as follows:

- lack of frankness by both parties
- timing and telephoning arrangements left unclarified

That the student is assessing the supervisor is not adequately recognised. Some supervisors forget (it may not even occur to them) that their students can make astute judgements about them based on their own experience of marking papers, counselling and managing others. Issues for the student are reliability, truthfulness, supportiveness (without developing dependency), and bad manners, e.g. the non-return of telephone messages and non-compliance with verbally agreed timetables such as, 'I'll have it ready by...'. A supervisor may claim to have read material and noted points on the draft but the student may quickly recognise hurried, glancing type comments for what they are. Lies and half lies are recognised as such by both students and supervisors.

- testing of the student's level of reading, literature searching and writing

It is worth noting here that early checks by supervisors on the student's source recording methods and bibliographic style will minimise frustrating time-wasting later in the project.

(iv) Middle period

On the assumption that a working relationship between supervisor and student has been established it becomes essential for both to find a balance with regard to time-keeping and method of structuring the thesis. The student must appreciate that he/she is but one of the supervisor's responsibilities while the supervisor should understand that comments such as 'I can pick holes in this', or 'I have spent hours on this' can lead to accumulated resentment when it is obvious to the student that few pages of the submitted draft have been turned and little constructive help is forthcoming.

The supervisor, from my observation, lives amongst chaos and frustration of which any single student forms but a small part. During the settling in and middle phases ambiguous and contradictory research data emerges creating a fog of ever-increasing density. Difficulties can be multiplied by the unarticulated preconceptions and expectations of both parties. Once these are recognised, it is then that two-way compromises and adjustments in the relationship are most likely to be determined. Both parties must realise that differences in working methods will remain and that common ground and common objectives rather than differences should feature. The two individuals are not marching to the same drum. If the students allow their style to be subsumed to someone else's they become clones of the supervisor. Will technology make the latter more likely? Clearly e-mail and web sites will assume a more central role in the relationship, but I believe face to face discussion should continue to be a core part of the relationship. If this need for personal contact is a personal idiosyncrasy then it is a further element of the relationship that will need to be addressed.

But, the exhilarating discovery following unfolding research outweighs the 'crosses' borne by both supervisor and student. The relationship is largely what the individual makes it. Focus and application to the task provide a force which outweighs by far many temporary (or sustained) limitations in relationships.

(v) The end stretch

For the final stage, parameters of assistance to the student have to be established. Should the supervisor 'take over' sections of the final draft? After all a thesis reflects on the supervisor, possibly to as great an extent as on the student. From a supervisor's viewpoint the thesis cannot go forward, let alone fail, so that final polishing and tightening for professional presentation closely involves both parties. Whose will prevails in the final draft? Probably the pattern of guidance has long been established but in the final stages the 'baby' becomes apparent as a whole and the view of 'this is mine' comes from both student and supervisor. Nonetheless, if the student is to leave the postgraduate apprenticeship as a fly-alone professional, they have to accept that they have to build the thesis to an acceptable standard and this may mean target submission deadlines are revised, but at least the student can be confident they are the principal contributor - the alternative is nagging doubts that will carry over into further academic work.

Who will be the examiners? This should be considered early rather than later owing to the personal view, if not the bias of many of the possible examiners. Once non-objective examiners are excluded the choice can be markedly reduced. In addition, such circumstances may force the student to be selectively judgemental in their interpretation of the data and their written expression. Strongly worded summaries may have to be avoided, for example, to avoid creating an unintended impression on examiners. Knowing that non-objectiveness is present and not knowing the examiners results in selective forms of writing. It is an area of thesis production and assessment that requires examination.

Unfortunate realities

Annual progress reports are collected by universities, but what do the responses to such questionnaires provide? Students are motivated to pass whilst supervisors are asked to criticise themselves. Frankness will seldom prevail. The process I have observed is flawed. It is similar to company exit-interviews - the employee will not be frank. He/she is dependent on the company for future references.

I did not have a choice of supervisor in any of my supervised research projects. Nor did I consider it a central factor. All I wanted was to be admitted to candidature and supervision is one of the conditions. After gaining admittance I have always felt that I was on my own. I am independent and prefer it that way. Supervision can be a nuisance, but that is a two-way stretch too. The relationship is a reciprocal as well as a collaborative one. I experienced one supervisor who had difficulty recognising the possibility existed that the material, if not the student, could provide a maturing and learning experience.

My ego has taken a lot of thumps and bumps. However, I retained both enough faith in each project and enough self-confidence to recognise and accept the validity of ego-deflating lessons provided by able supervisors.

In summary, until the parameters of both the roles and aims of both supervisor and student are objectively established and genuinely accepted by both, the relationship so vital to cooperative research, will remain fragile, emotional and unbalanced.

Learning to Think Like a Researcher

Jane Orton[*]
University of Melbourne

Introduction

Learning to do research, like learning any practice, means 'learning *to think like* a practitioner of the field' (Schön, 1987). In academic fields, this clearly entails considerable growth in learning about one's content area. However, considering the process of my own PhD and the experience of supervising a dozen thesis students since then, it would seem that successfully learning *to think like an educational researcher* most essentially requires developing cognitive and emotional skills, broadening fields of knowledge, and gaining a sense of possible research project *shapes* or structures. To help a student develop in these ways, a supervisor must take on a demanding and complex role as teacher-demonstrator-critic, and establish a relationship with the student which is both tough and loving. Tolerance is not helpful if work is below standard; criticism is punitive unless accompanied by assistance to improve. Content knowledge and goodwill towards novices are essential qualities in a supervisor, as are coaching skills and an understanding of different styles of learning.

Cognitive and emotional development

It would be hard to imagine a more concentrated period of cognitive development for me than the four years I spent on my PhD, and this, as much or more than the content itself, has been the enabling source of teaching and research ever since. Yet, as I have discovered in conversations then and later, cognitive development appears to be almost a taboo subject between supervisor and student. This silence is interpreted by the student as an unspoken expectation that he or she has the capacities to proceed with each step of the project, and if not, that this should not be mentioned. Thus when faced with

---

[*]   Jane received the award of PhD from La Trobe University in 1991.

questions which require them to develop beyond their current capacities, many students suffer considerable anguish. They spend hours worrying in secret that 'Maybe I'm not bright enough', rather than understanding the questions to signal entry into a new phase of learning, perhaps the most exciting periods of the whole undertaking, and certainly *normal*.

Exciting they may be, but glimpsing the advent of a whole new phase of learning does also seem to set off a natural law of conservation in many human beings. Particularly in new researchers just beginning their projects I find this quite noticeable, but it can also occur at any transition point throughout a project. If it is at the start, the student will typically arrive holding a narrowly defined and inadequate, but total, research plan, complete with conclusions. Invited to go away and open it up, he or she will return with some development of the background, still followed by the tightly bounded total plan. The student may remain wedded to the plan for quite a while, before abandoning it in favour of a much more mature proposal, something which suddenly shows the openness of a researcher's gaze.

One of the first steps in thinking like a researcher is thus developing some distance on the topic so that it can be opened up to critical scrutiny without disturbing personal equilibrium. This is an especially difficult first step for those researching their own practice arena, as I did and many education students also do. Inquiring into one's own practice necessitates relinquishing one of the base measures of actual practice, the capacity *to cope*: to do the best you can, get by, hang in there, get it together, see it through. Becoming reflective and critical requires holding up to scrutiny actions which were successful in these terms at the time, questioning their value and the validity of their foundations, admitting ignorance and opening one's professional behaviour up to doubt and uncertainty. Embarrassment, guilt, and an intolerance for colleagues or students can be further emotional baggage needing to be laid aside in order to gain a research perspective on familiar situations. Relinquishing their coping mentality and judgemental tendencies add up to students achieving a cognitive and emotional change of state whereby they come *to be in relation to* their problem without *being made up by* it (Kegan 1994). This transformation usually requires the extension of knowledge as well as psychological growth.

Knowledge

As I did at the time, most students who present for supervision in the field of language education and intercultural communication combine reservoirs of sophisticated linguistic and pedagogical knowledge and understanding with huge lacunae of social knowledge and understanding. They usually have only the most primitive idea of how organisations function and change, or of the processes of interpersonal relations and individual change, all of which will impinge to some or a great extent on their research. It is often only as they develop their knowledge in these related areas, and begin to admit the complexity of situations and the relativity of judgements, that they are able to gain a researcher's perspective on the practice arena they want to study.

Research also requires its own knowledge. I was fortunate, I see now, that my desire to use Action Research for my PhD raised so many concerns at the time that it sent me off to months of reading philosophy of the social sciences from which to construct a reliable methodological framework. Although always anxious about 'the politics of method', I enjoyed it even then, and it has been highly useful ever since. These days I am an unabashedly passionate advocate for the compulsory semester-long subject in research methodology taught in my Faculty. Private reading and a few hours of methods and techniques are not sufficient to counter the half-baked scientist norms - the manipulative interviews and surreptitious observation schedules planned in the name of 'objectivity' - that seem still to be the legacy of ill-remembered Year 9 Science, which most students otherwise bring to qualitative method design and ethics.

Project shapes

My experience as learner, researcher and supervisor have taught me that working within the content area of one's research, it is easy to get quite lost in detail unless one is also developing an increasingly strong sense of project *shape*. Talking about shape from the start, and working with students to develop their sense of the shaping process, are necessary, and need to be the major topic of a supervision session from time to time. Evans (1995) has been of great help in starting my own students off in developing a sense of thesis structure, not least those who did their prior studies overseas and have little background in Western academic style and expectations.

Relationship

Knowledge of the field and experience in researching it are obviously important strengths in a supervisor, and students are usually linked with a supervisor through their common core content area. But for a student to learn to think like a researcher, a supervisor has to take on a teaching task broader than that related simply to content or approach. It is a teaching task requiring attitudinal qualities, teaching skills, and energy: gifts to the student of *bothering* and *attention*; tolerance for their conservatism; respect for their courage to abandon the familiar and apparently certain; the technical competence to adjust teaching style to learning style; confidence in the learning process: a student does not need to start at the finishing line in order to end there; and the interpersonal skills to develop a relationship where matters like 'I don't know' and 'I don't understand' become discussable; and work which does not meet the standard can be named as such without debilitating embarrassment or guilt because help to improve is available. Understanding the swell of resistance which can rise when first faced with the demands of a new learning phase, supervisors also need to be tough to withstand the emotional ploys students commonly make use of at such periods.

Conclusion

In conclusion I would say that, if learning to think like a researcher requires the nurture of a supervisor with the skills of an educator, so too does learning to think like a supervisor. Most universities run short courses in supervision as part of professional development programs for staff. Being a practice, however, learning to be a good supervisor is more likely to be achieved through some kind of apprenticeship as well which models the skills and relationship to be developed.

References

Evans, D. 1995, *How To Write a Better Thesis or Report*, Melbourne, Melbourne University Press.
Kegan, R. 1994, *In Over Our Heads*, Cambridge, Harvard University Press.
Schön, D. A. 1987, *Educating the Reflective Practitioner*, San Francisco, Jossey Bass.

The Plain Truth is Out There

Nicholas Sun-Keung Pang*
The Chinese University of Hong Kong

I am grateful to have this opportunity to reflect on my experience of being an overseas PhD student in Australia.

Seeking the overseas experience

Dissonance arises when people face two equal and important choices and when opting for one action is at the expense of the other. Being offered entry to two PhD programs at the same moment, one in Hong Kong and one in Australia, my dissonance lasted until the final decision was made. Understanding the facts that a PhD program might take years to complete if I undertook a part-time research program alongside a full-time job in Hong Kong, and that my family would be suffering for as long as it took, I decided to go for full-time study overseas and intended to finish it as early as possible. Studying overseas also allowed me to start a new life and career, and to acquire extensive exposures and experiences in a new country and to widen my personal views and values towards life and the world. These were the simple motives for my decision but so important that they helped sustain me in coping with the hardships of PhD study.

One of the major reasons that I decided to have my doctoral study overseas was to expose myself to an environment in which English is the first language. It was really a great challenge to me, especially at the beginning of my PhD program. The first day when I was in Australia, I even couldn't understand what people were saying because of their Australian accents! To enhance my skills in reading, writing, listening and speaking English through practice (learning by doing) was the only way I could acquire all these skills. So, I totally immersed my whole life in Australia. I brushed up my English more than ten hours a day, seven days a week, almost nearly for the three years I was there. Learning took place when I read the newspapers, watched the TV and video programs (without Chinese sub-titles), and spoke to people when walking around the supermarkets and on the streets, and to

---

* Nicholas received the award of PhD from the University of Newcastle in 1996.

my neighbours. Another great challenge to me was to switch between the two languages appropriately.

Immersion was the basic technique I used to handle the complex and abstract concepts in the literature and my thesis. Through days or nights, even in dreams, I thought and expressed all the ideas in the same ways as the native speakers. In actual sense my thinking, feelings, emotions and even behaviour (writing) became part of the literature as if my 'whole body', physically and psychologically, was part of the theories.

I was absolutely free to read or not to read, to write or not to write. I was the one totally responsible for my progress. I didn't have to attend any lectures but I attended six Masters subjects. The subjects in educational administration allowed me to revise my knowledge of the literature and to think about what I had to do with my thesis. The subject in qualitative research methodology allowed me to widen my research skills and the one in educational policy allowed me to know more about education in Australia. Most important of all, attending these courses, I exposed myself to English and to people. I read a huge volume of papers and I wrote reports and papers pertinent to my thesis. With all the immersion my supervisors were astonished at my improvement in English.

Australia is a multi-cultural country. I met people from so many different countries. I was eager to make friends with other research students and it was important for me to realize that although I was seriously isolated in my own research, I was not alone in facing the difficulties arising from research study. To me there was no great distinction between being an overseas student and a local student in a PhD program, except at the first stage in which an overseas student might have higher pressure in induction and adaptation in a new environment. A short induction program or an orientation would benefit overseas postgraduate students.

Obtaining supervision

Expectations

In common sense, the criterion of a good supervisor should be more important than that of a good university, because the field of study may be so narrow and advanced that there is no suitable professor in a good university. It is always true that what makes a university or faculty prestigious is a distinguished professor. However, a distinguished professor may also be an absent professor and is not necessarily the best supervisor, though others may be impressed to hear that I have been working with him or her. Neither a good supervisor nor a good university was the criterion I used. Since I was overseas I was too remote to get full information in these two areas and my belief was that it is the candidate who makes a PhD thesis successful. A good supervisor may guide the candidate through the program, but would not do the research for him/her. I should be fully responsible for the quality of the thesis.

A PhD thesis aims at contribution to knowledge. The major challenge for me in the program was not only to convince the supervisors and the graduate committee of the university, but also the external examiners and, most important, the academic circle. Before the commencement of the PhD program, I always worried about whether I could have good understanding of, and insights into the literature and a good theory to be tested, rather than who would be my supervisors and what were their track records. So, without giving very serious considerations to these two areas, I just chose a university with a professor who could supervise me in my area of study.

Multiple supervisors

Because of the complexity and vigour of my research study, the department head recommended team-supervision for me and appointed three professors to supervise my doctoral research: a principal supervisor specialising in educational administration, one co-supervisor in educational policy and one in advanced statistics. The first idea came to my mind was that one good supervisor was just enough; two supervisors would create conflicts; and three would lead to confusions. Different professors, no matter in the same field or not, always have different views on an issue. Paradigm wars are very common when people exchange their views. Team-supervision was good for me to conduct inter-disciplinary research, however, handling a team of three supervisors might be another great challenge to me. I was already faced with many hardships in the doctoral research. I realized that failing to manage group dynamics within the team-supervision would inevitably ruin the thesis and my academic life. Fortunately, I survived the organic process of team-supervision. All four of us (the three supervisors and me) contributed to its smooth running and success. I would like to share with other supervisors and students the five principles that are crucial to the success of team-supervision and what I experienced in the process of team-supervision.

1. A good start. We established explicitly at the outset what I could expect from the supervisors and what the supervisors could expect in return. This included the arrangement of individual and group meetings and the kind of reports of progress to submit. More important, I spoke frankly to them about my fear of facing three supervisors and sought their advice about our relationships in the process of team-supervision.

2. Trust and respect. It was common that my supervisors had diverse views on my research and they tended to disagree. I gave full consideration to their criticisms and tried to fulfil the suggestions as far as possible. If there was no way to reach a compromise, I made the decisions for myself. I found that they always had some good theories behind their suggestions. I never played up their disagreements with each other.

3. Avoid the politics. Politics is everywhere and part of the life for everyone. The politics among the supervisors or within the Department had no room for me and vice versa. I thought it would definitely be a disaster if I got involved. Fortunately, the supervisors were good in keeping me away from the politics.

4. Distinguish between supervisors and friends. My supervisors arranged some social functions informally for other students and me. They had a clear distinction between social times and work times. With this principle in mind, I made no use of social times for the sake of my thesis, but I enriched my social life occasionally by inviting them to dine out.

5. Be sensible, reasonable and supportive. My supervisors realized that team-supervision might have incurred additional pressure on me. I was lucky that they were sensible and understanding and let me feel easy in the numerous contacts. Without their support I would never succeed in the PhD program.

So, now my belief is that it is *not only* my efforts that are crucial to the success of the PhD thesis, but also the efforts of my supervisors.

Progress - 'How good is my work?'

I think I experienced different phases in the candidature similar to other research students, and I experienced difficulties in all of them from time to time in:

(i)   proposing a research topic;
(ii)   organising ideas in the literature and building a framework for research;
(iii) designing the research and planning ahead to conduct it;
(iv)   co-ordinating the subjects in my study;
(v)   handling and analysing data;
(vi)   interpreting results and drawing substantive conclusions, and
(vii) organising chapters and writing the thesis.

These phases were not clear cut and developed linearly as well as cyclically, so that I was moving backward and forward. My emotion was entirely tied to my progress.

What made me feel I was making progress? There were four ways through which I could tell myself I was on the right track. First, through extensive reading of the literature. Second, I seriously cared about the feedback from my supervisors. Their constructive and useful criticisms kept me on the right track, and they provided feedback from different perspectives. Third, I attempted to get further feedback from attending public conferences and presenting papers during my candidature (more learning by doing) and the fourth was to submit papers to journals. It was good the Department had so many internal seminars to allow exchanges between the students and professors. I attended as many as I could. I learned their ways of expressing ideas and organising their projects. I trained myself in judging other's work. I would admire the brilliant and the clever, and sometimes when compared with other's work I could tell my work was not so bad.

To refresh myself I got away from the computer, made friends, I went out for study trips every year and joined the short courses offered in the ASCPRI programs.

There were a few negative feelings, but the most striking was the prolonged loneliness. Conducting PhD research in education where a team approach is seldom used, I had to follow my own area of specialization in isolation. Most of the time was spent in the library, in designing and administering surveys, in wrestling with computer analysis of the data, and often all through the night writing at a computer terminal. Other negative feelings emerged from time pressure which combined with confusion leads to frustration. In instances when the situation was hard to resolve there was disappointment, hopelessness and thoughts about giving up. I always asked: 'How good is my work?' No one could tell me but the supervisors - they were the next-of-kin in my academic life at that moment. They were kind and supportive and this helped me cope with the stress.

The more I specialized in the field the less chance I could share with other staff members and students so conferences and reviewer's comments became very important. Audience responses and queries could tell me how good was my work. Although it was stressful facing the public and open criticism it was sometimes very rewarding: 'Hey! Nicholas, you should improve the data analysis by multilevel methods'; 'Nicholas, your conclusions and suggestions might be too idealistic and the problems in schools may not be solved in these ways'; 'Mr Pang. Well done! I will surely cite your article in my paper' and; 'Congratulations! It is a good piece of work'. The audience was usually kind and generous. I sent several articles to journals for consideration. Sure, it was not an easy task. Nonetheless, whether they were accepted or rejected the reviewer's comments were very valuable. And bingo! *The Journal of Educational Administration* accepted an article and it was only about my pilot study!

What were the rewards? The answers are simple but significant. One was the recognition that came along with the award of the PhD degree, and publications in journals and books, and the other was the overseas experience. All these happenings are now only some ripples in memory - agonies and ecstasies. My reflections on being a PhD student overseas are only the plain truth of myself.

In the End, It's Up to Me

*Peter Beamish**
Avondale College

Seeking a supervisor

I suppose that I should have learnt more lessons from my Masters degree, but it had been a few years since I had completed it, and time encourages you to forget. Besides, I had just finished a twelve month back-packing trip around the world, which leaves one feeling slightly euphoric. I mean, if you can survive constant food poisoning, being robbed on five separate occasions, and having your car catch fire while driving down the autobahn in Germany, surely you can do and survive anything. So it was, with reckless abandon, that I started my PhD.

Two of the biggest decisions I had to make at the beginning of the research project were: What topic am I interested in researching and, as a consequence, who will be my supervisor? I adopted a proactive approach to these questions and started visiting the library to broaden my reading so I would be better informed on developments in my field of educational computing. I thought about what interested me, and what I would like to spend the next years of my life working on. I spoke to other students and some of the lecturers in the Faculty of Education at my local university and gradually began to focus on a range of topics.

I then started to think about a supervisor. I wished to remain at the University of Newcastle, and at the time they had no senior lecturing staff in educational computing. I had established a good rapport with my supervisor during my Masters degree. Although he was strong on research methodology, he was not working in my area and I perceived him to be somewhat resistant to technological change as he refused to use voice mail and was still using DOS while most (like me) were considering Windows 95. The solution was two supervisors. One working in educational computing and my previous supervisor as the senior supervisor. Fortunately, a clear demarcation soon developed between my supervisors and my PhD studies were fully under way.

*   Peter's thesis has been examined and he will receive the award of PhD from the University of Newcastle in 1999

Are these guys doing enough?

I had started with a surge of energy to find a topic, and get a supervisor on board. Once that had been accomplished I thought that the research program would slowly but surely unfold. I started having fortnightly meetings with my supervisors and my immediate reaction was: 'These guys are not doing enough! I'm doing all the hard work and they sit back and reflect on my seemingly inadequate efforts'. They appeared content to give advice about how to make choices, find useful information, correct my misunderstandings, and get me back on course. I came to meetings with questions and dilemmas, and left with suggestions and a whole lot more work to do. I thought, if they have all the good ideas, why don't they help work on the solutions? Our meetings could then adopt a team approach in which we pooled our resources and findings. This would be much more profitable and a much better use of my time.

Then one day after a meeting it hit me. I was driving in my car thinking how I wished my supervisors would do more when it became clear. I am ultimately responsible for the success of my research program! Although supervisors give advice and direction, counsel and encouragement, they do not provide the energy, drive and momentum necessary for the ultimate success of the study. My supervisors were slowly but surely working to raise my level of responsibility and accountability. They were working in the best Vygotskian tradition, as more capable researchers, raising my levels of awareness and performance.

The exact nature of good feedback changes as a PhD project progresses. The feedback that I found particularly useful reflected this progression as follows:

- providing a good sounding-board for ideas and critical evaluation of direction (most students need to be encouraged to kick on after the initial euphoria has passed);
- pointing out directions and references;
- extremely critical eye for methodological considerations;
- monitoring data collection;
- editing the drafts, and
- joint authoring of papers.

Feedback generally took the form of discussions in one supervisor's office. This was good and bad. Good in that it allowed an exchange of ideas and modification of suggestions as problems were discussed. Bad in that you did not have a record of discussions apart from the notes you scribbled. Written feedback is helpful because you can refer to it later. I thought about audio recording the conversations but never actually did it.

Whatever the nature of the feedback, I prefer the supervisor to be frank. Although we all enjoy positive feedback (I know I do) if I'm heading for disaster, I prefer to know. Also feedback needs to be punctual. Although the supervisor has a million things on the go, at times your project cannot proceed until you have sorted out a problem. I do not expect supervisors to drop everything, but if they cannot help you in the short term, they need to communicate this and make arrangements for a meeting in the not too distant future.

Supervisors help students enormously by modelling effective research practice. As I read my supervisors' theses (at first for political correctness and later out of genuine interest), and the journal articles they had written, attended conferences with them, and discussed other research projects they were working on, I began to appreciate more fully the way that research is done, and the contribution it makes to the general progression of knowledge and the specific development of better classroom practice. I began to appreciate, not only how my own research should be conducted, but the contribution that it could make. These lessons are invaluable and if this instruction is not happening students should beg to be included in more of these activities.

Managing time

An area in which I found my supervisors to be of little help was in the area of time management. As well as working on a PhD program, I was also working full time as a lecturer in a private college. I had received a promotion to Head of Department and had to cope with an increased administrative load. Family commitments increased with the arrival of our two children (as I am writing this I can hear my three year old son and two year old daughter creating havoc in the family room). I owner-built our house, and continued to serve on the boards of several community projects and foundations. Of course my supervisors were sympathetic when I told them I was busy, but who isn't? My supervisors often shared tricks as to how they approached a busy schedules, however unless you adopt the same value system and priorities as theirs you will differ. Having two supervisors makes the dilemma worse in that you have two different sets of expectations based on two different sets of priority systems. While not denying the need for a genuine work ethic and some hard yards along the way, maintaining the balance in your life during a PhD candidature is difficult. How one copes with these time pressures does not come from your supervisors but ultimately comes down to personal decisions and priorities.

Supervisors can be away for a variety of reasons including conferences, sabbaticals and holidays. Reasons for, and length of absence, determine expectations about accessibility during these absences. I do not think you can prescribe any hard and fast rules but expectations should be negotiated. I would not expect any help during holidays but planning for their absence is important. Good supervisors will help you structure your work around their absence and negotiate with you the level of support you will need while they are away. I found that it is important that during long absences communication is not terminated and strategies I used included e-mail, express post and fax. I also took advantage of cheap phone deals which assisted when their travels took them out of the state.

Give and take

Traits that, for me, are important in a supervisor include the following:

That they

- are enthusiastic about the student's research project;
- develop a professional/academic relationship while showing a personal interest;
- give the student the impression that their work contributes to knowledge and understanding, and
- are knowledgeable, flexible and have a sense of humour.

Working on a PhD is a very demanding but rewarding experience that provides opportunities for professional and personal growth. I thank the supervisors who have worked with me over the years and guided me on my journey of discovery. For the student, its not all a matter of take. Not many relationships, academic, professional or personal, are unidirectional. It is often tempting for students to think they are a burden to their supervisors, however they may have a lot to offer them. In fact students may even be able to teach supervisors something, for example, expose them to a wider body of literature than they may have occasion to read, bring them up-to-date with technology, challenge them with problems they can not solve immediately, co-author papers and offer friendship. All of these things can put that extra glint in a supervisor's eye. I hope I have on occasion!

PART IV:
Ethics of Supervision

Some Ethical Issues in the Supervision of Educational Research

Martin Bibby
University of New South Wales

This chapter explores some of the ethical issues which supervisors and their research students in education face. It examines some of the choices they have to make, and the ethical considerations that constrain their actions. Since education research is not just one thing, but includes a variety of complexly inter-related sub-disciplines, this discussion is generalised and abstract.[1]

Relations of trust

It is useful to begin with a comparison between the supervisor/student relationship and that between professionals and clients. In preferring this to the master/apprentice and school teacher/student comparisons, I note that supervising differs from other forms of teaching, including apprenticeship, in several respects. An apprentice is employed by the tradesman, and is paid for her/his work. A school student is a child, compelled to attend school, and not in a position to negotiate the content of her/his learning. Research students are adults; they may be older than their supervisor. They choose to do research degrees for purposes of their own, and they are entitled to have these purposes taken seriously in the choice of research topic and the manner of supervision. They come to mutually agreed arrangements with their supervisors, and they proceed in partnership, each with responsibilities to the other. In keeping with this, I shall refer to the supervisor and his/her student as 'the partners'.

The relationship between a professional and her/his client is commonly held to be a fiduciary one. That is, it is characterised by mutual requirements of trustworthiness, in which neither side has total dominance. On the one hand, the professional is not simply an agent of the client, a hired gun, expected to do what the client wants and having no moral responsibility for the result. Lawyers for example are not merely tools of their clients, helping them to achieve whatever they want. Their clients do make the essential decisions on whether to proceed with an action or a contract. Lawyers are expected to volunteer all information that is relevant to a decision, and not, for instance, to press a client to sue an opponent without a full and truthful exposure of the chances of success. However, although professionals' ethical responsibilities to their clients normally take precedence over their own interests, they have responsibilities to their profession and to the communities in which they work which may conflict with their clients' interests. The lawyer must decline to do what the client wants if the action is illegal or immoral. Supervisors, similarly, have responsibilities to universities and to society which restrict the extent to which they should accede to their students' wishes.

On the other hand, a professional relationship is not purely paternalistic, with the decisions and the moral responsibility being taken by the professional alone. Professionals do not take action even in the interests of their clients without consulting their clients' wishes. Lawyers, doctors and engineers are expected to provide their clients with alternatives, and advice on the likely outcomes. The final choice is up to the client, since it is the client's life that is affected (Bayles 1989, pp. 69-79).

So it is with supervisors and their students. Supervisors and students come to mutual agreement on the topic of the thesis and on the arrangements for supervision. As the thesis progresses, choices may have to be made about whether to follow up one issue or another, whether to take the time to deal with some difficulty or merely to note its existence, or whether the candidate will have to take chances in order to finish work within the time s/he can make available. The supervisor gives advice, but in the end it is up to the candidate to decide.

The relationship of mutual trust characterises well the ethical obligations of professional to client and client to professional.

> A client wants the professional to use expertise to analyse the problem, formulate alternative plans or courses of action, determine their probable consequences, make recommendations, or carry out certain activities (audit, surgery) on his or her behalf. A professional's obligations to a client are those necessary to deserve the client's trust that these activities will be performed in a manner to promote the client's interests—including the freedom to make decisions regarding his or her life. (Bayles 1989, pp. 79f)

At the start of the candidature, the student is heavily dependent on the supervisor. The choice of a suitable topic for the thesis is crucial to its success. Both the candidate and the supervisor will be working on this topic for as long as the candidature lasts, which in the case of a part-time PhD may be as long as eight years. The candidate usually arrives with a topic area on which s/he wants to work. Indeed, supervisors are usually chosen because of their expertise in that area. Supervisors must provide students with topics which can be finished in the available time, and which are complex and difficult enough to enable them to make a contribution to knowledge commensurate with the level of the degree. The student's understanding of the methodology appropriate to the topic has to be assessed, also his/her awareness of the literature and of relevant issues in the various branches of education. The supervisor must be made aware of any difficulties the student will have in studying—relevant family circumstances, requirements of part or full time work, lack of facility in the language of instruction. It may be desirable to prescribe that the student take various courses of study, read literature which is tangential to the topic of the thesis or engage in regular conversation in English. The supervisor must also advise whether there is someone else available who is more suited to supervise the thesis than s/he, whether s/he has too much other work to do to be able to supervise a student with this particular combination of needs for assistance, or even whether the student has any hope of completing the degree. Thus the student right from the start must trust the supervisor with a good deal of information, knowing that the outcome may be that s/he sends him away.

As the candidature proceeds, students become more independent. However, progress must be checked. Advice will be needed on overcoming difficulties, on avoiding false trails. Candidates have to trust their supervisors with their ideas, their discoveries of promising avenues for the research to develop. They need to know when they have done enough work to pass, or when they need the remaining time to write their thesis up. At the end of the thesis (and in some sub-disciplines, all the way through) the supervisor must be trusted to make enough time to read drafts carefully and discuss them fully, to advise about format, structure, ordering of ideas, and even grammar. The supervisor must be trusted to determine when the thesis is fit for examination, and to recommend examiners who will be fair. Finally, after the thesis is complete, the supervisor may be asked to provide the candidate with a reference in relation to a job application or an application for promotion. That is a great deal of trust to place in someone whom you may hardly know.

Supervisors in turn must trust their students. Their reputations as supervisors are in their students' hands. They will trust the student with their ideas on matters that they discuss. The student will find out what research they are working on, what ideas they have for further work, what thoughts they have on other matters related to the thesis. Supervisors need to be able to plan their life and work, and so to know what they are letting themselves in for. Each student must be trusted to be honest about his/her needs.

According to Bayles (p. 81), the implication of the fiduciary relation between professional and client is that professionals owe their clients honesty, candour, competence, diligence, loyalty, fairness and discretion. I will use these categories to structure my remarks.

Honesty in supervising relations

Honesty is desirable because it is required for the maintenance of trust. When deceit is exposed, the relationship between the partners may be expected to be endangered. The student is so reliant on the supervisor for guidance (and not only in the early stages of the thesis) that an inability to trust leaves him uncertain and insecure. I have seen students become so suspicious of their supervisors' motives that they interpret everything that they do in the worst possible light. The supervisor likewise can become unwilling to offer the student anything other than the most formal advice.

By depriving deceived persons of the knowledge of the circumstances in which their actions are taken, deceivers take it upon themselves to make decisions for them, to determine the values by which their lives are lived. This is contrary to that respect for persons as moral agents which is the foundation of morality.

Honesty in supervision will involve the partners sorting out who has the right to use what ideas. Bayles compares plagiarising with theft (Bayles 1989, p. 81). It is, of course, not always easy to disentangle the contribution of the student from that of the supervisor, whether to a key idea or to a paper submitted for publication. The AARE Code of Ethics declares that:

> Intellectual ownership is a function of creative contribution. It is not a function of effort expended, nor of formal relationship or status. All those and only those who have made substantial creative contributions to a product are entitled to be listed as authors of that product. These may include research assistants and/or students. Authorship and principal authorship are not warranted by legal or contractual responsibility for or authority over the process that generates an intellectual product. (Supervisors of students' research, for instance, do not have an automatic right to authorship.) (AARE 1995 p. 8)

Thus supervisors are declared not to have an automatic right to principal authorship when they have contributed to the creative work. The presumption, indeed, is against it. For a PhD is supposed to be an original work which makes a substantial contribution to knowledge. It is difficult to see how a work which meets these requirements could have been substantially done by the supervisor, or even how the supervisor can be entitled to authorship at all.

At the same time, thesis writing is not the candidate's unaided work. Depending on the sub-discipline (a complicating factor of some significance) the supervisor will help to sort out the topic to be researched, help the student gain access to the literature, provide critical input or even direction into the method of research, make critical comments and propose or demand further research as the results start to emerge, draw the student's attention to relevant published material, and provide advice about presentation and validity of arguments towards the end of the process. It would be wrong of the student to pass off the work as her/his own unaided research. Some proper acknowledgment is required.

These functions of the supervisor are well known. The stipulations on the PhD have to be read with them in mind, as do lists of publications.[2] There is, however, a difference between a publication which results from a thesis, where the work of the supervisor is limited to the standard procedures, and one where an academic is a genuine joint researcher. It would be better if academics' *curricula vitarum* had a separate heading for publications of students which result from supervised research, rather than, in the present misleading practice, having them included in the principal list of publications where first or joint authorship is claimed.

The acknowledgment of students' ideas in lectures and publications is a related requirement of honesty.[3] Whatever is decided about these matters, they should be discussed with the candidate early in the supervision, along with the ownership of copyright, patents, software and other intellectual property.

Honesty is also required in the writing of references. This is owed to the reader and the student alike. While that point is not likely to be contentious, it becomes a problem in circumstances of high unemployment. If one's students are to have a chance of employment or promotion, do they not need glowing references? If colleagues are known, or suspected, of giving exaggerated references, is not a bit of truth-stretching permissible?

This response is typical of crude utilitarianism.[4] Crude utilitarianism involves using short term and limited consequences to judge a proposed action, and further, concentrating on the effects that favour the outcome desired. To be a defensible moral theory, utilitarianism must take into account the long term and widespread consequences on a society of the adoption of practices.[5]

In the case at hand, the issue of glowing references to students who are not worthy of them weakens the institution of seeking and giving references to the point where it is nearly useless. References are diminished in use from the most important criterion in appointment and promotion to the least. And thus their use as an important indication of which candidate is most fit for a job is destroyed.

Candour and supervision

Honesty only requires that a person does not deliberately deceive someone else. Candour goes beyond honesty, in that the candid person provides all the information that is important for a client's decisions, without having to be asked (Bayles 1989, pp. 83ff). Candid supervisors will disclose to students the uncertainty of outcome of a research degree, their chances of success, the usefulness of the degree in relation to their purposes in taking it, the amount of preliminary work needed in order to be able to commence the research, the extent of the existing literature and the implications of that for the research. They will explain the extent of their competence, and the pressures on their time, including the number of other research students they have. Candour requires also some disclosure to the prospective research student of the nature and state of education research and of its reputation amongst other academics.

Candid supervisors will inform their students about their rates of progress as candidature proceeds. Candour is also involved in not extending a student's candidature unreasonably. A student who is unlikely to complete the thesis successfully should be told, as soon as this is apparent. (There needs, naturally, to be opportunity for students to improve or overcome difficulties affecting their work.)

If honesty requires truthful references, candour requires that the student be given some understanding of whether their supervisor's reference is likely to be helpful in their obtaining a post—and which posts. This is a matter that can cause some embarrassment and hostility. Yet there is no respect for persons in allowing someone to think their supervisor is writing good references for them when s/he is not. Once the student finds out, as they inevitably will, a sharp deterioration in relationships may be expected.

Candour is, of course, a requirement on the student too. Should something go wrong with the student's relations with research subjects, or with, say, the principal of a school where research is being carried out, the supervisor will need to know quickly. Attempts to conceal the full gravity of the situation will put the supervisor in a false position in dealing with the offended people.

More mundanely, the supervisor is entitled to know what the student hopes to gain from doing the degree, and any circumstances that might impede that student's progress. The student should be open about any difficulties with the work or with the supervision, or ethical or methodological problems with the research plans.

Competence and diligence

The extent of background needed to perform competently is likely to be a sore point. Competent education research requires a substantial knowledge of at least one sub-discipline and a good knowledge of others. It requires time, and motivation to complete a long and arduous process. A research thesis requires these things of both the student and the supervisor

Supervisors, too, have difficulty keeping up. No one can read all the research on education, nor all the research in any foundation discipline that is relevant to education, (such as all the work in history that bears on the history of education). One could perhaps hope to read all the philosophy of education that is published in English each year. No one can read all the work published in educational psychology.

This is no trivial matter. I have heard many papers given at conferences where the researcher appears unaware of work done in other sub-disciplines which bears upon his/her own work. Researchers can repeat research done years ago, or make presuppositions which are known to be false, or, even worse, try to prove what is known to be false.

Supervisors and students can try to avoid being caught out by attending conferences and by discussing work with colleagues. Theses can be discussed with colleagues in their early stages and as they develop. Competence requires the willingness to listen to their objections and take them seriously. It is obviously undesirable that the first time a student hears of an objection to their thesis is when the examiner recommends that it be re-written.

Diligence is a virtue that gives rise to fewer moral conflicts. There is pressure on some academics to take on more students than they can handle. It is up to supervisors to ensure that they have the time necessary to perform their role properly. Regular meetings with students, rapid return of drafts, thorough criticism, careful advice and keeping up with the literature are what is required. The provision of adequate training in research theory and methods fits in here, including ensuring that candidates have a good understanding of the various relevant views and disputes about research. The academic also needs to be up to date with university procedures and requirements on the degree.

Diligence by students is obviously basic to completion of the degree. However, they also owe it to their supervisors not to waste their time by needing explanations to be given many times or in other ways being unprepared for their consultations.

Loyalty and fairness

The partners owe loyalty to each other. There can be no trust without this. However, the obligation to be loyal is often over-ridden by the requirements of fairness. For instance, supervisors should press for funds to be provided for their students where these are important for the research, or where students need them to attend a conference that will assist their work. Supervisors should press their students' cases even when they themselves have a case for spending the funds, if the students' needs are greater. A university department, however, may have to choose between two students. There is no lack of loyalty if a supervisor decides that the second student has the better case, even if that person is not the supervisor's own student. It is a harder judgement when the choice is between the supervisor and the student. Supervisors may prefer their colleagues to make the decision in such cases, to avoid conflicts of interest.

No such easy route is available for conflicting demands for time. There are limits to the amount of time a student may reasonably claim. Supervisors are expected to do their own research, supervise other students, prepare classes, and make contributions to public life. They are also entitled to time with their families and for leisure. They must decide what is fair to their various students and themselves. They are not the servants of their students, at their beck and call. In making demands on their time, students must be fair to the supervisors too.

What, though, if a supervisor were approached by a book editor with an offer to publish a paper on the topic of the student's thesis, where the student knows more about the topic than the supervisor does? Here loyalty and fairness are on the same side. The editor should be told about the student.[6]

Loyalty can conflict with candour, too. Supervisors are expected to report to their heads of department or deans at fixed intervals about the progress of their students. The trust placed in the supervisor by an employer demands that the report be candid, but loyalty to the student may tempt the supervisor not to reveal difficulties that the student faces.[7] In general, this temptation should be resisted. Such reports are intended to ensure that help is provided to candidates, not to provide the opportunity to end their candidature.[8]

In some cases the partners may be married to each other, or be parent and child. This has the potential to create very difficult situations through conflicting loyalties, and it should be avoided if possible. Friendship, though, is another matter. The partners will often become friends during the candidature, and this situation creates a second set of loyalties on top of those owed in virtue of the supervision arrangements. Fairness over-rides these loyalties too. In general, justice is a fundamental value, and as such, over-rides all others.

Loyalty to colleagues can be a matter of concern. There is a temptation to involve research students in the politics of the education faculty or department; to engage them in ideological disputes, or if not that, to enlist them on the 'right' side. This may be seen as part of their induction into academic life.

It is true that such tensions are part of academic life, and, I think, that students should become aware of them. Since one of the functions of the PhD is as a gateway to a university position, it is perhaps part of the supervisor's task to help students understand what they are getting themselves into if they take on an academic career—or any career. However, that does not mean that the supervisor should be a bad role model. It is better to talk accurately and fairly about what colleagues are doing where this is relevant to the student's choices, and leave the judgements to the student. There is a place for showing a good deal of compassion, too, and understanding of the pressures of life; as well as a time when internal whistle-blowing is desirable—as sometimes it will be. Students should learn by example here. Students might also be taught the prudential wisdom of keeping their hands clean.

It is common and appropriate for the research student to be consulted before examiners of his/her thesis are appointed. The prime requirements are that examiners should know the area of research, know what standard is required of a pass or a grade of honours, and are themselves fair. The requirement of expertise is naturally dealt with at the start of the candidacy, with the candidate encouraged towards an area where it is available. Still, expertise is a matter of degree, theses are original, and it would be absurd to prevent a candidate from pursuing new and important lines of research on the grounds that there are no potential examiners working on the same material.

There is plainly not just one standard operating in education. The different sub-disciplines have different requirements, and there is a degree of arbitrariness in attempts at comparison—though there is no shortage of complaints about the standards of other people's research. Within each sub-discipline, however, standards also have come to vary widely. Accordingly it would be possible to improve the chances that a marginal student will pass by arranging for examiners with lower expectations to be appointed. This, however, would be unfair to the institutions that may employ or promote the candidate, to his own future students or subordinates, and to the candidate, who may gain an exaggerated impression of her/his competence. In the long run it does great damage to the reputation of education as a discipline. It is, however, reasonable that the examiners should share the partners' view on the methodology of the research.

Equally, choosing persons with toughest standards may be unfair to all but the best candidates. There needs to be some more discussion about standards of degrees across Australia, to obtain some agreement on what is expected. Otherwise we shall be at the mercy of governments pressing for higher success rates and shorter completion times, and the PhD will lose its value. Already, appointment committees are looking for publications as proof of the quality of the PhD.

Should one of the examiners be a person who is likely to oppose the candidate's views? This used to be an expectation, and it was designed to ensure that the standard was maintained. Supposedly, if a candidate could persuade an unsympathetic examiner that the thesis should be passed, then it must be of high quality. I cannot see, however, that this is necessarily the case. An examiner is as likely to treat a thesis s/he disagrees with more lightly than others, fearing that s/he may be prejudiced against it.

There is a reasonable expectation that supervisors will offer candidates advice about their careers. Care should be taken that that advice is offered even handedly—without favouritism or preference on the basis of gender, colour, social class, religion, sexual orientation, marital status, ethnic background, or national origin.

Advice, though, is one thing. Assistance is another. A supervisor is not in a position to promise her/his student favourable treatment in a job application. Devising criteria for appointment in order to ensure that only a favoured candidate is likely to fulfil them is not only dishonest, it is disloyal to the employing institution, since it is thereby deprived of the best available staff member. A contrasting trap here is exploiting candidates, for example burdening them with administrative tasks. Thesis candidates, with their dependence on the goodwill of the supervisor, are not in a good position to refuse what they are asked to do. In general, no administrative work should be given unless the candidates are explicitly paid for it. Supervisors, in consultation with their candidates, have an obligation to protect them against such exploitation, and to ensure that they are not accepting too much employment because they feel vulnerable if they refuse.

It is probably better, also, not to accept a candidate as a subject for experiments, even when he volunteers for this purpose; nor to accept his relatives and friends, nor his own students, if he is a teacher.

Discretion and supervision

The main demands on the discretion of the partners are the temptation to gossip and breach of confidence. Breach of confidence and gossip are betrayals of the partner's trust; they threaten to destroy the relationship between them and the supervisor.

It is undesirable for a supervisor to have sexual relationships with a candidate, for as with student teacher relationships at a younger level, the supervisor can never be entirely sure that the candidate is acting in freedom. Further, the supervisor will be in difficulties fostering the candidate's career—it will be impossible to act without giving the appearance at least of favouritism. Wherever possible, if such relationships start to develop, the candidate should be transferred to another supervisor.

The National Tertiary Education Union asserts in its Code of Ethics that small presents by students may be accepted by an academic, provided there is no suggestion of favours in return. Matters are particularly delicate where cultural differences are present—ensuring that there are no misunderstandings without giving offence calls for a degree of tact, especially since in some cultures giving presents to one's teacher is a mark of respect, and in others, bribes are a way of life. In my view, it is better to refuse all gifts until after the degree has been awarded, to avoid any possible misunderstanding.

The ethics of research

Discussion of the ethics of education research is properly part of the supervision process. Supervisors who ignored it would be telling their students that moral issues do not matter; or worse, that there are no moral issues in the research that they are doing. Further, a research degree is widely used not just as an end in itself or professional development for school teaching, but as a qualification for an academic or a senior administrative job. Allowing a candidate to enter either profession with an immoral approach to research stirs up trouble for the future; fostering such a candidate contributes to a decline in morality in education.

What should be included in the discussion of ethics? Actions and attitudes of the supervisor make a natural starting point. Where ethical issues are involved in the student's or the supervisor's research or in the supervisor's actions, they should be discussed with the student. The supervisor's attitude to the university ethics committee (whose consent is usually required for research on human subjects) and to the procedures and forms they require will be important too.

It might be objected that, unlike the situation in other disciplines, education research students are usually mature, with several years of teaching experience. Accordingly they can be expected to have a well-developed morality, and be accustomed to dealing with the moral dilemmas of the classroom and the profession. My experience of teaching professional ethics to postgraduate students, however, is that moral issues are often not well handled. The major problem is that crude utilitarianism of which I wrote above, which takes account of only a few of the immediate consequences of an action and ignores effects on schools and on society. Such comments such as 'Where else can we get students from?', or 'The benefits of this research will far outweigh any concerns about deception', or 'If we tell the subjects that they have been deceived, it will get about and we won't be able to continue our research with other subjects' are an indication of an intention to ignore subjects' rights and harm to society. The Australian Association for Research in Education's Code of Ethics is firmly opposed to such an approach.

> Subordinates, students or others may not be compelled or pressured to participate in research. Persons should know when they are to be participants in research, be asked for their informed consent, and be entitled to withdraw at any time ... Deception is an attack on the autonomy and integrity of participants. Such deception is scarcely ever justified ...

(p. 3; See also Bibby, Martin (ed.) 1997, *Ethics and Education Research,* p.117.)

Ethics committee documents are an indication of what matters the university treats most seriously. One of the issues that might be expected to arise in such discussion is the appropriateness of university procedures to education research. I argued (Bibby 1997b) that education researchers should not seek to isolate their ethics procedures from those of other researchers, on the grounds that a weakening of procedures for the (usually innocuous) research in education would have flow-on effects for research in other fields. It is true that research in education usually carries minimal risk of harm. However, education researchers cannot prevent their advocacy of lesser standards for 'safe' research from having impact on other disciplines.

This issue should be discussed with the candidate, along with the issues of doing research on children and teenagers and on disadvantaged minorities. Supervisors should also take the time to discuss with their students the ethical issues raised by their own research. Ethical issues involved in their research should be raised from time to time in staff members' contributions to research seminars and in discussions there of students' research. Issues not only of research methods but of the social responsibility of doing the research at all should be raised as appropriate. To avoid those issues is to deny responsibility for society; it is to fail as a professional.

A segment on the ethics of research should be part of standard subjects in research methods. This might be based on an accepted code of research ethics, and should at least aim to make the candidate aware of the rights of participants and the ethics of publication. In addition to these compulsory components, it is desirable that a climate of moral concern be created. Subjects in professional ethics, which are increasingly available as part of Master of Education and Master of Education Administration courses, should include segments on the ethics of research. Research students could be encouraged to attend papers on research ethics. They should be brought into discussions on the ethical issues as they arise in the universities, and be encouraged to contribute to the construction of codes of ethics or their revisions.

It might be appropriate at the end of the candidature if the student were asked by the Dean or the Head of Department to make some written comment on the features of the research process, its procedures and support, and any problems encountered. This would include any ethical concerns the student may have. The request would be best made after the examination of the thesis is complete.

Impotence and the driven snow

'Only the impotent are pure'. This quotation from Australia's former prime minister Gough Whitlam sums up a possible response to the demands of ethics committees, the ethical standards expected in research, and my remarks in this paper on the ethical demands on supervisors and their students. Supervisors can only do so much, make so many sacrifices in the interests of what they believe in, spend so much time with students, engage in so much argument with colleagues. Supervision of student research competes with other tasks in the academic's crowded work life. Governments press for early completion and high success rates, and for greater 'productivity'. Rejecting students has become expensive. Students have limited time to complete a degree, and will often have a job and a family making demands on their time. The standards required may be seen as irksome. Does there not come a time when the harm done in trying to maintain standards is greater than that done be letting in a few exceptions?

These pressures threaten standards, education policy and the quality of future academics, teachers and administrators. They limit what supervisors can do for their students.

The problem of dirty hands was an issue much discussed in the 1970s (e.g. Walzer 1973, Howard 1977, Williams 1978, Lukes 1986, Coady 1993). It concerned the committing of very great evil in order to prevent worse, with the principal example being the dropping of the atomic bomb on Hiroshima. I draw on the conclusions of that debate. 1. If evil actions are to be justified by their consequences in preventing evil, then they have to be successful. 2. The evil doer, and indeed all involved, is obliged to work to ensure that the situation where the choice of evils has to be made does not recur. 3. The immoral action is not justified if there is some other, less evil action, which will achieve the same end.

When applied to the lesser immoralities of university life, these points tell strongly in favour of sticking to driven snow (or totally pure) standards. The cost of developing competence in cheating is that one must become a cheat. Moreover, once people become cheats, they then tend to reach for deceit wherever it might be useful. As increasing numbers of people 'play the game' of getting their students through and publishing as much as possible, standards in education research will decrease, and the standard of education in schools will follow it. Universities will gain a poor reputation with their former students, and government pressures will increase.

Thus the consequences of soiling one's hands are not in the end an increase in the general good. If only the impotent are pure, the potent are only potent for harm. I do not believe, however, that Whitlam's point is correct. Persons of competence and integrity gain respect and trust. They are potent for good.

Notes

1.   By sub-disciplines I mean educational psychology, comparative education, the history, philosophy, sociology, economics and politics of education and education administration.

2. There are differences between the sub-disciplines here. In some, joint authorship with their research students, is almost never claimed. In others, it appears to be done as a matter of course.
3. I owe my awareness of this to Professor David Armstrong, former Professor of Philosophy at Sydney University, whose careful practice of acknowledgement was exemplary.
4. I owe this term to Dr. Kathie Forster, of the University of Technology, Sydney.
5. For further discussion of moral theories in a context of education research, see Bibby (1997a).
6. Here joint publication may be the way out.
7. I owe this point to Dr. Allyson Holbrook.
8. I did have occasion once to conceal the area of a student's work from my Head of School and Dean. They had objected to his working on the rights of homosexual school teachers on the grounds that such a discussion ought not to take place in a university!

References

The Australian Association for Research in Education 1995, *Code of Ethics for Research in Education*, Coldstream, Victoria, AARE.

Bayles, M. D. 1989, *Professional Ethics*, Belmont, Calif. Wadsworth, 2nd ed.

Bibby, M. 1997a, 'Introduction', *Ethics and Education Research*, RARE No. 4, Coldstream, Victoria, AARE.

Bibby, M. 1997b, 'The medical model and informed consent', in M. Bibby (ed.), *Ethics and Education Research*, RARE No. 4, Coldstream, Victoria, AARE.

Bibby, R. M. 1985, 'Aims and Rights', *Educational Philosophy and Theory*, 17 (2), pp. 1-12.

Bridges, D. 1986, 'Dealing with controversy in the school curriculum' in J. Wellington (ed.), *Controversial Issues in the Curriculum*, Oxford, Blackwell.

Coady, C. A. J. 1993, 'Politics and the problem of dirty hands', in P. Singer (ed.), *A Companion to Ethics*, Oxford, Blackwell, pp. 373-383.

Howard, W. K. 1977, 'Must public hands be dirty?', *Journal of Value Inquiry*, 11(1), pp. 29-40.

Lukes, S. 1986, 'Marxism and dirty hands', *Social Philosophy and Policy*, 3 (4), pp. 204-223.

National Tertiary Education Union 1998, *Code of Ethics*, East Melbourne, NTEU.

Walzer, M. 1973, 'Political action: The problem of dirty hands', *Philosophy and Public Affairs*, 2 (2), pp. 160-180.

Williams, B. 1978, 'Politics and moral character', in S. Hampshire (ed.), *Public and Private Morality*, Cambridge, Cambridge University Press.

Acknowledgements

I would like to thank the editors of this volume and an anonymous referee for their helpful comments on a draft of this chapter. They are not to be blamed for the faults that doubtless remain. I would like also to thank my research and coursework students over many years of teaching the ethics and the social philosophy of education, on whom I have tried out my ideas. Their indirect contribution to this material has been profound.

PART V:
The Future:
Reconceptualisation and
Challenge

Off-campus Doctoral Research and Study in Australia: Emerging Issues and Practices

Terry Evans
Deakin University

Margot Pearson
Australian National University

Introduction

In this chapter we describe both the broad context of Australian doctoral education within which off-campus doctoral research in education has emerged since the establishment of doctoral degrees in Australia, and also the trends which now shape further development. On this basis, we then draw the main implications and explore some of the issues for 'students' and 'supervisors' as they undertake their work together.

We argue that the future of postgraduate research in Australia is going to be based on research students who complete their doctoral research and study in varying forms of 'flexible' or 'mixed-mode' study. Doctoral students will choose to be full or part-time, on or off campus depending on the nature of their research, their personal needs and employment commitments. They may be principally off-campus, but incorporate some periods on-campus, possibly full-time for a period. They may be based on-campus but choose to spend significant parts of their candidature in the workplace and often abroad. In professional arenas the research will normally be based within the student's professional practice. We suggest that there are some important policy and planning initiatives required to create the best possible conditions to ensure that the research conducted is of a high quality and addresses the relevant scholarly, professional and national needs.

In a field such as education the supposedly traditional approach of full-time on-campus study and research for young researchers preparing for initial career entry, has never been appropriate, nor practised widely. Yet the concept of the traditional supervisor who either offers close supervision at the bench (the 'apprentice' model frequent in the sciences), or allows the student freedom of independent study from the beginning (the 'coming of age' model frequent in the social sciences and humanities), still dominates our thinking (Moses 1985). In education the role of the supervisor should not be expected to follow either model, or their extremes whether some form of 'overseeing' or benign neglect. A supervisor's role should be one of providing a 'critical friend' or mentor ; or perhaps to re-cast the North American university term 'adviser'. We would prefer to conceptualise a role for the supervisor based on a systematic analysis of the needs, strengths and capacities of mature professional 'students' and of the professional contexts in which they work.

Context: Changes in postgraduate research education nationally

Since 1989, the increasing numbers of people participating in higher education and the expansion of the university sector has been reflected in rising numbers of postgraduate students: there were 14,751 higher degree research students in 1989 rising to 33,560 in 1996 (DEETYA 1996, p. 17). This growth has occurred in all institutions, but most doctoral study is still concentrated in the established research-based institutions as might be expected (Appendix A *Table: Postgraduate and doctoral students by state and institution 1996*).

Doctoral study is a relatively recent aspect of tertiary education in Australia. The first doctoral degrees in Australia were awarded after the second World War, and doctoral study was, prior to 1989, confined to a small elite university system. In the main, doctoral study in Australia followed the British model which itself is a combination of the disciplinary department system which spread to England from Scotland, and the emphasis on personal tutorial relationships which characterised teaching in the English university college system. This is an approach discussed by Clark as an extension of a specialised BA program (or a 'B. A. plus some research time' according to Johnson, quoted in Clark 1995, p. 79). Echoes of this model as the system 'norm' linger in the rules and handbooks of many institutions in Australia, with an emphasis on residency requirements, regular contact with the supervisor, and concerns about mode of attendance. This latter condition was identified as particularly problematic for part-time candidates in the Australian Vice-Chancellors' Committee (AVCC) Code of Practice for Higher Degrees (1990). It was stated in this code that for admission:

> Since part-time students often have other obligations, the criteria could include: availability for study and interaction with the supervisor, level of motivation, evidence of maturity, and capacity to cope. (AVCC 1990, p. 5)

However with the overall growth of the higher education system the doctoral student population has become more diverse in many respects and the practice of supervision more flexible.

Characteristics of the doctoral population

An analysis of the 1996 doctoral student population (Pearson & Ford 1997) revealed the diversity of individual students in respect of age, sex and modes of enrolment, as well as differences among the broad fields of study (BFOS as defined by Department of Employment, Education, Training and Youth Affairs (DEETYA) 1996). The different profiles across the BFOS are of interest because they challenge perspectives on supervision based on an assumption that most doctoral students are either in the BFOS of Science or in the BFOS of Arts, Humanities and Social Sciences. Yet in 1996 46% of the doctoral students were in the other BFOS which could be loosely categorised as professional fields. It is this distribution which explains how Education doctoral students can seem quite different from the total doctoral population in many respects as described in Table 1, but yet share important characteristics with other fields. Education as a field is distinctive but not unique.

Table 1   A comparison of characteristics of education doctoral students with the total 1996 doctoral population

Characteristic	% All doctoral students	% Education doctoral students
Under 30 years	35%	4%
30 years +	65%	96%
Female	41%	52%
External	3%	13%
Part-time	36%	63%
International	13%	7%
Total enrolments	22,696	2,145

The great majority of Education doctoral students are over 30 years of age, whereas the figure is smaller for the total population, though still larger than is often supposed as shown in Table 2. Sixty five percent - nearly two-thirds of all doctoral students - are 30 years of age or older. In all BFOS except Science, those under 30 are in the minority. Some of the older doctoral students will be professionals returning to study, some will have been mature-aged undergraduates (Bazeley, et al. 1996). Some will be university staff upgrading their qualifications, as has been a feature of university life for many years. It has always been customary for staff without higher degrees to complete them while teaching, and tutoring has long been a means to finance doctoral study - for example Deakin University had 157 staff enrolled in higher degrees in 1995, of whom 100 were pursuing doctoral degrees, and of these 45 were enrolled in other institutions (Deakin 1996).

Table 2   The distribution of doctoral students in Australian institutions by age and sex, 1996

Age	Under 30	30-39	40-49	50-59	60-64	65+	Total
Female	3,282	2,993	2,250	695	61	62	9,343
Male	4,659	4,918	2,864	760	76	76	13,353
Total	7,941	7,911	5,114	1,455	137	138	22,696
%	35.0	34.9	22.5	6.4	0.6	0.6	100

Source: Adapted from Pearson & Ford, 1997, p. 8.

The difference in age distribution for education doctoral students is not only one of numbers. The modal age group is 40-49 years as shown in Figure 1, a characteristic shared with Architecture and Building, though to a lesser extent for the latter. The pattern of distribution across age groups is similar for men and women in both fields. Although as shown in Table 2, overall numbers for women doctoral students peak in the under 30 year old age group in contrast to the figures for men whose numbers peak in the 30-39 age group, patterns of age distribution across BFOS are still similar for men and women within other well populated BFOS. While Science doctoral students are still overall predominantly male and younger with 56% being under 30 years of age, women Science doctoral students are also concentrated in the under 30 year old age group. In Arts, Humanities and Social Science where more doctoral students are women than men, the modal age group for both sexes is 30-39 years (Appendix B, and Pearson & Ford 1997, pp. 127-131).

Significantly more education doctoral students are enrolled as external students as a percentage of their field of study and in terms of actual numbers (282 out of 737 for all BFOS). In respect of part-time enrolments, there are more in the field of Education as a percentage of enrolments in that field, but not in terms of actual numbers of official part-time doctoral enrolments which totalled 8,062 or 36%, in 1996. As might be expected there are fewer part-time doctoral students enrolled in the field of Science (23%), in contrast to: Health (34%); Arts, Humanities and Social Science (39%); and Business, Administration, Economics (54%). However, the official figures for 1996 from the statistics provided by DEETYA, from which these percentages are calculated, underplay the extent of 'flexible' enrolments. A difficulty with the present data collection and thinking is that the definitions are fixed while practice is not. Not only has the growth of part-time enrolments created an effective 'open' campus (Evans 1995), but in practice students can and do change their type enrolment from external, to part-time and full-time, and combinations thereof, during the course of their candidature. Provisions for such flexibility are written into some institutional rules (e.g. Charles Sturt University), and the practice is widespread. In addition, many institutions (e.g. Griffith, University of Queensland, University of Technology, Sydney) have provisions for off-campus study and research which do not constitute 'external' enrolment so that the official DEETYA figures for external study do not capture the larger number of students who are based off-campus much of the time. This means that mixed enrolment, which comprises students moving in and out of part-time and full-time enrolment, and continuous on-/off-campus enrolment is more of a reality than official statistics acknowledge.

Figure 1   Age distribution of men and women doctoral students in education

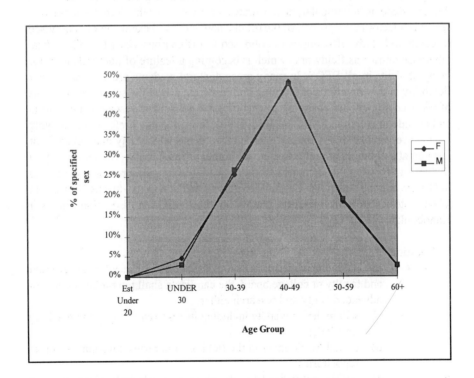

Another small but sizeable group of doctoral students are international (13% of total doctoral enrolments: 2,171 male, 874 female. *Selected HE Student Statistics*

1996, DEETYA). Education has a small number in comparison with other BFOS—only 5% of the total international doctoral enrolments (Pearson & Ford 1997, p. 125). This group of doctoral students is likely to grow in size overall, but not all of them will be studying within Australia. Although academic networks have always operated across national boundaries through visits of colleagues, academic exchanges, hosting of students for short periods during the PhD candidature, and employment of postdoctoral fellows, networking is now seen as important for the overall research and education program linked to the growth of globalisation (Grigg 1996, Back, Davis & Olsen 1996). This networking has come to include 'off-shore' programs and candidates, with a growing interest in more flexible arrangements which include distance enrolment, or mixed mode study whereby limited time is spent in Australia.

The trend to more off-campus research and study

The preceding description of the doctoral population in general, and Education doctoral students in particular, demonstrates the diversity of the doctoral population which is a factor in the growth of the official and unofficial extension of supervised research and study off-campus (as opposed to off-campus visits to collect data, otherwise known as fieldwork) which is becoming a feature of doctoral study for many students in all BFOS. In many areas doctoral students are seeking greater flexibility in the conditions of learning and research; and at the same time patterns of research activity are changing to encompass a network of research sites within and outside universities (ARC/NBEET 1996). Students may prefer to be carrying out their research at their workplace, or in other arenas which may necessitate their locating at a distance; or prefer to study at home, or in a library. The University of Sydney, a diverse multi-campus institution, with teaching and research campuses in Darwin and the Australian Capital Territory in addition to its various New South Wales sites, states the situation simply in their rules on 'Location' in their Handbook:

Location
12. (1) Subject to the annual approval of the supervisor, head of department and faculty or college board, the candidate shall pursue the course of advanced study and research either:
a) within the University including its research stations and teaching hospitals;
b) on fieldwork either in the field or in libraries, museums or other repositories;
c) within industrial laboratories or research institutions or other institutions considered by the faculty or college board concerned to provide adequate facilities for that candidature; or
d) within a professional working environment;

and shall attend the University for such consultation with the supervisor and shall participate in such departmental and faculty or college seminars as shall annually be specified. (University of Sydney 1995, p. 39)

Some of this flexibility has always been practised, but unacknowledged in institutional rules, nor as already indicated, in official data collection. Now even further flexibility in location has become possible with the feasibility of synchronous and asynchronous interaction mediated through computer and communications technologies. These technologies allow for more flexible strategies for students seeking to communicate with their supervisors and the institution from off-campus. Others, in contrast, will be seeking expanded access to expertise and experience globally, through e-mail correspondence, Web browsing, list servers and 'chat' groups. Such uses of technology for communication are the more important given the increasing mobility of academic staff and the use of supervisors external to universities. Many such supervisors and advisors may be based in industry, professions and research organisations.

The need to access expertise off-campus is also growing with changes in the patterns of research activity. Clark (1996) argues that a significant pressure for change in higher education is substantive growth which is driven by the proliferating base of academic knowledge and disciplinary fragmentation. This substantive growth is 'knowledge-led and generated largely by research' (p. 424). As an example of this growth he cites the development of a classification scheme for review journals that includes over 4,500 subtopics arranged under 62 major topic areas (p. 421). In another context Clark also highlights an extension to substantive growth in professional fields as:

...each profession or would-be profession develops a research wing. As hordes of knowledge workers in the general labor force have come to claim a research role, they too generate specialised literatures. Such self-amplifying production of basic and applied research turns substantive growth into a societal phenomenon rather than just characteristic of research-based higher education. (Clark 1995, p. 194)

This professional growth generates interest in doctoral study from potential students who do not necessarily expect to proceed to an academic career. They can be professionals seeking to consolidate their experiential knowledge for personal satisfaction. They may be responding to a perceived market demand for 'expert' professionals in the workplace (Haworth 1996, p. 393).

In Australia in more established fields there is pressure to introduce students to the culture of industry where they are likely to be employed (Clarke 1996, pp. 6-12). Government schemes to promote industry-related research include the Australian Postgraduate Research Awards (Industry) Scheme which was launched in 1990 to strengthen industry-university linkages, and the Cooperative Research Centre Scheme (CRCs) which has as one of its objectives:

> to promote the active involvement of researchers from outside the higher education system in educational activities, thus stimulating a broader experience in education and training, particularly in graduate programs to offer graduate students opportunities to be involved in major cooperative, user oriented research programs. (Steering Committee Report 1995, p. 39)

These developments are part of a profound change in the production of knowledge and the role of the universities according to Scott (1997). There is a shift taking place he argues in knowledge production where the distinction between applied and pure is becoming obsolete. The collaborative approach of the researcher and the user of the research working together, encouraged in CRCs, may be the way of the future.

For many doctoral students in professional fields such changes are already a feature of their candidature. In 1996, in Australia, for example, 4,445 doctoral students (20% of all enrolments) were enrolled in some or all of the broad fields of study of Architecture, Business and Economics, Education, and Law. In these fields those who are employed, already are, or are being, socialised into the culture of their profession; many would be researching on their practice in their own profession and/or their own workplace. The implications of this for professional fields such as education is discussed by Brennan (1995). She raises a number of issues to do with the particular difficulties associated with workplace research including the ethics and politics of pursuing investigative work 'made *public*' (her italics); and the need for developing appropriate methodologies and criteria for 'worthwhile knowledge'. There is a danger that in addressing issues both of confidentiality and intellectual property (for the student's employer or profession), and of representation and ethical care, the research will cease to be rigorous, or accepted as such. Addressing such concerns she cautions is critical as:

> The danger here is that universities will merely replace one pantheon of methodological frameworks with another -- reified as 'practitioner research' -- which may then be used to continue the expert-practitioner hierarchy without problematising the nature of knowledge and the interests at stake in its construction. (p. 22)

It is also in professional and applied areas, and the new humanities, that less traditional practices and innovations in thesis output (stories and creative production in contrast to a written thesis) are more likely to emerge (Brew 1996, Hodge 1995). Particularly this is so where there is an attempt to give a 'voice' to research participants, or to use audio and visual media.

The nature and extent of off-campus supervised research and study in education

From the discussion so far it is clear that postgraduate research in education does not need to be separated from postgraduate research more generally. Whether on-campus or off-campus, faculties, departments and schools of education have often been at the forefront of developments in higher degrees, both research and coursework. This is a statement which probably holds true in most countries of the world and over a long period of time. The roots of these connections can be traced back through the strong relationships between higher education (colleges and universities) and the preparation and professional development of one of the largest and most significant professions for national and cultural development—teaching. Distance education has played a strong part in this work, especially in those crucial times of colonial development in the early part of the twentieth century of which Australia is a good example (see Evans & Nation 1989, Evans & Nation 1993).

We would argue that, unless a government deploys disincentives, a fundamental aspect of future postgraduate research in Australia rests on research students who complete their work in forms of 'flexible' or 'mixed-mode' study. Mostly this will be part-time and principally off-campus, but may incorporate some periods on-campus, possibly full-time for a period. The research will typically be professionally or workplace related, and it is in this respect that the growth in professional doctorates can be seen to be particularly significant. We would suggest that there will need to be some important policy and planning initiatives to create the best possible conditions to ensure that the research conducted is of a high quality and addresses the relevant scholarly, professional and national needs.

Especially, this will require a greater understanding of the diversity of postgraduate research students' needs, interests and contexts spanning a broader range of social, economic and geographical circumstances. In professional disciplines (as in industry-based research), where forms of entry and forms of supervision are opening-up to allow students with a broader range of qualifications (often requiring professional experience) to be supervised by people with research experience beyond the academy, there is a need to be more open to the possibilities and resources of the students' contexts. In the future there will be proportionally fewer 'young' students prepared to commit themselves to full-time study/research whilst eking out an existence on a scholarship. University staff will find themselves dealing with students as old or older than themselves, who juggle work and family commitments alongside their research, and may well earn more than their supervisors!

The shift in perspective required of supervisors and universities (libraries, computer centres, research office, etc) is quite significant and means dealing with students more as colleagues or partners, than as juniors or 'students'. It also means dealing with some different candidate orientations to the doctoral credential and to the research they wish to do. The potential for high quality postgraduate research, which both draws on the richness of the students' contexts and also seeks to address research questions and issues in those contexts, seems substantial. In order to realise this potential another piece of our British colonial heritage will need to be reconstructed, namely, the research only doctorate examined through a thesis. In other parts of the world, for example North America, the doctorate has been one of coursework and research, although the dissertation (as doctoral theses are called there) still looms large over the examination process, although usually of less 'blockbuster' proportion than within the British-inspired tradition.

In many respects, both part-time and off-campus research students have existed at the margins of established research degree traditions, although this has typically been through informal or *de facto* means, for example, university staff members 'working' full-time at their university. The burgeoning number of off-campus, professional postgraduate students invites new ways of structuring research degrees and also new ways of supervising and supporting the research conducted. Clearly, there are the previously mentioned personal and professional contexts which need to be taken into account in terms of managing supervision, but there are also possibilities of turning these aspects into advantages. The growth in 'professional' doctorates such as the Doctor of Education (EdD), most of which contain a proportion of coursework in addition to research, provide a way to address the needs of the practitioner who does not necessarily intend to become an academic. Jongeling (1996) has given a detailed discussion of professional doctorates, suggesting that they are very similar to PhDs, and therefore questions their value. However, the American experience would indicate that both degrees may co-exist. According to Haworth (1996), there has been an escalation of doctoral enrolments in professional and 'practitioner-oriented' fields of study in the United States of America, in contrast to traditional arts and science, from the 1970s to the present, to the extent that they now comprise the majority of degrees conferred. While this growth has not been accompanied by a greater demand for professional doctorates, the biggest single group of professional doctorates continue to be EdD degrees (pp. 391-2).

The Deakin University EdD program is illustrative of the potential of professional doctorates to be configured differently both in terms of their research orientation and their 'supervision' off-campus. Drawing on previous papers (Evans 1995, Evans & Green 1995), the Deakin EdD can be distinguished from most other similarly-designated doctoral programs in Australia by its distinctive character as a *research*-oriented degree. It combines a structured sequence of research activities culuminating in the presentation of doctoral proposal document at a formally-constituted colloquium. This is followed by research, generally focused within the workplace or profession, which is examined through a research folio which is centred on a dissertation. The Deakin EdD involves a different understanding of research, its nature and purpose(s), and rather than directed towards making a 'significant contribution to knowledge' as for the PhD, the EdD is intended to contribute to and enhance *both* knowledge *and* practice in regard to the professional (educational) contexts of the candidates. Rather than focussed on, or addressed to, a research topic, in the conventional academic-intellectual sense, it is tied more directly to a specific place or site of educational-institutional work and its associated needs or problems which research can inform (see Brennan 1995, Brennan & Walker 1994).

On the basis of the experience of these initiatives for reconstructing the traditional notions of the PhD and its students, we are now in a position in Education to explore some of the possibilities which forms of open and distance education, particularly in the contemporary flexible learning and computer-based delivery forms, can afford. Evans and Nation (1993) argue that there is a form of convergence occurring between distance education and mainstream education brought about through the development of new educational technologies. Others before had seen distance education shifting from the 'margins to the mainstream' (Smith & Kelly 1987, Campion 1988). A weakness with the convergence argument, as Evans and Nation suggest, is that it implies a focusing or centring of educational activity, whereas much policy, practice and rhetoric seems to reflect diversity, choice and opening educational space. It is in this context that most of the new forms of doctoral research and the increasing numbers of postgraduate research students need to find their futures.

In many respects, as doctoral degrees are understood as 'research' degrees, this means ostensibly that they have no curriculum or teaching. Even the new professional doctorates are typically substantially research-based. Consequently, there are more 'open' possibilities for both individual tailoring of a student's work (research) to their particular professional needs and other circumstances, and also fewer institutional encumbrances than is the case for coursework programs with their accredited curricula and, often, course materials. This is not to deny that 'supervisors' are teachers of their research students in some ways, and that the curriculum can be seen to be both research (methodology and practice) and the substantive field of inquiry. But it seems to be the case that, both historically and contemporarily, there has been more opportunity to be 'flexible' and responsive to students' needs, interests and contexts, than is the case with, say, first year psychology, accounting or chemistry. We would suggest that this opportunity has rarely been taken, but that for the future, those institutions which do take the opportunity, especially in fields of education, are likely to experience greater success than those which do not.

Supervision issues

One might expect that the shift towards, and greater involvement in, forms of off-campus postgraduate research raises some important issues for the nature, quality and sustenance of supervision. However, as Evans & Green (1995) elucidate, there are many issues concerning higher degree by research supervision which have been left unscrutinised despite the burgeoning of this field of practice for academics over the past decades. They describe the 'absent presence' of pedagogy in the 'supervision' relationship thus:

> Postgraduate education is about *research* first and foremost, more often than not within circumstances of mentioning and apprenticeship, and about *learning*—that is, learning about research, as well as how to do research and how to be a researcher; this, in addition to, or complementary of, work in a specific discipline or realm of knowledge and praxis. Supervisors in this perspective are not so much 'teachers' as they are 'researchers', and certainly their role and status as researchers takes precedence over their identity and work as teachers. (Evans & Green 1995, p. 2)

They cite Connell's (1985) work as an important example of a teacher/scholar/supervisor stimulating a debate about the nature and purpose of supervision:

> Supervising a research higher degree is the most advanced level of teaching in our education system. It is certainly one of the most complex and problematic—as shown by the very high drop-out rate of students at this level. It is also one of the least discussed. (Connell 1985, p. 38)

We take the view that these and other issues of higher degree by research 'supervision' require urgent attention and that scholars in education are particularly well-equipped, if not obliged, to make a significant contribution. Beyond this we would argue that the shift to off-campus supervision is not so much a further complication to these issues, but rather an opportunity to reflect critically on the nature and purpose of 'supervision' with a view to theorising and improving practice. It seems important to understand the nature and purpose of 'supervision' in higher degree research—including the emerging demands for workplace-based and/or industry-related research—before one then considers any translation to off-campus supervision in general.

As Evans & Green (1995) reveal, supervision has never been an adequate description of the work of higher degree by research 'supervisors'. Apart from the teaching role which Connell foregrounded, there are also the mentor and 'master' (as in master and apprentice) roles. However, for those 'students' who are highly experienced in their professions or industries (some may even be academics themselves, some may have longstanding research positions), the role may be more one of a 'critical friend' guiding the 'student' through the scholarly maze to the doctoral examination and graduation. Or maybe as a 'gate-keeper of science' (Mulkay 1972) who ensures that the 'student' completes all the necessary conditions before entry. Our point here is to show that the term 'supervisor' is something of a misnomer, and also that the work of a 'supervisor' is quite complex. It also seems the case that, given the wide disparity in experience and backgrounds of the 'students'—it is worth noting the language, cultural and political diversities of international students—not to mention that of the supervisors, then one can expect that negotiation is an important part of the supervisor–student relationship, too.

The shift to off-campus and part-time supervision means that any pretence that supervision can be understood as 'peering over the shoulder' of the student has long gone. Of course, it has generally been the case that—especially outside the physical and natural sciences laboratories—the full-time 'on-campus' doctoral student's research ('fieldwork') has been conducted beyond the supervisor's gaze. However, the majority of other work connected with the planning, preparation, reviewing literature, writing-up etc, has typically been conducted on-campus, and if not directly within the supervisor's gaze, certainly with the illusion that there has been close 'supervising'. The reality is that such an on-campus student may well have had a regular meeting with the supervisor, and perhaps other casual encounters of the kind that the corridor, photocopier or tearoom provide, but the majority of the research (learning?) is a private and solitary activity which no-one 'supervises' or 'oversees'. Consequently, those involved in the management and supervision of off-campus and part-time higher degrees by research confront two broad concerns: one is the 'real' concern for the provision of supervision and support 'at a distance'; the other is the concern for coping with the illusion that on-campus students are supervised more or less continuously and that, therefore, off-campus students incur a deficit or disadvantage which renders them highly vulnerable to failure or non-completion.

It is arguable that, in dealing with these two areas of concern, two broad areas of strength have been overlooked: one resides in the relatively higher average levels of experience and maturity that off-campus part-time students have over their full-time counterparts; and the other resides in the resources (professional, intellectual and material) which off-campus part-time students typically have in their workplaces. They are also strengths which are particularly evident in education and the growth in professional doctorates, such as the EdD, highlights them.

Student issues

For students there are a number of issues which are significant for all forms of doctoral study, but which can be acute for those who are not on campus all the time. When the numbers of doctoral students were small, the tutor-style relationship inherited from the British system could work well. It was part of an approach to education which was informal and personal. In the present complex, open and flexible environment for doctoral study and research, students demand more structure, accountability and equitable access to resources. In a group discussion with research students reported in Pearson & Ford (1997) they asked for:

- resources: computer, fax, e-mail, photocopier, conference funding;
- clear guidelines about what is expected of the student, not just what rules the student must conform to /clear information about what the student is or isn't entitled to, so the student can form realistic expectations;

- supervisors who are committed to the student and accountable to the institution, and
- supervision which occurs - 'how it is done is less important than the fact it is done'.
  (Edited from a workshop statement from an interstate group of ten research students at a Postgraduate Conference 1996, p. 87)

Such a list is not surprising when we contrast the views of doctoral students and supervisors. Studies that compare perspectives (Cullen, Pearson, Saha & Spear 1994, Powles 1996, Russell 1996) show that students often have different ideas from their supervisors about how much help they are getting and frequency of contact, whether on or off-campus. This can be voiced by students as a lack of 'support'. One explanation for this perceived lack could be the difference in focus of supervisors and of students found by Russell (1996) in his study of doctoral students in Education, Humanities, Law and Theology. He found that whereas students were more likely to emphasise the day-to-day aspects of their work, the supervisors had more concern for the broader context within which the work was placed (p. 17). Another part of the explanation is the nature of the student passage. Becoming an expert in one's own topic can be stimulating and isolating and the experience can be intense and emotional even for those who are mature and professionally competent (Cullen, Pearson, Saha & Spear 1994, pp. 92-97). Communications and the quality of the supervision are therefore of particular significance for doctoral students.

Communications issues

Communications are usually seen to be more significant for those who are off-campus and appear to be isolated. Isolation is however a complex issue. Not all off-campus students will see themselves as isolated, and their perceptions will depend on the circumstances in which they are studying and researching. Part-time students for example may be intellectually isolated but not professionally or socially. Taylor (1995) suggests that there is a change in educational preferences taking place as some students decide to stay in their existing community, and have their education imported, instead of coming to university to join a university community. This former population can include students at work, and international students who increasingly are demanding to continue graduate study in their home country with visits to Australia or elsewhere for specific projects or research tasks. Rather than assume isolation and difficulties, a more productive approach is to focus on what is essential for effective supervision and a successful candidature. Doctoral students need engagement with researchers in relevant areas, access to expertise and intellectual leadership from some supervisory figure or process, and some form of social/emotional support. This can happen through a number of means, only one of which is physical attendance on campus. The significant issue is not location, but how to foster effective communications and maintain dialogue among students, their peers, supervisors and other relevant experts by various means.

One way forward is to exploit computer and communications technologies. Students and supervisors are using mediated communication through:

- Telephone;
- e-mail/telephone, and
- Online discussions and bulletin boards.

Often students and supervisors use both the telephone and/or e-mail communications to structure meetings in person. From the student perspective such approaches can give them more control of the situation. They can set up visits in advance via e-mail, with mailed material for discussion, making actual interactions off- and on-campus more efficient. Such means are often supplemented by face-to-face communications when the occasion arises as at conferences, or through visits from the supervisor to the student. The advent of more robust desktop videoconferencing could become another useful strategy. These methods of communications enable ongoing conversations which can continue regardless of where the student or the supervisor is located at any particular time during the student's candidature.

The move to greater use of communications and information technology for research, and to communicate with others, is making access to the technology a necessity. Yet not all doctoral students have such access and it should not be assumed. Some institutions such as Deakin and Edith Cowan have set up systems which have especially designed user-friendly interfaces for students. Deakin University provides its off-campus students with a CD-ROM 'Learning Toolkit' which, when loaded on to a student's computer, provides access not only to email, the Internet, library access and help desk support, but also to postgraduate conferencing facilities.

Quality of supervision issues

For students the quality of their supervision is important, however independent they are and expect to be. As indicated from the group discussion reported above, students expect commitment and accountability. The supervisor is their institutional link, as well as an intellectual leader. This may seem a less than inspiring role for some supervisors, but without access to clear guidelines, rules and expectations, the doctoral student can find being independent very difficult, and especially if they are not in constant day-to-day contact, through which much of what they need to know can be picked up through incidental informal contact. Structure and flexibility go together for students. Many institutions are recognising this and setting out in readable handbooks their policies and procedures, and codes of practice. In 'good' practice examples (e.g. University of Sydney, University of Queensland) who is accountable for what institutionally is spelt out. Helping students manage their candidature, whether in relation to complying with institutional requirements, or in finding specialist expertise, or in clarifying methodological problems, is itself a sign of 'commitment' for them.

At the same time not all assistance will come from the individual supervisor. Where students are mature professionals, some of their need for intellectual exchange can be met most productively from peer exchange convened by the supervisor, or by themselves. A feature of the current environment is a number of innovative approaches to group supervision (Pearson & Ford 1997):

- virtual discussion groups;
- national conferences within disciplinary fields (e.g. Housing and Urban Studies, Economics);
- conferences convened by postgraduate student associations (e.g. Deakin, Griffith, Central Queensland University);
- annual residentials for course cohorts (e.g. Education, University of New England).

Such approaches give students a broader experience base. They can find out more about methodological issues from other students to allay anxiety and tease out the issues and possibilities. Sharing experience provides emotional/intellectual support. Contact with other researchers, the more junior and the established, will expand their intellectual horizons. These approaches provide that critical mass for intellectual development which otherwise can be absent for an off-campus student, or indeed for an on-campus student where there are small numbers on campus. Group supervision can offer an introduction to the research culture of their discipline. It is in such settings that students can explore the nuances of disciplinary and professional academic practice, which will include matters of ownership of data and authorship. These group initiatives counterbalance the dispersion of students which occurs when they are part-time, work-based, and with adult responsibilities which also demand their attention and time. They are significant for providing that engagement with their intellectual and professional community which is an important part of their professional education (Pearson 1996).

Conclusion

The categories of 'supervisor', 'student', 'on-campus' and 'off-campus' are somewhat fluid in postgraduate research. This creates misleading statements in policies and guidelines which assume the categories are fixed, stable and mutually exclusive. The increasing popularity of off-campus, part-time study has roots in the 'flexible', if marginal, practices of institutions since the inception of doctoral degrees. Doctoral students have always been involved in what is a form of open, flexible and independent learning; but this has been masked by the British model with an emphasis on individual and often intense personal relationships, or apprentice-style arrangements at the bench.

As we argued at the outset, in professional arenas such as education the traditional approach has never been appropriate, nor practised widely. In education we must re-cast the role of the supervisor from that of the 'overseer' to one which is more akin to the 'critical friend' or mentor ; or perhaps to re-cast the North American university term 'adviser'. Such a re-casting should be based on a systematic analysis of the needs, strengths and capacities of mature professional 'students' and of the professional contexts in which they work. This requires building research, supervision and communication arrangements which not only fit the students' needs and requirements, but maximise the use of their intellectual and experiential resources producing research outcomes which together develop the discipline and enhance educational practice.

References

ARC/NBEET 1996, *Patterns of Research Activity in Australian Universities*, Commissioned Report 47, Canberra, Australian Government Publishing Service.

AVCC 1990, *Code of Practice for Maintaining and Monitoring Academic Quality and Standards in Higher Degrees,* Canberra, AVCC.

Back, K., Davis, D. & Olsen, A. 1996, *Internationalisation and Higher Education: Goals and Strategies,* Higher Education Division DEETYA, Canberra, Australian Government Publishing Service.

Bazeley, P., Kemp, L., Stevens, K., Asmar, C., Grbich, C., Marsh, H. & Bhathal, R. 1996, *Waiting in the Wings: A Study of Early Career Academic Researchers in Australia,* ARC Commissioned Report No 50. Canberra, Australian Government Publishing Service.

Brennan, M. & Walker, R. 1994, 'Educational research in the workplace: Developing a professional doctorate', in R. Burgess & M. Schratz (eds), *International Perspectives in Postgraduate Education and Training*, Innsbruck, Austrian Academic Press, pp. 220-233.

Brennan, M. 1995, 'Education doctorates: Reconstructing professional partnerships around research?', *The Australian Universities Review*, 38 (2), pp. 20-22.

Brew, A. 1966, 'An original contribution to knowledge - challenges to supervisors of research degrees', paper presented at *1996 National Conference: Quality in Postgraduate research - Is it Happening*, Adelaide, April.

Campion, M. & Kelly, M. 1988, 'Integration of external studies and campus-based education in Australian higher education: The myth and the promise', *Distance Education*, 9 (2), pp. 171-201.

Clark, B. R. 1995, *Places of Inquiry: Research and Advanced Education in Modern Universities,* Berkeley, University of California Press.

Clark, B. R. 1996, 'Substantive growth and innovative organisation: New categories for higher education research', *Higher Education*, 32, pp. 417-430.

Clarke, J. 1996, 'Preparation of PhDs for the real world', Paper presented at Second Seminar of Deans and Directors of Graduate Studies in Australian Universities, Adelaide.

Connell, R. W. 1985, 'How to supervise a PhD', *Vestes*, 2, pp. 38-41.

Cooperative Research Centres Program Evaluation 1995, *Changing Research Culture Australia - 1995, Report of the CRC Program Evaluation Steering Committee*, Canberra, Australian Government Publishing Service.

Cullen, D., Pearson, M., Saha, L. J. & Spear, R. H. 1994, *Establishing Effective PhD Supervision*, Canberra, Australian Government Publishing Service.

Deakin University 1996, Student enrolment and performance statistics, Internal Report, Office of the Pro Vice-Chancellor (Research), Victoria.

DEETYA 1996, *Selected HE Student Statistics 1996*, Canberra, Australian Government Publishing Service.

Evans, T. D. 1995, 'Postgraduate research supervision in the emerging 'open' universities', *The Australian Universities Review*, 38 (2), pp. 23-27.

Evans, T. D. & Green, W. 1995, 'Dancing at a distance? Postgraduate studies, supervision, and distance education', Paper presented Australian Association for Research in Education Conference, Hobart, November.

Evans, T. D. & Nation, D. 1989, 'Primary teachers upgrading through distance education', in H. Edwards & S. Barraclough (eds), *Research & Development in Higher Education vol. 11,* Higher Education, Melbourne, Research and Development Society of Australia, pp. 138-140.

Evans, T. D. & Nation, D. E. 1993, 'Educating teachers at a distance in Australia: Some history, research results and recent trend', H. Perraton (ed.), *Distance Education for Teacher Training*, London, Routledge, pp. 261-286.

Evans, T. D. & Nation, D. E. 1993, 'Educational technologies: Reforming open and distance education', in T. Evans & D. E. Nation (eds), *Reforming Open and Distance Education,* London, Kogan Page, pp. 196-214.

Grigg, L. 1996, *The Internationalisation of Australian Higher Education: An Evaluation of the contribution of the Overseas Postgraduate Research Scholarships Scheme*, Higher Education Division DEETYA, AGPS, Canberra.

Haworth, Jennifer G. 1996, 'Doctoral programs' in J. C. Smart (ed.), *American Higher Education, in Higher Education: Handbook of Theory and Research,* Vol XI, New York, Agathon Press.

Hodge, B. 1995, 'Monstrous knowledge: Doing PhDs in the new humanities', *The Australian Universities Review*, 38 (2), pp. 35-39.

Jongeling, S. B. 1996, 'Professional doctorates in Australian universities', Paper presented Second Seminar of Deans and Directors of Graduate Studies in Australian Universities, Adelaide, April.

Mulkay, M. J. 1972, *The Social Process of Innovation*, London, MacMillan.

Moses, I. 1985, *Supervising Postgraduates*, HERDSA, Canberra.

Pearson, M. 1996, 'Professionalising PhD education to enhance the quality of the student experience', *Higher Education*, 32, pp. 303-320.

Pearson, M. & Ford, L. 1997, *Open and Flexible PhD Study and Research*, DEETYA, Canberra, Australian Government Publishing Service.

Russell, A. 1996, 'Postgraduate research: Student and supervisor views', Paper presented at *1996 National Conference: Quality in Postgraduate Research - Is it Happening?*, Adelaide.

Scott, P. 1997, 'The changing role of the university in the production of new knowledge', *Tertiary Education and Management,* 3 (1), pp. 5-14.

Smith, P. & Kelly, M. (eds), 1987, *Distance Education and the Mainstream,* London, Croom Helm.

Taylor, P. 1995, 'Postgraduate education and open learning: Anticipating a new order?', *The Australian Universities Review, 38* (2), pp. 28-31.

University of Sydney 1995, *Postgraduate Studies Handbook* 1995, Sydney, University of Sydney.

Acknowledgements

The data presented in this paper come from a study reported as *Open and Flexible PhD Study and Research 1997,* which was funded by the Evaluations and Investigations Program, Higher Education Division, DEETYA.

Appendix A   Australian postgraduate and doctoral students by state and institution, 1996

State/ Institution	Total Post Graduate	Doctoral Only	Percentage PhD of Postgraduate %
NEW SOUTH WALES			
Australian Film, Television and Radio School	-	-	-
Avondale College	41	-	-
Charles Sturt University	3,751	119	3
Macquarie University	4,923	631	13
National Institute of Dramatic Art	15	-	-
Southern Cross University	1,420	133	9
University of New England	4,429	485	11
University of New South Wales	8,320	1,704	20
University of Newcastle	1,859	415	22
University of Sydney	7,510	2,336	31
University of Technology, Sydney	5,510	384	7
University of Western Sydney	4,215	438	10
University of Wollongong	3,224	633	20
Total New South Wales	**45,217**	**7,278**	**16**
VICTORIA			
Deakin University	6,047	408	7
La Trobe University	4,206	732	17
Marcus Oldham Farm Management	-	-	-
Monash University	8,178	1,622	20
Royal Melbourne Institute of Technology	6,118	443	7
Swinburne University of Technology	2,088	167	8
University of Ballarat	566	35	6
University of Melbourne	8,661	1,789	21
Victoria University of Technology	2,931	303	10
Total Victoria	**38,795**	**5,499**	**14**
QUEENSLAND			
Central Queensland University	1,816	78	4
Griffith University	2,817	581	21
James Cook University of North	1,308	456	35
Queensland University of Technology	5,735	506	9
University of Queensland	5,441	2,152	40
University of Southern Queensland	2,103	73	3
Total Queensland	**19,220**	**3,846**	**20**

Continued....

WESTERN AUSTRALIA			
Curtin University of Technology	4,121	551	13
Edith Cowan University	2,762	161	6
Murdoch University	1,651	508	31
University of Western Australia	2,541	1,008	40
Total Western Australia	**11,075**	**2,228**	**20**
SOUTH AUSTRALIA			
Flinders University of South Australia	1,833	465	25
University of Adelaide	2,793	946	34
University of South Australia	4,429	449	10
Total South Australia	**9,055**	**1,860**	**21**
TASMANIA			
Australian Maritime College	137	1	1
University of Tasmania	1,639	545	33
Total Tasmania	**1,776**	**546**	**31**
NORTHERN TERRITORY			
Batchelor College	14	-	-
Northern Territory University	746	111	15
Total Northern Territory	**760**	**111**	**15**
AUSTRALIAN CAPITAL TERRITORY			
Australian Defence Force Academy	431	121	28
Australian National University	2,338	1,063	45
University of Canberra	1,773	89	5
Total Australian Capital Territory	**4,542**	**1,273**	**28**
MULTI-STATE			
Australian Catholic University	2,055	55	3
Total Multi-State	**2,055**	**55**	**3**
TOTAL	**132,495**	**22,696**	17

Source: DEETYA Aggregated Data Sets, 1996

Appendix B

Australian doctoral students by broad field of study and age range, 1996

Field of study/age	Under 30	30-39	40-49	50-59	60+	Totals
Agriculture	41%	41%	17%	2%	1%	853
Architecture, Building	16%	38%	39%	7%	1%	222
Arts, Humanities and Social Sciences	25%	35%	28%	10%	3%	5,742
Business, Admin., Economics	17%	41%	35%	7%	1%	1,787
Education	4%	26%	48%	19%	3%	2,145
Engineering, Surveying	42%	42%	13%	2%	1%	2,318
Health	37%	39%	20%	4%	1%	2,687
Law, Legal Studies	18%	43%	27%	10%	2%	295
Science	56%	31%	11%	2%	1%	6,445
Veterinary Science	47%	40%	10%	2%	0%	202

Source: Pearson & Ford 1997, p. 12.

Educational Research, Disciplinarity and Postgraduate Pedagogy: On the Subject of Supervision

Bill Green
The University of New England

Alison Lee
University of Technology Sydney

Subject to education?

What does it mean to be a postgraduate student in education - that is to be pursuing advanced research training in education as a field of study? More provocatively perhaps: What is involved in becoming, as it were, 'subject-ed' to education? These are crucial and increasingly pressing questions, made all the more so because of the contemporary crisis of higher education and the university, in Australia and elsewhere. Funding has become restricted and highly focused and new imperatives of accountability and efficiency have all but overwhelmed the academic-educational agenda, along with new logics of competitive performativity. Importantly, this develops alongside a heightened concern with postgraduate study as an institutional(ised) object of desire, and indeed graduate education as a necessary symbolic *and* economic investment, nationally, institutionally and individually. In faculties and schools of education, this is as marked and urgent as anywhere else in the university, because of the very precariousness of education's identity, authority and indeed legitimacy within the power-knowledge complex of the Academy. Due consideration needs to be given here to increasing numbers of increasingly diverse students in higher education, the emergence of the unified national system, and the arrival of the former CAE's into the domain of research and research training. These developments have put on the agenda new urgent questions concerning the proper object of educational research, characteristically disrupting some of the traditional disciplinary formations and structures of the modern research university.

Postgraduate research training can be conceptualised as a particularly intense engagement within the nexus of research, teaching and study, which Clark (1994, 1997), has argued as integral to the modern idea and practice of the university, more particularly in its elite formations. Within this nexus it is arguably the third of these ('study') that has perhaps become most problematical, and most charged with a sense of danger and disarray. This is perhaps not so surprising since, as we have argued elsewhere, pedagogy—understood expressly as a particular relationship between teaching and learning—has to date characteristically been overlooked and marginalised in both the theory and the practice of advanced research education. Moreover, it is more particularly the subject of 'study' (the 'student') that is effectively missing from the official scene of teaching and research. That is, whereas one binary works to privilege 'research' over 'teaching', especially in recent times, another sets this 'production' emphasis against that of 'consumption', as realised in and through 'study'. There is a powerful irony here, however. Academic 'being' is thus effectively foregrounded, and indeed valorised, at the relative expense of academic 'becoming'. Yet how *is* academic identity formed? How does such a full-fledged, properly authorised and licensed identity come to *be*? This matter is a notable absence in much of the available work on postgraduate studies and advanced research education. How might this 'becoming - academic' be understood, other than in terms of deficiency or lack, or as necessarily incomplete? Yet what we have called the subject of study evokes precisely the figure of the 'other' that lies at the very heart of (postgraduate) pedagogy. Since, as Readings (1996, p. 161) argues, the very 'condition of pedagogical practice is ... "an infinite attention to the other" ', it is the student's experience and perspective—both literally and symbolically—that needs to be drawn more explicitly into account here.

A question posed by this chapter, located as it is within a book dedicated to postgraduate education in the field of education is: what makes advanced research training in education different and distinctive? And what kinds of professional and intellectual identities are being formed in the crucible of educational research in current times? In addressing this question, we argue that it is necessary to bring to bear an historical perspective on the emergence and consolidation of education as a field of study during this century, and its on-going formalisation and disciplinisation according to the structural and functional imperatives of the modern university in an age of disciplinarity. In taking a curriculum-historical and genealogical perspective on the field of education, we seek to interrupt some taken-for-granted assumptions about the objects and practices of educational research training.

The chapter forms a part of a larger project of inquiry into doctoral research education in the Humanities and Social Sciences, focusing on English, Sociology and Education.[1] Of each of these three 'disciplines' we ask the question: what is it that current practices of research training, and particularly the practices of supervision pedagogy, are setting out to produce, in terms of objects of study, as well as capacities and identities, or forms of subjectivity? How do these practices shape the kinds of persons who become researchers, scholars, academics and professionals in their respective fields and, in turn, how are the fields themselves shaped and renewed through the practices of postgraduate pedagogy? What is the particular relationship of research, teaching and study in postgraduate education in each of these fields? What is the relationship between research training and disciplinary reproduction and the production of the new, the changing of the 'research frontier' (Swoboda 1979, p. 53)?

In the case of the field of education, these questions take on a particular resonance, since 'education' refers to both the field of inquiry of the research and the sets of practices of supervision and study undertaken within the research degree. In support of the latter point, Bob Connell (1985, p. 38) has aptly described postgraduate research supervision as 'the most advanced level of teaching in our education system', and further, as 'a genuinely complex teaching task'. Elsewhere, we have argued that understanding supervision as teaching—or rather, at once more broadly and more precisely, as *pedagogy*—is far from straightforward, or uncontroversial. Indeed, a deepseated prejudice exists in the modern university, which systematically privileges research over teaching, disciplinarity over pedagogy (Green and Lee 1995, Lee and Green 1997). Connell's early intervention is particularly important, it seems to us, because it put on the agenda a distinctively *educational* orientation—that is, a language and a perspective that is drawn specifically from the disciplinary discourse of education, as a significant form of study in its own right.

At the same time, education as a specialist field of study has remained marginal to the heroic sweep of disciplinary specialisation in the modern university; 'an inferior form of disciplinary life', and 'best disregarded in serious academic company', as Hoskin (1993 p. 272, p. 271) notes provocatively. Hoskin goes on to argue, however, in an important historical account, that, rather than being subordinate, education is 'superordinate' within modern disciplinary economies and hence within the project of the modern university. That is, he traces the birth of disciplinarity in the second half of the eighteenth century and its spread in the nineteenth century to small but crucial changes in pedagogical practices. Thus, according to Hoskin, the only way to understand the genesis of disciplinarity and the subsequent apparently inexorable growth of disciplinarity's power is to understand the power of education.

There are two complementary points of focus for this paper, therefore: that of the role of educational theorising in understanding and thus constituting the objects and practices of postgraduate research education, and that of the specificity and distinctiveness of education as a specialist field of enquiry, and hence the particularity of being 'subjected' to Education—of becoming formed as a particular kind of knowing subject, through the representations of education that form its contemporary objects of inquiry.

Disciplinarity and Pedagogy

It is important, at the outset, to be clear what we mean when we refer here to *disciplinarity*. Following Messer-Davidow and her colleagues, we understand 'disciplinarity' as that which 'makes for disciplinary knowledge as such', that is 'the possibility conditions of disciplines' (Messer-Davidow, Shumway and Sylvan 1993, pp. 1-2). What is it that makes 'disciplines', and disciplinary knowledge, possible? Moreover, the study of disciplinarity is about the ways in which knowledge is socially constructed, authorised, and organised, and hence involves a distinctive attitude towards knowledge as well as its enabling technologies. Hence, 'disciplinarity is about the coherence of a set of otherwise disparate elements: objects of study, methods of analysis, scholars, students, journals ...'. Further, disciplinarity is 'the means by which ensembles of diverse parts are brought together into particular types of knowledge relations with each other'. Importantly, this is always to be seen as 'a historically contingent, adventitious coherence of dispersed elements' (Messer-Davidow et al. 1993, p. 3). Disciplinarity must therefore be understood not so much in transcendentally epistemological terms as pragmatically and politically, and above all materially and historically. 'Disciplining' (and hence differentiating) knowledge and its associated forms of identity is a social practice, and hence it cannot be conceived outside of the social dynamics of power and desire.

In stressing the contingency and historicity of disciplines and disciplinarity, it is possible to grasp the manner in which relatively unstable and arbitrary coalitions are formed, on the basis of material rewards and related forms of association. These then become contexts and forums for certain kinds of knowledge production and reproduction. Over time, they may become increasingly abstract, formalised, institutionalised and reified. However they have no necessary or 'ideal' identity or authority, except that which tradition grants them. Messer-Davidow et al. point to processes and practices whereby disciplines maintain and renew themselves—for instance, through various kinds of 'boundary-work'. They explicitly include supervision and pedagogy within what they call 'socializing practices': 'the particular kinds of work performed by students in learning their disciplines and scholars or scientists in practising theirs' (Messer-Davidow et al. 1993, p. 15). Advanced research education is clearly a crucial context in this regard, especially the characteristically intense, often privatised and even traumatic pedagogic relationship arguably at the very heart of doctoral work.

Of course, supervision is both more and less, very often, than this; and opportunities for other kinds of relationships and performances of pedagogy *and* of research are extremely important, for instance the *seminar*. As we have noted elsewhere:

> The seminar is a powerful means whereby what counts as academic-intellectual work is represented and authorised. This does not just involve the presentation itself, [...] but crucially also the exchange afterwards, in the manner in which individuals of varying authority and expertise engage with the presenter or with each other and the manner in which the presenter responds to and transacts with others in the session. It is for students a matter often of watching and learning how to be, how to interact and intervene, how to introduce and develop a commentary however attenuated it might need to be in the circumstances, how to work with difference and

disputation, how to speak and when, even how to hold one's body or deploy certain mannerisms and gestures ... (Green and Lee 1995, p. 41)

'Supervision', that is, is always much more than the (stereo)typical one-to-one relationship of academic supervisor and postgraduate student—even when opportunities for such interaction and display are limited. Yet what is at issue, always, is the production, silent or otherwise, of a certain kind of regulated, 'disciplined' subject.

At this point it is impossible to go past Bernstein's now classic account of educational knowledge, and specifically his observation that what he calls 'collection codes'—in our terms, here, disciplinary forms of knowledge and identity—are quintessentially hierarchical in their organisation such that 'the ultimate mystery of the subject is revealed very late in the educational life' (Bernstein 1971, p. 57). Importantly this is only when the subject is 'made safe', or more or less thoroughly 'socialised' into the self-referential culture of the discipline in question. The paradox is, of course, the successful candidate is also *enabled* in this process, authorised to speak, in and through and also *for* the discipline, in a properly 'disciplined', (re)productive manner. Henceforth the now self-supervising subject, because he or she can play by *the* rules, is also able to play *with* the rules. Whether this in fact happens, of course, is debatable. Yet an authorised academic identity has been formed, the work of the Institution is thereby confirmed, and educational life goes on.

Elsewhere (Lee and Green 1997) we have sought to describe the complex, contradictory relationship between pedagogy and disciplinarity in the (post)modern university. Up until quite recently, what seemed the unassailable norm in university research and advanced graduate education was the disciplinary structure of knowledge (re)production. Yet, as we argued, this needed to be re-assessed *historically*, and understood therefore as arising out of quite specific and delimited historical conditions and configurations. At issue, accordingly, was the need to re-think 'a set of taken-for-granted assumptions concerning the relations between disciplinarity and pedagogy' in the university, and more specifically 'the primacy of the former over the latter and the relegation of pedagogy—matters of teaching and learning, and education more broadly—to the margins' (Lee and Green 1997, p. 3). Our particular concern, in accordance with the important work of Hoskin (1993), was to draw attention to 'the historical nexus of modernity and disciplinarity' (Lee and Green 1997, p. 9), and to assert and affirm the significance of educational practice in this regard.

In the light of this previous work, and in relation to the larger project outlined above, it is worth briefly reflecting, here, on Education as a distinctive field of study within the university—as a 'discipline'. In doing so, we caution that our work in foregrounding pedagogy at the (relative) expense of disciplinarity—that is, to strategically subordinate disciplinarity to pedagogy—has not meant a simple re-positioning and thereby privileging of the professional and institutional study of Education within the symbolic and material economy of the university. Our concern, rather, is with pedagogy as *practice*, and hence with how the university operates as a site of and for education, across the disciplines and fields of study.

Education as 'discipline'

In a recent account of multidisciplinary research in language and literacy education (Beach et al. 1992), Jerome Harste notes that all too often the *specificity* of education as a field of study has been ignored, or glossed over, the result being the perpetuation of the unfortunate 'illusion that others—other researchers, other disciplines—have faced and solved language education's research problems'. Accordingly, as he continues: 'All we need to do is search these disciplines out and adopt their procedures to address our own needs'. This is for him clearly unsatisfactory. Recalling an earlier argument of his own, he describes '[t]he agenda ahead for educators of all kinds' as one of 'develop[ing] a research methodology for their discipline' (Harste 1992, p. xi). Elsewhere in the same volume, in seeking 'to make problematic the relationship between education and the disciplines from which we traditionally "borrow" ', Siegel (1992, p. 374) asks what would it mean 'to take seriously the idea of education as a basic rather than an applied field'? This line of enquiry and argument has obvious implications for postgraduate research education, not just in language and literacy education but in educational research more generally. The graduate student needs to come to an informed understanding of *educational* research—research in and as education, and hence of the distinctive manner in which educational research is practised, in addressing educational issues and problems. In Harste's (1992, xi) terms: 'Basic research in education is different from basic research in psychology, sociology, or linguistics ...'.

That immediately raises some fundamental issues, to do precisely with the disciplinary identity and integrity of education as a university field of study. It is important to bear in mind that not only is it the case that 'questions of disciplinarity quickly become questions of politics and questions of institutional structure' (Levine and Kaplan 1997, p. 3), but also that there may well be a disjunction between '[t]he discipline as training program' and 'the discipline as research frontier' (Swoboda 1979, p. 53)—altogether necessary qualifications, if not entirely uncontentious in themselves. Nonetheless, we need to develop an informed sense of the distinctiveness of educational research and its characteristic forms of maintenance and renewal, notwithstanding due recognition of 'the arbitrariness of disciplinary boundaries and the potential intellectual distortions that derive from those boundaries' (Levine and Kaplan 1997, p. 3). In particular, it is appropriate and important to ask questions of the historical relationship between disciplinarity and professional practice.

Connell's magisterial study of education's formative role and significance in the course and shape of the twentieth century is both directly pertinent here and instructive (Connell 1980). As he writes:

> The development of education as a professional discipline has been substantially an achievement of the twentieth century. The coincidence of the Herbartian and the child study movements at the turn of the century provided a growing body of knowledge from research, school practice, and theory relevant to the changing situation of the time. The subsequent expansion of educational psychology and later additions from educational sociology increased the body of knowledge. (Connell 1980, p. 16)

Connell locates the study of education firmly and directly within the context of professional practice:

> Like the study of engineering and medicine, the study of education has usually been carried on in institutions concerned with the training and refreshing of members for the profession. The needs of the practice of education have therefore generally had an effect on the nature of the research and thinking that has gone into the study of education.

This, as he observes, has been a mutually 'reciprocal exercise in relevance', with on the one hand 'the needs of the profession' keeping theorists and researchers 'reasonably close to the classroom' and, on the other, theorists and researchers 'help[ing] to push the classroom teacher into breaking with the traditional recipes for classroom practice which are inclined to linger on in a conservative profession' (Connell 1980, p. 16). The point we want to draw attention to, here, is the linking of education as a university field of study to engineering and medicine, as expressly 'professional disciplines'.[2]

That is, in fact, an intriguing set of articulations and associations, from an historical and institutional point of view. While medicine has long been associated with the university, engineering is only more recently so, relatively speaking. Moreover, what is often overlooked is that originally and traditionally the university was expressly a context for professional studies, with regard specifically to the so-called 'higher faculties' of theology, law and medicine. It was only with the advent of the modern university, in institutions such as Halle and more particularly Berlin, in the latter part of the eighteenth century and the early nineteenth century, that the university curriculum was reorganised and reconceptualised in terms of the disciplinisation of knowledge. This became, increasingly, a defining feature of the modern university, although the relationship of the professional disciplines to the professions they replenish has remained throughout most of this century a very close and complex one (Swoboda 1979).

There is a significant tension here, and a certain irony, between the project of the neo-Humboldtian (or modern) university and its practice and institutionalisation.[3] As we have written elsewhere:

Whereas what might be called the 'Humboldtian' vision of the university was predicated on a holistic view of knowledge and scholarship, and on principles of unity and even a (manly) 'heroism', the programmatic realisation of this vision across the nineteenth century was something quite different. This was the great age of disciplinarity, of disciplinary power and a central feature of the new disciplinary organisation of knowledge and power was *differentiation*—the generation of grids of specification and practices of specialisation. (Lee and Green 1997, p. 11)

Accordingly, as Wittrock (1993, p. 315) writes:

[T]he Humboldtian university, inspired by holistic thinking in broad historical cultural categories and informed by a type of philosophy which rejected narrow-minded specialisation, turned out to be the ideal and archetypical home for scientific activities which were, if anything, based on opposite conceptions.

The result of this was that, by the mid-nineteenth century, scholarship and study was increasingly organised into narrowed 'disciplinary channels oriented towards research, discovery and specialisation' (Wittrock 1993, pp. 311-312, citing R. Stephen Turner). Hence 'the nineteenth-century university was decisively marked by the power of disciplinarity (and therefore by distinctive albeit contradictory pedagogic practices and regimes' (Lee and Green 1997, p. 11). In Swoboda's (1979, p. 59) terms: 'What we now call disciplines and specialities are a product of the nineteenth century'—a phenomenon that arguably persists, exacerbated and escalating, to the present day.

What does this mean for education? Swoboda's (1979) historical account of 'interdisciplinarity' and the disciplines is directly pertinent in this regard. He makes specific reference to education as a field of study in the American university, having argued that disciplinary formations and structures had quickly become normative and all-pervasive, to the point where such an overarching orientation was in many instances counter-productive, intellectually and pedagogically. Research was increasingly and systematically privileged over teaching, and a considerable potential for conflict and tension generated accordingly between what he calls 'the externally directed (teaching) and internally directed (research) roles of disciplines' (Swoboda 1979, p. 76). The point to emphasise is that, in contrast with what might be called here 'pre-modern' forms of the university, this was directly related to the disciplinary focus and character of the modern(ist) university. 'Research' became paradigmatic and, indeed, transcendental, at least in Europe and the United States, and less so and later in Britain and Australia (Scott 1995).

Swoboda's account is consistent with his observation that 'an important feature of the development of disciplines [is] that at their highest level they remain primarily self-contained and self-regulating activities' (Swoboda 1979, p. 74). This meant, among other things, a privileging of the doctorate as the primary mechanism of self regulation and reproduction. Accordingly:

> Teaching activities of disciplines ... played a relatively minor part in the internal dynamics of academic structures. Here research continued to exert the most important influence. By the turn of the century, the doctorate had become the ticket of admission to membership in American academic life. The doctorate, of course, certified not teaching ability but the ability to do research—and research of a strictly disciplinary nature at that. (Swoboda 1979, p. 77)

This meant that, on the one hand, teaching was effectively undervalued—and arguably in advanced research education as well, and, on the other, certain kinds of 'disciplining' occurred, perhaps at the expense of a more appropriate pursuit of certain forms of knowledge and professional practice.

It is in this context that Swoboda makes specific reference to education: 'Even academic areas that by definition would seem to call for an interdisciplinary approach—such as education—have been recast in a disciplinary mold' (Swoboda 1979, p. 81). He goes on to provide a quite devastating account of the field's disciplinary formalisation, suggesting that its legitimation and consolidation ran hand-in-hand with its movement towards differentiation and specialisation and even, in some respects, its effective marginalisation:

> [T]he strict disciplinary emphasis inevitably meant that the new discipline could only justify itself by a clear separation of the process and content of education. Questions of process were declared to lie in the special discipline of education; issues of content were subject to the sovereign laws of other disciplines. Education separate from its contents became an increasingly dogmatic, isolated, and trivial enterprise, until a great deal of its research became a parody of science, the worse for being an unconscious parody. (Swoboda 1979, pp. 81-82)

This account is certainly rather harsh and even quite unsympathetic. All the same, it contains more than a grain of truth, and is at least consistent with a recurring and arguably still largely current perception of education in the university, framed as that is by orthodox and institutionalised understandings of knowledge and research, especially as organised and authorised by the traditional 'meta-disciplinary' perspectives of philosophy and psychology.

Indeed, such understandings may themselves have contributed to the marginalisation of education, at least according to one account over two decades ago of the formation of education as a university field of study (Hardie 1974).

Pointing to the field's origins in philosophy and psychology, in accordance with 'the German pattern', he writes: 'Philosophy, and particularly moral philosophy, was considered to determine the end of education, and psychology was considered to provide the means by which that end was to be realised' (Hardie 1974, p. 90). Further:

> The success or failure of the study of education was thus almost inevitably linked with the fortunes of philosophy and psychology, and I believe the low esteem in which the study of education is often held today is an unfortunate result of the disillusionment which has become widespread with regard to these two subjects. (Hardie 1974, p. 90)

Indeed, Hardie subsequently speaks (p. 94) of ' "guilt by association" '! His concern is with asserting the significance and integrity of education as 'a university subject in its own right', and moreover an empirical, 'experimental' subject which may indeed now lay rightful claim 'to be one of the most promising and exciting subjects in the university' (Hardie 1974, p. 101).[4] But what is more particularly relevant to our purposes here is his positioning of education *within* philosophy, by which he is referring to the German philosophical tradition that arguably underpins the very structure of the modern university:

> While the subject of education or pedagogy could be considered new to [late-nineteenth century] universities in the United States and in Great Britain, it had for some time been included under the subject of philosophy in some German universities. (Hardie 1974, p. 90)

There are a number of observations that can be made here. First, we need to bear in mind that philosophy has had in effect a privileged position, not just in the university but in doctoral education; after all, the 'PhD' stands in for 'Doctor of Philosophy'. Philosophy thus serves as an overarching, unifying meta-discipline. Second, what might be called the professionalisation of the Academy goes hand-in-hand with the growth and consolidation of disciplinarity and formalisation. This might go part of the way to explaining recent moves in fields such as the Humanities and Social Sciences, in direct response to the emergence of the Professional Doctorate, particularly in non-traditional areas, to (re-)assert and (re)claim the notion of erstwhile disciplinary doctorates (PhDs) as being themselves *professional* doctorates. The profession in this case is that of the academic, generally speaking, but more specifically the professional historian, sociologist, economist, etc.

A question that might be asked at this point is what the implications are of this ongoing formalisation and abstraction for educational research—its 'disciplining', as it were. This becomes all the more interesting and pressing when Connell's earlier assertions about the links between formal educational research and education as a field of study, on the one hand, and educational-institutional practice and the teaching profession, on the other. It is akin, perhaps, to the process of transformation and compromise that has been observed in the emergence and consolidation of school-subjects (Goodson, 1988)—a congruence and an analogy that certainly warrants some further investigation.

At this point, however, it is useful to turn to a more recent attempt to account for education as a distinctive field of study and research, specifically in the context of the university. Lingard and Blackmore (1997) review different perspectives and debates in this regard, and conclude that education is best understood as 'a "research field" rather than a "research discipline with its boundaries and distinctive features" ... determined, by and large, by its focus on education' (Lingard and Blackmore 1997, p. 2). Hence they point to what they describe as 'the multidisciplinary character of educational research'. For our purposes here, understanding education as a *multi-discipline* in this fashion is quite problematic. Advanced research education in the field is thereby normatively positioned as, in the first instance, oriented towards the traditional PhD and hence towards the traditional disciplinary doctorate. This is indicated in the following:

> Reflecting its multidisciplinary character, educational research ... includes such approaches as philosophy of education, educational psychology, sociology and anthropology of education, educational policy and administration, and the economics of education. (Lingard and Blackmore 1997, p. 3)

Therefore, understood in this way (still) within the meta-organising terms of disciplinarity, education as a field of study falls into the same category as other 'fields', effectively albeit implicitly marginalising pedagogy and practice alike. Although account may well be taken of other, more specific foci such as curriculum and pedagogy, as well as the study of social and administrative 'contexts', the implication remains that these are best conceived in appropriately 'disciplined' (i.e. disciplinary?) terms. Yet: 'Education as a research field has symbiotic links to educational practice and the institutions and policies within which such practice occurs' (Lingard and Blackmore 1997, p. 4). Furthermore, as they observe, there is a notable tension between the 'multidisciplinary' orientation of educational research and its own contextualisation within changing material and discursive circumstances, *including* the challenges to disciplinarity associated with poststructuralism and what has been called the 'modernism-postmodernism' debate (Green 1993). For us, however, these 'tensions' present a real difficulty, and mark a significant contradiction in the contemporary self-understanding of educational research.

At fundamental issue here is the question of disciplinarity itself, which we want to argue is not to be understood in traditional terms, but rather as referring to the manner in which knowledge (and its associated forms of identity) is organised and (re)produced as a social-discursive practice. What needs to be accounted for is the way in which boundaries are formed around particular matrices of knowledge, power and desire, in all their undecidability and instability in what are now widely acknowledged to be postmodern times and conditions. The Foucaultian overtones of 'discipline' cannot be ignored here, although it is likely that other more 'energetic' perspectives are also needed (e.g. Deleuzian emphases on 'assemblages' and 'intensities'). Furthermore, what needs to be appreciated here is the likelihood that educational research (training) might well be better or more appropriately conceptualised as 'interdisciplinary' or 'transdisciplinary' in character and orientation, and even (in some instances at least) as 'pre-disciplinary'—that is, as emergent and loosely and heterogenously organised, in accordance with the relatively unique circumstances of its genesis and generation. This latter pertains more particularly to the *practice* of curriculum and pedagogy. The former aligns educational research with work in cultural studies and the 'New Humanities' (Hodge 1995, Readings 1996, Pinar et al. 1995). In such a perspective, disciplinarity as such becomes problematic and often explicitly thematised. As Hodge writes, such work characteristically

> deconstructs [the system of disciplinarity's] taken-for-grantedness, the unquestioned sense that the boundaries around the existing disciplines are inherent features of knowledge. It also inspects the disciplinary processes themselves, to see the work they do in constructing and forming human subjects, and constructing also the objects of knowledge that define their institutional existence as authorised knowers. (Hodge 1995, p. 35)

This phenomenon is increasingly evident in doctoral work in educational studies, in the form of 'alternative' dissertations, often drawing on new patterns and arrangements of 'text' and 'commentary' and avowedly rhetorical in their attitude.

The rise of the Education Doctorate in recent times can also be seen as a direct response to some of the problems and possibilities associated with these developments, and as constituting in certain important respects a critique of the dominant form of the PhD, as the preferred credential in educational research. That is to say, it turns out that education constitutes a particularly fascinating forum for debates over 'disciplinary' versus 'professional' forms of doctoral study. Indeed, it might be better to describe doctoral study in education as an exemplary *hybrid* in this regard, and as at once 'disciplinary' and 'professional' in its orientation and its character. There are, of course, important implications in this for supervision, and it is to this matter that we now turn, in conclusion.

Supervising subjectivity

'Supervision' carries powerful overtones of 'overseeing' (of 'looking over' and 'looking after') production and development with regard to academic knowledge and identity. All higher research degrees, and especially those associated with doctoral work, are required by formal legislation to be subject to 'supervision', which means that both the student (the 'candidate') and the dissertation are to be constructed under the authorised and authorising gaze of an already-established, hopefully active researcher-academic, as it were standing in for the field of study in question and for the Academy more generally. The supervisor-supervisee relationship is one, moreover, which has both a literal or actual, empirical dimension—these people, in this institution, engaged in these particular exchanges—and a symbolic dimension, which involves negotiating among other things '[t]he idealism and paranoic excess' (Hodge 1995, p. 36) all too often characteristic of doctoral candidature. It is for this reason that bureaucratic ('policy') solutions to the problem of postgraduate supervision are not enough, and indeed may exacerbate the specific dilemmas and difficulties associated with postgraduate research education. This is particularly a risk if such rational(ist) initiatives are not supplemented and informed by due regard for the complexities and mysteries of pedagogic practice, understood precisely as an (re-)in(tro)duction into the Symbolic Order[5]. This is not to ignore or to gloss over the practical forms and requirements of authorisation and credentialling, nor to slight the forms of technical training that are also associated with advanced-level postgraduate study. It is, rather, to place the emphasis more firmly and squarely on the discursive production of subjectivity, in the specific context of doctoral study.

Let us assume that what is at stake in doctoral work and postgraduate supervision, over and beyond the much-vaunted contribution to knowledge, is precisely the (re)production of an intelligible academic identity—a certain kind of (licensed) personage. In the field of education, this is someone who, increasingly, can operate with initiative and authority in an emergent 'learning society', inside *and* outside of formal educational institutions. It may be possible to imagine a continuum of subject-positions here, from one whose primary reference-point is outside, oriented to other disciplinary communities and formations, to one more specifically oriented to educational phenomena *per se*. This means due attention to the specificities of workplace and institution, and due regard for practice and profession. What for instance makes schooling a distinctive social institution? How might one come to understand the complexities and specificities of classrooms and schools, as sites of educational practice, or to appreciate those associated with teaching and teacher education? How might one come to a properly and distinctively *educational* understanding of what is involved in what has been called 'public pedagogy' or 'cultural pedagogy'? Does it make sense, and if so in what ways, to conceive of television as curriculum? Further, following Bernstein and others, what is at risk in the specific forms of 'disciplining' associated with education? To what extent does doctoral training and the discipline of research construct the phenomena in a particular way, thereby changing them irrevocably?

These are important questions. They suggest a different, at once less utilitarian and more critical-reflexive view of supervision and candidature from what seems the usual course of things in the theory and practice of higher education. Drawing in specific consideration of pedagogy and subjectivity means taking up a more flexible stance towards disciplinarity—installing it, as Readings (1996, p. 177) suggests, as 'a permanent question'—and the nexus of knowledge and identity in academic work. It means, above all else, attending to supervision as a matter of on-going negotiation and explicit dialogue with regard to the social and institutional dynamics of power and desire. What that means, in 'practice', remains a challenge, certainly, but we would argue that an important and necessary beginning rests with acknowledging the contradictory tensions and perplexing difficulties associated with supervising subjectivity and managing the Symbolic.

Notes:

1   Re-Thinking Postgraduate Pedagogy: On the History and Praxis of the PhD in Australia', Australian Research Council Large Grant, 1997-1999. Chief Investigators: Alison Lee, Bill Green and Lesley Johnson. We want to acknowledge feedback and helpful suggestions from our colleague Lesley Johnson in the preparation of this paper.

2   Note also the following observation, with specific regard to the Australian context: 'Teacher training was never accepted at the Universities of Sydney or Melbourne in the same manner as the professional training courses such as Medicine, Law or Engineering. This has been seen as closely related to the low status of teachers in the community compared with these more prestigious professions. Teaching was associated with the public service and apprenticeship training' (Bessant and Holbrook 1995, pp. 266).

3   What should also be noted, in this context, is the Humboldtian emphasis on the subordination of the student (and the teacher) to knowledge, and hence of pedagogy to what later becomes disciplinarity: 'At the higher level ... both teacher and student have their justification in the common pursuit of knowledge' (von Humboldt 1970, p. 243 [orig pub 1809/1810]).

4   Ironically, Hardie's attempted intervention into the debate over status and specificity of education as a field of study was premised on just the sort of enterprise of which Swoboda was so critical--that is, the reduction of educational studies to 'a parody of science, the worse for being an unconscious parody'. On the significance for the Australian scene of North American models of the university and of educational research, see Connell (1980) and also Bessant and Holbrook (1995).

5   A difficult notion, we acknowledge. It relates to our emerging understanding of disciplinarity as a cultural-symbolic practice, and of the relationship between knowledge and language, drawing on work in poststructuralism and psychoanalysis. It is premised on the idea that subjectivity is constructed in and through a series of engagements with the Symbolic Order, rather than just one primary engagement in early childhood, as in the conventional Lacanian account (Lemaire 1977, pp. 78-92). For a more specific orientation to curriculum and schooling, see Donald (1992, pp. 45-46).

References

Beach, R., Green, J. L., Kamil, M. L. and Shanahan, T. (eds), 1992, *Multidisciplinary Perspectives on Literacy Research*, Urbana, Illinois, National Conference on Research in English and the National Council of Teachers of English.

Bernstein, B. 1971, 'On the classification and framing of educational knowledge', in M. F. D. Young (ed.), 1971, *Knowledge and Control: New Directions for the Sociology of Education*, London, Collier-Macmillan, pp. 47-69.

Bessant, B. and Holbrook, A. 1995, *Reflections on Educational Research in Australia: A History of the Australian Association for Research in Education*, Coldstream, Victoria, Australian Association for Research in Education Inc.

Clark, B. R. 1994, 'The Research-teaching-study nexus in modern systems of higher education', *Higher Education Policy*, 7 (1), pp. 11-17.

Clark, B. R. 1997, 'The Modern integration of research activities with teaching and learning', *Journal of Higher Education*, 68 (3), pp. 241-255.

Connell, R. 1985, 'How to supervise a PhD', *Vestes*, (2), pp. 38-41.

Connell, W. F. 1980, *A History of Education in the Twentieth Century World*, Canberra, Curriculum Development Centre.

Donald, J. 1992, *Sentimental Education: Schooling, Popular Culture and the Regulation of Liberty*, London, Verso.

Goodson, I. 1988, *The Making of Curriculum*, London, The Falmer Press.

Green, B. and Lee, A. 1995, 'Theorising postgraduate pedagogy', *Australian Universities Review*, 38 (2), pp. 40-45.

Green, B. 1993, 'Literacy studies and curriculum theorizing; or, the insistence of the letter', in B. Green (ed.), *The Insistence of the Letter: Literacy Studies and Curriculum Theorizing*, London, The Falmer Press, pp. 195-225.

Hardie, C. D. 1974, 'One hundred years of the university study of education', *The Australian University*, 12 (2), pp. 89-102.

Harste, J. 1992, 'Preface', in Richard Beach et al. *Multidisciplinary Perspectives on Literacy Research*, Urbana, Illinois, National Conference on Research in English and the National Council of Teachers of English, pp. ix-xiii.

Hoskin, K. W. 1993, 'Education and the genesis of disciplinarity: The unexpected reversal', in E. Messer-Davidow, D. R. Shumway and D. L. Sylvan (eds), *Knowledges: Historical and Critical Studies in Disciplinarity*, Charlottesville and London, University Press of Virginia, pp. 271-304.

Lee, A. and Green, B. 1997, 'Pedagogy and disciplinarity in the "New University"' *UTS Review*, 3 (1), pp. 1-25.

Lemaire, A. 1977, *Jacques Lacan*, trans. D. Macey, London, Henley and Boston, Routledge & Kegan Paul [Revised 2nd edition].

Levine, G. and Kaplan, E. A. 1997, 'Introduction', in E. A. Kaplan and G. Levine (eds), *The Politics of Research*, New Brunswick, NJ, Rutgers University Press, pp. 1-18.

Lingard, B. and Blackmore, J. 1997, 'The performative state and the state of educational research', *Australian Educational Researcher*, 24 (3), pp. 1-20.

Messer-Davidow, E., Shumway, D. R. and Sylvan, D. L. (eds), 1993, *Knowledges: Historical and Critical Studies in Disciplinarity*, Charlottesville and London, University Press of Virginia.

Pinar, W. F., Reynolds, W. M., Slattery, P. and Taubman, P. 1995, *Understanding Curriculum: An Introduction to the Study of Historical and Contemporary Curriculum Discourses*, New York, Peter Lang.

Readings, B. 1996, *The University in Ruins*, Cambridge, Mass., Harvard University Press.

Scott, P. 1995 *The Meanings of Mass Higher Education*, Buckingham, The Society for Research into Higher Education & Open University Press.

Siegel, M. 1992, 'Multidisciplinary research on literacy and the possibility of educational change', in R. Beach et al. 1992, *Multidisciplinary Perspectives on Literacy Research*, Urbana, Illinois, National Conference on Research in English and the National Council of Teachers of English, pp. 373-384.

Swoboda, W. W. 1979, 'Disciplines and interdisciplinarity: A historical perspective', in J. J. Kockelmans (ed.), *Interdisciplinarity and Higher Education*, University Park and London, The Pennsylvania State University Press, pp. 49-92.

von Humboldt, W. 1970, 'On the Spirit and the organisational framework of intellectual institutions in Berlin', *Minerva*, 8 (2), pp. 242-250.

Wittrock, B. 1993, 'The modern university: Three transformations', in S. Rothblatt and B. Wittrock (eds), *The European and American University since 1800: Historical and Sociological Essays*, Cambridge, Cambridge University Press, pp. 303-362.

1. 'Re-Thinking Postgraduate Pedagogy: On the History and Praxis of the PhD in Australia', Australian Research Council Large Grant, 1997-1999. Chief Investigators: Alison Lee, Bill Green and Lesley Johnson. We want to acknowledge feedback and helpful suggestions from our colleague Lesley Johnson in the preparation of this paper.

2. Note also the following observation, with specific regard to the Australian context: 'Teacher training was never accepted at the Universities of Sydney or Melbourne in the same manner as the professional training courses such as Medicine, Law or Engineering. This has been seen as closely related to the low status of teachers in the community compared with these more prestigious professions. Teaching was associated with the public service and apprenticeship training' (Bessant and Holbrook 1995, pp. 266).

3. What should also be noted, in this context, is the Humboldtian emphasis on the subordination of the student (and the teacher) to knowledge, and hence of pedagogy to what later becomes disciplinarity: 'At the higher level, ... both teacher and

student have their justification in the common pursuit of knowledge' (von Humboldt 1970, p. 243 [orig pub 1809/1810]).

4. Ironically, Hardie's attempted intervention into the debate over status and specificity of education as a field of study was premised on just the sort of enterprise of which Swoboda was so critical––that is, the reduction of educational studies to 'a parody of science, the worse for being an unconscious parody'. On the significance for the Australian scene of North American models of the university and of educational research, see Connell (1980) and also Bessant and Holbrook (1995).

5. A difficult notion, we acknowledge. It relates to our emerging understanding of disciplinarity as a cultural-symbolic practice, and of the relationship between knowledge and language, drawing on work in poststructuralism and psychoanalysis. It is premised on the idea that subjectivity is constructed in and through a *series* of engagements with the Symbolic Order, rather than just one primary engagement in early childhood, as in the conventional Lacanian account (Lemaire 1977, pp. 78-92). For a more specific orientation to curriculum and schooling, see Donald (1992, pp. 45-46).

SUBJECT INDEX

Subject Index

Contributors

Sandra Acker

Sandra Acker is a Professor in the Department of Sociology and Equity Studies in Education at the Ontario Institute for Studies in Education of the University of Toronto. Her research and teaching interests include women and education, teacher education, thesis supervision, careers of teachers and academics, and workplace cultures in schools and universities. Publications include *The Realities of Teachers' Work: Never a Dull Moment* (Cassell, 1999), *Gendered Education* (Open University Press, 1994), and *Teachers, Gender and Careers* (Falmer Press, 1989). Her current research is on the experiences of university academics in the four professional fields of education, social work, pharmacy and dentistry.

Tania Aspland

Tania Aspland is a PhD student within the Graduate School of Education at the University of Queensland. She also teaches curriculum theory and pedagogical studies at Queensland University of Technology. Her teaching and research interests focus on generating better practices in the areas of culturally responsive teaching, supervision and learning within school and university contexts. She has recent publications in the fields of curriculum leadership, action research, NESB students in Australian university contexts, and higher degree teaching and supervision.

Ray Barker

Since 1996 Ray Barker has been attached to the Faculty of Education at the University of Newcastle in an Honorary capacity. Ray's current academic interests include occupational education, the history of enterprises, and the history of education. His most recent publications are in the areas of exploring the dimensions of 'other' education in Australia (including mapping informal and occupational education in the Hunter region). His PhD thesis was in an allied area: 'The Education and Training of Apprentices and Engineering Technicians in the Metal Trades in New South Wales 1947-1972: An Historical Study of Sectional Influence', and was awarded the Newcastle IER Prize.

Peter Beamish

Peter Beamish is currently Senior Lecturer in the Faculty of Mathematics and Computing at Avondale College. Peter taught in secondary schools in New South Wales for six years. His research interests include the study of the use of computers in the classroom to enhance student learning, with a particular focus on the use of computer applications to enhance constructivism in the classroom and he has a number of publications in this field. His PhD thesis entitled 'Databases and Student Learning: A Multilevel Analysis of the Use of Databases in the Classroom' focused on this topic and was submitted for examination in August 1998.

Martin Bibby

Martin Bibby is a Senior Lecturer at the University of New South Wales, where he teaches professional ethics and philosophy of education. Martin chaired the AARE committee that produced the AARE Code of Ethics and he recently edited *Ethics and Education Research* (AARE, 1997).

Robin Burns

Robin Burns is a Senior Lecturer in the Graduate School of Education, La Trobe University. Her major research interests are the sociology of knowledge and she is currently working on an ethnography of field science in remote areas, namely the lived experience of women living and working in Antarctica. Recent publications include chapters in *Education into the Twenty-First Century: Dangerous Terrain for Women?* (Falmer Press, 1998), and *The Health Promoting School. Policy, Programmes and Practice in Australia* (Harcourt Brace, 1998).

Barbara Comber

Barbara Comber is Director of the Language and Literacy Research Centre at the University of South Australia. Her interests include teachers' work, social justice, critical literacies, public education, school-based collaborative research, tertiary pedagogies and literacies and developing multi-media research and educational artefacts and sites. She is currently editing two books, 'Negotiating Critical Literacies in Classrooms' (with Anne Simpson) and 'Inquiry into what?: Empowering Today's Young People, Tomorrow's Citizens Using Whole Language'(with Sibel Boran). Her PhD thesis was entitled 'The discursive construction of literacy in a disadvantaged school', and employed ethnographic and poststructuralist discourse analytic methods.

Terry Evans

Terry Evans is Director of Research in the Faculty of Education at Deakin University. He is the author of *Understanding Learners in Open and Distance Education.* (Kogan Page, 1994) and the co-editor of nine books including *Opening Education: Policies and Practices From Open and Distance Education* (with D. Nation, Routledge, 1996) and *Shifting Borders: Globalisation, Localisation and Open and Distance Education* (with L. Rowan & L. Bartlett, Deakin University Press, 1997).

Bill Green

Bill Green is Professor of Curriculum Studies at the University of New England. His research interests are in curriculum and literacy studies, curriculum history, English teaching, technology and cultural studies, and postgraduate research education. Until recently he was on the Editorial Executive of the *Australian Educational Researcher.* In 1998 (with Alison Lee) he co-edited *Postgraduate Studies/Postgraduate Pedagogy* a collection of essays on new challenges and practices in Australian doctoral education (Centre for Language and Literacy and the University Graduate School, University of Technology Sydney).

Martin Hayden

Martin Hayden is Professor and Director of Teaching and Learning at Southern Cross University, New South Wales. His areas of research interest include student participation in higher education, the nature of the academic profession, and issues of teaching and learning in higher education.

Allyson Holbrook

Allyson Holbrook is a Senior Lecturer in the Faculty of Education at the University of Newcastle. Much of her current research has been in the area of history of education, particularly the history of occupational education, youth transition from school to work, and the history of educational research. She is currently President of the Australia and New Zealand History of Education Society (ANZHES). Her other main research and teaching areas are Qualitative Research Methods and Futures in Education. Allyson has taken an active role in promoting educational research through executive positions in such organizations as ANZHES, AARE and the Newcastle Institute for Educational Research.

Sue Johnston

Sue Johnston is Professor and Director of the Teaching and Learning Centre at the University of New England in Armidale. She began her career as a school teacher and then moved to teacher education at QUT. After four years directing a higher education teaching and learning centre at the University of Canberra, she moved to UNE at the beginning of 1998. The Teaching and Learning Centre at UNE fulfils a diverse set of functions, including academic development, academic skills support for students, multimedia production, distance education operations and support for teaching and learning initiatives across the university. Sue's research interests have been closely associated with her other responsibilities and have focused on educational change, professional development, teacher thinking, and postgraduate supervision.

Garry Kidd

Garry Kidd is an Assistant Professor in the Department of Psychology at Bond University. His research has been concerned with learning styles, career and tertiary course choice, and the measurement and stability of occupational interests among Australian adolescents. More recently, he has commenced a three year longitudinal study of Year 10 students' occupational interests, career beliefs and indecisiveness, and post secondary destinations. Garry received the AARE Outstanding Thesis Award in 1992 for his doctoral dissertation entitled: 'Tertiary Course Choice: Interests as Predictors'.

234

Sally Knowles

Sally Knowles works in the Teaching and Learning Centre at Murdoch University. She co-ordinates and teaches intensive academic programs for international postgraduate students and runs discipline-based thesis writing workshops. Her research interests include postgraduate writing and supervision, genre analysis, and feminist pedagogies. Her interest in feedback is based on her own need to obtain feedback on her writing and her role in helping students to develop their own strategies for academic writing and research.

Rolene Lamm

Rolene Lamm is currently completing a PhD on tertiary supervision at La Trobe University. Rolene taught secondary school English language and literature both in Australia and abroad. These teaching experiences led to her interest and further research in the area of reading difficulties, and the academic underachiever. The latter became the focus of her MEd research. Rolene has been an educational consultant in school curriculum and student achievement. In recent years Rolene has been involved in a number of research projects on issues relating to higher degree studies and tertiary supervision and has published in this area.

Alison Lee

Alison Lee is a Senior Lecturer in the Faculty of Education, University of Technology Sydney. Her research interests include literacy studies, critical discourse analysis, gender and education, higher education policy and postgraduate research education. In 1998 (with Bill Green) she co-edited *Postgraduate Studies/Postgraduate Pedagogy*, a collection of essays on new challenges and practices in Australian doctoral education (Centre for Language and Literacy and the University Graduate School, UTS).

Ramon Lewis

Ramon Lewis is a Senior Lecturer in the Graduate School of Education at La Trobe University where he has specialised in the area of quantitative research methodology for over 20 years. His major research interests are classroom discipline, and adult and adolescent coping. He has published 5 books, 2 psychometric scales and numerous articles in these areas. Among his most recent publications are the second edition of *The discipline dilemma* (ACER, 1997), and (with E. Frydenberg) the *Coping Scale for Adults* (ACER, 1997). In addition to his academic position, Dr Lewis teaches part time or consults with schools in a bid to explore the gap between theory and practice.

Jane Orton

Jane Orton is a Senior Lecturer in the Department of Language, Literacy and Arts Education at the University of Melbourne, where she co-ordinates studies in modern languages education. She is currently Director of a NALSAS project designing and producing a Graduate Certificate in Advanced Chinese for delivery over the

Internet. Jane's research interests are in intercultural communication between Australians and Chinese in workplace settings and she has published in this area. Her PhD thesis, 'Educating the Reflective Practitioner in China', was awarded by La Trobe University in 1991 and won the La Trobe University Annual Award for exemplary thesis writing and research in the field of Education in the School of Education, 1991.

Nicholas Pang

Nicholas Sun-Keung Pang is Assistant Professor in the Department of Educational Administration and Policy at the Chinese University of Hong Kong. His research interests include educational administration and policy, organizational theories, quality school education, educational research methodology and applied statistics. He has published widely in Educational Administration and Management journals. His doctoral thesis was entitled 'Organizational Values and Cultures of Excellent Schools in Hong Kong'.

Sharon Parry

Sharon Parry is a member of staff of the Centre for Teaching and Learning at Southern Cross University, New South Wales. Her doctoral thesis concerned disciplinary differentiation in the nature of doctoral study. She has a special interest in the nature of academic profession and how its norms are learned, and she publishes in this area.

Margot Pearson

Margot Pearson is Director of the Centre for Educational Development and Academic Methods at the Australian National University. She has published widely in the area of postgraduate research supervision, including *Establishing Effective PhD Supervision* (with D. Cullen, L. J. Saha, & R. H. Spear, AGPS, 1994), and *Open and Flexible PhD Study and Research* (with L. Ford, DEETYA 1997).

Ilana Snyder

Ilana Snyder is a Senior Lecturer in the Faculty of Education, Monash University. She is the author *of Hypertext: the Electronic Labyrinth* (Melbourne University Press 1996) and the editor of *Page to Screen: Taking Literacy into the Electronic Era* (Allen & Unwin, 1997). With Colin Lankshear and Bill Green, she is co-authoring a book for Allen and Unwin based on *Digital Rhetorics,* a DEETYA project on literacy and technology. The title of her PhD thesis was: 'The Impact of Word Processors on Students' Writing. A Comparative Study of the Effects of Pens and Word Processors on Writing Context, Process and Product'.

About the AARE Doctoral Thesis Award

This award is intended as recognition of excellence in educational research by doctoral students and is seen by the Australian Association for Research in Education (AARE) as a way of recognising the high quality contribution made to educational knowledge by graduate students, and at the same time promoting dissemination and furthering of research.

The main criterion for assessment of excellence in doctoral research for the award is the contribution made to theoretical, empirical, and/or methodological knowledge in education. In particular, preference is given to studies which have made a conceptual advance in educational theory, policy and practice; which point to methods of improving educational practice or pioneer innovation; which contribute through disciplined research to knowledge on which new educational practices may be based, or which contribute to advances in methodology of educational research, evaluation and dissemination.

Other criteria include originality and thoroughness in carrying through the research, and the quality of presentation of the work. Other things being equal, theses which are judged to be readily adaptable to scholarly and professional dissemination will be preferred.

The award committee comprises six persons appointed by the AARE executive, and in making selection the committee may seek opinions from assessors. Institutions can not make more than one nomination a year. The award-winning thesis is chosen from a short listing of six. In exceptional circumstances the committee might award a tie (as was the case in 1996 and 1997).

	Award Recipient(s)	Special Commendation
1989	Dr L. English	Dr G. Cooper, Dr C. Wilson
1990	Dr A. MacKinnon	Dr R. Fielding
1991	Dr I. Snyder	-
1992	Dr G. Kidd	Dr J. Orton
1993	Dr M. McCorriston	-
1994	Dr P. Chandler	-
1995	Dr S. Dockett	-
1996	Dr A. Hickling-Hudson	-
	Dr R. Stancliffe	-
1997	Dr B. Comber	-
	Dr S. Marginson	-
1998	Dr L. Baker RSJ	Dr J. MacCallum